IIBA® International Institute of Business Analysis

A Guide to the
Business Analysis Body of Knowledge® (BABOK® Guide)

Version 2.0

www.theiiba.org

Table of Contents

Preface

IIBA® was founded in Toronto, Canada in October of 2003 to support the business analysis community by:

▶ Creating and developing awareness and recognition of the value and contribution of the Business Analyst.

▶ Defining the *Business Analysis Body of Knowledge®* (*BABOK®*).

▶ Providing a forum for knowledge sharing and contribution to the business analysis profession.

▶ Publicly recognizing and certifying qualified practitioners through an internationally acknowledged certification program.

The Body of Knowledge Committee was formed in October of 2004 to define and draft a global standard for the practice of business analysis. In January of 2005, IIBA® released version 1.0 of *A Guide to the Business Analysis Body of Knowledge®* (*BABOK® Guide*) for feedback and comment. That version included an outline of the proposed content and some key definitions. Version 1.4 was released in October of 2005, with draft content in some knowledge areas. Version 1.6, which included detailed information regarding most of the knowledge areas, was published in draft form in June of 2006 and updated to incorporate errata in October of 2008.

This publication supersedes *A Guide to the Business Analysis Body of Knowledge®, Version 1.6*. Following the publication of version 1.6, IIBA® sought out a number of recognized experts in business analysis and related fields and solicited their feedback on the content of that edition. Their comments were used to plan the scope of this revision. IIBA® volunteers then worked to define a structure for version 2.0 and developed the revised text, which was made available to the business analysis community for review in 2008. During that exposure period, IIBA® also solicited feedback from industry experts and business analysis practitioners through a formal review process. IIBA® received thousands of comments during this process, and this document has been revised to incorporate as many of those comments as possible.

The *BABOK® Guide* contains a description of generally accepted practices in the field of business analysis. The content included in this release has been verified through reviews by practitioners, surveys of the business analysis community, and consultations with recognized experts in the field. The data available to IIBA® demonstrate that the tasks and techniques described in this publication are in use by a majority of business analysis practitioners. As a result, we can have confidence that the tasks and techniques described in the *BABOK® Guide* should be applicable in most contexts where business analysis is performed, most of the time.

The *BABOK® Guide* should not be construed to mandate that the practices described in this publication should be followed under all circumstances. Any set of practices must be tailored to the specific conditions under which business analysis is being performed. In addition, practices which are not generally accepted by the business analysis community at the time of publication may be equally effective, or more effective, than the practices described in the *BABOK® Guide*. As such practices become generally accepted, and as data is collected to verify their effectiveness, they will be incorporated into future editions of this publication. IIBA® encourages all practitioners of business analysis to be open to new approaches and new ideas, and wishes to encourage innovation in the practice of business analysis.

The goal of this revision was to:

▶ Complete the description of all knowledge areas.

▶ Simplify the structure to make it easier to understand and apply.

▶ Improve the consistency and quality of text and illustrations.

▶ Integrate the knowledge areas and eliminate areas of overlap.

▶ Improve consistency with other generally accepted standards relating to the practice of business analysis.

▶ Extend the coverage of the *BABOK® Guide* to describe business analysis in contexts beyond traditional approaches to custom software application development, including but not limited to agile methodologies, Business Process Management, and commercial-off-the-shelf (COTS) application assessment and implementation.

▶ Clarify the relationship between business analysis and other disciplines, particularly project management, testing, and usability and information architecture.

▶ Focus on the practice of business analysis in the context of the individual initiative, with material on strategic or enterprise-wide business analysis separated for inclusion in a future application extension.

The major changes in this release include:

▶ Changes throughout to address the goals described above.

▶ All content has been revised and edited, and much of it has been rewritten.

▶ Many of the tasks found in version 1.6 have been consolidated, resulting in a reduction from 77 tasks to 32.

▶ Tasks in the *Requirements Planning and Management* Knowledge Area have been reallocated to *Business Analysis Planning and Monitoring* and *Requirements Management and Communication.*

▶ Three other knowledge areas have been renamed to better reflect their purpose.

▶ Techniques apply across multiple Knowledge Areas.

▶ Inputs and Outputs have been defined for all tasks.

IIBA® would like to extend its thanks and the thanks of the business analysis community to all those who volunteered their time and effort to the development of this revision, as well as those who provided informal feedback to us in other ways.

Introduction

1.1   What is the Business Analysis Body of Knowledge?

A Guide to the Business Analysis Body of Knowledge® (BABOK® Guide) is a globally recognized standard for the practice of business analysis. The *BABOK® Guide* describes business analysis areas of knowledge, their associated activities and tasks, and the skills necessary to be effective in their execution.

The primary purpose of the *BABOK® Guide* is to define the profession of business analysis. It serves as a baseline that practitioners can agree upon in order to discuss the work they do and to ensure that they have the skills they need to effectively perform the role, and defines the skills and knowledge that people who work with and employ business analysts should expect a skilled practitioner to demonstrate. It is a framework that describes the business analysis tasks that must be performed in order to understand how a solution will deliver value to the sponsoring organization. The form those tasks take, the order they are performed in, the relative importance of the tasks, and other things may vary, but each task contributes in some fashion, directly or indirectly, to that overall goal.

This chapter provides an introduction to key concepts in the field of business analysis and describes the structure of the remainder of the *BABOK® Guide*. Chapters 2 through 7 define the tasks that a business analyst must be capable of performing. Chapter 8 describes the competencies that support the effective performance of business analysis, and Chapter 9 describes a number of generally accepted techniques that support the practice of business analysis.

1.2   What is Business Analysis?

Business analysis is the set of tasks and techniques used to work as a liaison among stakeholders in order to understand the structure, policies, and operations of an organization, and to recommend solutions that enable the organization to achieve its goals.

Business analysis involves understanding how organizations function to accomplish their purposes, and defining the capabilities an organization requires to provide products and services to external stakeholders. It includes the definition of organizational goals, how those goals connect to specific objectives, determining the courses of action that an organization has to undertake to achieve those goals and objectives, and defining how the various organizational units and stakeholders within and outside of that organization interact.

Business analysis may be performed to understand the current state of an organization or to serve as a basis for the later identification of business needs. In most cases, however, business analysis is performed to define and validate solutions that meet business needs, goals, or objectives.

Business analysts must analyze and synthesize information provided by a large number of people who interact with the business, such as customers, staff, IT professionals, and executives. The business analyst is responsible for eliciting the actual needs of stakeholders, not simply their expressed desires. In many cases, the business analyst will also work to facilitate communication between organizational units. In particular, business analysts often play a central role in aligning the needs of business units with the capabilities delivered by information technology, and may serve as a "translator" between those groups.

A *business analyst* is any person who performs business analysis activities, no matter what their job title or organizational role may be. Business analysis practitioners include not only people with the job title of business analyst, but may also include business systems analysts, systems analysts, requirements engineers, process analysts, product managers, product owners, enterprise analysts, business architects, management consultants, or any other person who performs the tasks described in the *BABOK® Guide*, including those who also perform related disciplines such as project management, software development, quality assurance, and interaction design.

1.3   Key Concepts

1.3.1   Domains

A domain is the area undergoing analysis. It may correspond to the boundaries of an organization or organizational unit, as well as key stakeholders outside those boundaries and interactions with those stakeholders.

1.3.2   Solutions

A solution is a set of changes to the current state of an organization that are made in order to enable that organization to meet a business need, solve a problem, or take advantage of an opportunity. The scope of the solution is usually narrower than the scope of the domain within which it is implemented, and will serve as the basis for the scope of a project to implement that solution or its components.

Most solutions are a system of interacting solution components, each of which are potentially solutions in their own right. Examples of solutions and solution components include software applications, web services, business processes, the business rules that govern that process, an information technology application, a revised organizational structure, outsourcing, insourcing, redefining job roles, or any other method of creating a capability needed by an organization.

Business analysis helps organizations define the optimal solution for their needs, given the set of constraints (including time, budget, regulations, and others) under which that organization operates.

1.3.3   Requirements

A requirement[1] is:

1. A condition or capability needed by a stakeholder to solve a problem or achieve an objective.

2. A condition or capability that must be met or possessed by a solution or solution component to satisfy a contract, standard, specification, or other formally imposed documents.

---

1   Based on IEEE 610.12-1990: *IEEE Standard Glossary of Software Engineering Terminology.*

3.   A documented representation of a condition or capability as in (1) or (2).

As implied by this definition, a requirement may be unstated, implied by or derived from other requirements, or directly stated and managed. One of the key objectives of business analysis is to ensure that requirements are visible to and understood by all stakeholders.

The term "requirement" is one that generates a lot of discussion within the business analysis community. Many of these debates focus on what should or should not be considered a requirement, and what are the necessary characteristics of a requirement. When reading the *BABOK® Guide*, however, it is vital that "requirement" be understood in the broadest possible sense. Requirements include, but are not limited to, past, present, and future conditions or capabilities in an enterprise and descriptions of organizational structures, roles, processes, policies, rules, and information systems. A requirement may describe the current or the future state of any aspect of the enterprise.

Much of the existing literature on business analysis is written with the assumption that requirements only describe an information technology system that is being considered for implementation. Other definitions may include future state business functions as well, or restrict the meaning of the term to define the ends stakeholders are seeking to achieve and not the means by which those ends are achieved. While all of these different uses of the term are reasonable and defensible, and the *BABOK® Guide*'s usage of the term includes those meanings, they are significantly narrower than the way the term is used here.

Similarly, we do not assume that requirements are analyzed at any particular level of detail, other than to say that they should be assessed to whatever level of depth is necessary for understanding and action. In the context of a Business Process Management initiative, the requirements may be a description of the business processes currently in use in an organization. On other projects, the business analyst may choose to develop requirements to describe the current state of the enterprise (which is in itself a solution to existing or past business needs) before investigating changes to that solution needed to meet changing business conditions.

.1   Requirements Classification Scheme

For the purposes of the *BABOK® Guide*, the following classification scheme is used to describe requirements:

▶   **Business Requirements** are higher-level statements of the goals, objectives, or needs of the enterprise. They describe the reasons why a project has been initiated, the objectives that the project will achieve, and the metrics that will be used to measure its success. Business requirements describe needs of the organization as a whole, and not groups or stakeholders within it. They are developed and defined through *enterprise analysis*.

▶   **Stakeholder Requirements** are statements of the needs of a particular stakeholder or class of stakeholders. They describe the needs that a given stakeholder has and how that stakeholder will interact with a solution. Stakeholder requirements serve as a bridge between business requirements and the various classes of solution requirements. They are developed and defined through *requirements analysis*.

▶ **Solution Requirements** describe the characteristics of a solution that meet business requirements and stakeholder requirements. They are developed and defined through *requirements analysis*. They are frequently divided into sub-categories, particularly when the requirements describe a software solution:

  ▷ **Functional Requirements** describe the behavior and information that the solution will manage. They describe capabilities the system will be able to perform in terms of behaviors or operations—specific information technology application actions or responses.

  ▷ **Non-functional Requirements** capture conditions that do not directly relate to the behavior or functionality of the solution, but rather describe environmental conditions under which the solution must remain effective or qualities that the systems must have. They are also known as quality or supplementary requirements. These can include requirements related to capacity, speed, security, availability and the information architecture and presentation of the user interface.

▶ **Transition Requirements** describe capabilities that the solution must have in order to facilitate transition from the current state of the enterprise to a desired future state, but that will not be needed once that transition is complete. They are differentiated from other requirements types because they are always temporary in nature and because they cannot be developed until both an existing and new solution are defined. They typically cover data conversion from existing systems, skill gaps that must be addressed, and other related changes to reach the desired future state. They are developed and defined through *solution assessment and validation*.

1.4 Knowledge Areas

Knowledge areas define what a practitioner of business analysis needs to understand and the tasks a practitioner must be able to perform.

Business analysts are likely to perform tasks from all knowledge areas in rapid succession, iteratively, or simultaneously. Tasks may be performed in any order as long as the required inputs are available. In principle, a business analysis effort may start with any task, although the most likely candidates are *Define Business Need (5.1)* or *Evaluate Solution Performance (7.6)*.

Knowledge areas are not intended to represent phases in a project. It is certainly possible and permissible to proceed from performing enterprise analysis activities, to requirements analysis activities, to solution assessment and validation activities, and treat each as a distinct phase in a project. However, the *BABOK® Guide* does not require that you do so, and it should not be construed as a methodology for the performance of business analysis.

Business Analysis Planning and Monitoring (*Chapter 2*) is the knowledge area that covers how business analysts determine which activities are necessary in order to complete a business analysis effort. It covers identification of stakeholders, selection of business analysis techniques, the process that will be used to manage requirements, and how to assess the progress of the work. The tasks in this knowledge area govern the performance of all other business analysis tasks.

Elicitation (*Chapter 3*) describes how business analysts work with stakeholders to identify and understand their needs and concerns, and understand the environment in which they work. The purpose of elicitation is to ensure that a stakeholder's actual underlying needs are understood, rather than their stated or superficial desires.

Requirements Management and Communication (*Chapter 4*) describes how business analysts manage conflicts, issues and changes in order to ensure that stakeholders and the project team remain in agreement on the solution scope, how requirements are communicated to stakeholders, and how knowledge gained by the business analyst is maintained for future use.

Enterprise Analysis (*Chapter 5*) describes how business analysts identify a business need, refine and clarify the definition of that need, and define a solution scope that can feasibly be implemented by the business. This knowledge area describes problem definition and analysis, business case development, feasibility studies, and the definition of solution scope.

Requirements Analysis (*Chapter 6*) describes how business analysts prioritize and progressively elaborate stakeholder and solution requirements in order to enable the project team to implement a solution that will meet the needs of the sponsoring organization and stakeholders. It involves analyzing stakeholder needs to define solutions that meet those needs, assessing the current state of the business to identify and recommend improvements, and the verification and validation of the resulting requirements.

Figure 1–1: Relationships Between Knowledge Areas

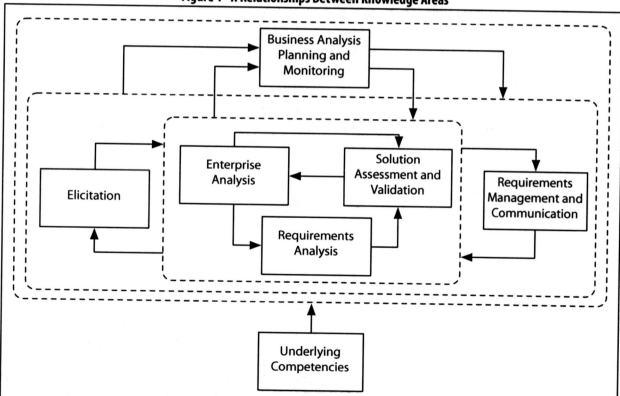

Solution Assessment and Validation (*Chapter 7*) describes how business analysts assess proposed solutions to determine which solution best fits the business need, identify gaps and shortcomings in solutions, and determine necessary workarounds or changes to the solution. It also describes how business analysts assess deployed solutions to see how well they met the original need so that the sponsoring organization can assess the performance and effectiveness of the solution.

Underlying Competencies (*Chapter 8*) describes the behaviors, knowledge, and other characteristics that support the effective performance of business analysis.

1.5 Tasks

Each knowledge area describes the tasks performed by business analysts to accomplish the purpose of that knowledge area. Each task in the *BABOK® Guide* is presented in the following format:

1.5.1 Purpose

Each task has a purpose. The purpose is a short description of the reason for a business analyst to perform the task and the value created through performing the task.

1.5.2 Description

A task is an essential piece of work that must be performed as part of business analysis. Each task should be performed at least once during the vast majority of business analysis initiatives, but there is no upper limit to the number of times any task may be performed.

Tasks may be performed at any scale. Each task may be performed over periods ranging from several months in time to a few minutes. For example, a business case may be a document several hundred pages long, justifying a multi-billion dollar investment, or a single sentence explaining the benefit that a change will produce for a single individual.

A task has the following characteristics:

▶ A task accomplishes a result in an output that creates value to the sponsoring organization—that is, if a task is performed it should produce some demonstrable positive outcome which is useful, specific, visible and measurable.

▶ A task is complete—in principle, successor tasks that make use of outputs should be able to be performed by a different person or group.

▶ A task is a necessary part of the purpose of the Knowledge Area with which it is associated.

The *BABOK® Guide* does not prescribe a process or an order in which tasks are performed. Some ordering of tasks is inevitable, as certain tasks produce outputs that are required inputs for other tasks. However, it is important to keep in mind that the *BABOK® Guide* only prescribes that the input must exist. The input may be incomplete or subject to change and revision, which may cause the task to be performed multiple times. Iterative or agile lifecycles may require that tasks in all knowledge areas be performed in parallel, and lifecycles with clearly defined phases will still require tasks from multiple knowledge areas to be performed in every phase. Tasks may be performed in any order, as long as the necessary inputs to a task are present.

The description of a task explains in greater detail why the task is performed, what the task is, and the results the task should accomplish.

1.5.3   Input

An input represents the information and preconditions necessary for a task to begin. Inputs may be:

► Explicitly generated outside the scope of business analysis (e.g., construction of a software application).

► Generated by a business analysis task.

There is no assumption that the presence of an input or an output means that the associated deliverable is complete or in its final state. The input only needs to be sufficiently complete to allow successive work to begin. Any number of instances of an input may exist during the lifecycle of an initiative.

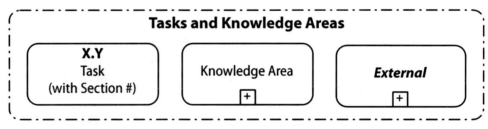

Figure 1–2: Task Input/Output Diagrams

.1   Requirements

Requirements are a special case as an input or output, which should not be surprising given their importance to business analysis. They are the only input or output that is not produced by a single task. Requirements can be classified in a number of different ways and exist in any of a number of different states. When listed as an input or output in this section of the task, the following format will be used to indicate the classification and state of a requirement or set of requirements:

Classification Requirements [State or States]. If no classification or states are listed, any or all requirements may be used as an input or output. For example, **Requirements [Stated]** means that the requirement may have any classification, whereas **Business**

Requirements would mean that the business requirements may be in any possible state (e.g. verified, prioritized, stated, or combinations thereof).

States may also be combined in some cases. For example, **Requirements [Prioritized and Verified]** should be read to indicate that the requirements have been both prioritized and verified. **Requirements [Prioritized or Verified]** means that the requirements may be prioritized, verified, or both.

In general text, the state will be written first, followed by the classification (e.g. stated requirements, verified business requirements, etc.) Again, if no state or classification is indicated, it means that the requirement is not restricted to any particular state or classification.

1.5.4   Elements

The format and structure of this section is unique to each task. The elements section describes key concepts that are needed to understand how to perform the task.

1.5.5   Techniques

Each task contains a listing of relevant techniques. Some techniques are specific to the performance of a single task, while others are relevant to the performance of a large number of tasks (and are listed in *Chapter 9: Techniques*). If a particular task can use both kinds of techniques, the ones found in Chapter 9 will be listed under a "General Techniques" subsection. If there are no subsections, then all techniques may be found in Chapter 9. For additional information, see *Techniques (1.6)*.

1.5.6   Stakeholders

Each task includes a listing of generic stakeholders who are likely to participate in the execution of that task or who will be affected by it. A generic stakeholder represents a class of people that the business analyst is likely to interact with in a specific way. The *BABOK® Guide* does not mandate that these roles be filled for any given initiative. Any stakeholder can be a source of requirements, assumptions, or constraints.

This list is not intended to be an exhaustive list of all possible stakeholder classifications, as it would simply not be possible to compile such a listing. Some additional examples of people who fit into each of these generic roles are provided in *Figure 1–3*. In most cases, there will be multiple stakeholder roles found within each category. Similarly, a single individual may fill more than one role.

.1   Business Analyst

By definition, the business analyst is a stakeholder in all business analysis activities. The *BABOK® Guide* is written with the presumption that the business analysis is responsible and accountable for the execution of these activities. In some cases, the business analyst may also be responsible for the performance of activities that fall under another stakeholder role. The most common roles to be assigned to business analysts, in addition to the business analysis role, are the Domain Subject Matter Expert, Implementation Subject Matter Expert, Project Manager, and Tester. Guidance on performing these additional roles falls outside the scope of the *BABOK® Guide*, as these roles are not part of the discipline of business analysis.

Figure 1–3: Examples of Generic Stakeholders

Generic Stakeholder	Examples and Alternate Roles
Business Analyst	Business Systems Analyst, Systems Analyst, Process Analyst, Consultant, Product Owner, etc.
Customer	Segmented by market, geography, industry, etc.
Domain SME	Broken out by organizational unit, job role, etc.
End User	Broken out by organizational unit, job role, etc.
Implementation SME	Project Librarian, Change Manager, Configuration Manager, Solution Architect, Developer, DBA, Information Architect, Usability Analyst, Trainer, Organizational Change Consultant, etc.
Operational Support	Help Desk, Network Technicians, Release Manager
Project Manager	Scrum Master, Team Leader
Supplier	Providers, Consultants, etc.
Tester	Quality Assurance Analyst
Regulator	Government, Regulatory Bodies, Auditors
Sponsor	Managers, Executives, Product Managers, Process Owners

.2 Customer

A customer is a stakeholder outside the boundary of a given organization or organizational unit. Customers make use of products or services produced by the organization and may have contractual or moral rights that the organization is obliged to meet.

.3 Domain Subject Matter Expert (SME)

A domain subject matter expert is any individual with in-depth knowledge of a topic relevant to the business need or solution scope. This role is often filled by people who will also be end users or people who will be indirect users of the solution, such as managers, process owners, legal staff (who may act as proxies for Regulators), consultants, and others.

.4 End User

End users are stakeholders who will directly interact with the solution. The term is most frequently used in a software development context, where end users are those who will actually use the software application that is being developed, but in the broader context of a solution they can include all participants in a business process.

.5 Implementation Subject Matter Expert (SME)

Implementation subject matter experts are responsible for designing and implementing potential solutions. The implementation subject matter experts will provide specialist expertise on the design and construction of the solution components that fall outside the scope of business analysis.

While it is not possible to define a listing of implementation subject matter expert roles that is appropriate for all initiatives, some of the most common roles are:

Developers/Software Engineers

Developers are responsible for the construction of software applications. Areas of expertise among developers or software engineers include particular languages or application components. Good software development practices will significantly reduce the cost to build an application, the predictability of the development process, and the ability to implement changes in the functionality supported by an application.

Organizational Change Management Professionals

Organizational change management professionals are responsible for facilitating acceptance and adoption of new solutions and overcoming resistance to change. Areas of expertise among change management professionals include industry and cultural expertise. Good change management can help to create advocates for change within an organization.

System Architects

System architects are responsible for dividing a software application into components and defining the interactions between them. Areas of expertise among system architects include understanding of methodologies and of solutions offered by specific vendors. Good system architecture will facilitate rapid development of solutions and reuse of components in other solutions.

Trainers

Trainers are responsible for ensuring that the end users of a solution understand how it is supposed to work and are able to use it effectively. Areas of expertise among trainers may include classroom-based or online education. Effective training will facilitate acceptance and adoption of a solution.

Usability Professionals

Usability professionals are responsible for the external interaction design of technology solutions and for making those solutions as simple to use as is feasible. Areas of expertise among usability professionals include user interface designers and information architects. Good usability will increase productivity, customer satisfaction, and reduce cost in solution maintenance and training.

.6   Project Manager

Project managers are responsible for managing the work required to deliver a solution that meets a business need, and for ensuring that the project's objectives are met while balancing the project constraints, including scope, budget, schedule, resources, quality, risk, and others.

.7   Tester

Testers are responsible for determining how to verify that the solution meets the solution requirements defined by the business analyst, as well as conducting the verification process. Testers also seek to ensure that the solution meets applicable quality standards and that the risk of defects of failures is understood and minimized.

.8   Regulator

Regulators are responsible for the definition and enforcement of standards. Standards may be those that the team developing the solution is required to follow, standards the solution must meet, or both. Regulators may enforce legislation, corporate governance standards, audit standards, or standards defined by organizational centers of competency.

.9 Sponsor

Sponsors are responsible for initiating the effort to define a business need and develop a solution that meets that need. They authorize work to be performed and control the budget for the initiative.

.10 Supplier

A supplier is a stakeholder outside the boundary of a given organization or organizational unit. Suppliers provide products or services to the organization and may have contractual or moral rights and obligations that must be considered.

1.5.7 Output

An output is a necessary result of the work described in the task. Outputs are created, transformed or change state as a result of the successful completion of a task. Although a particular output is created and maintained by a single task, a task can have multiple outputs.

An output may be a deliverable or be a part of a larger deliverable. The form of an output is dependent on the type of initiative underway, standards adopted by the organization, and best judgment of the business analyst as to an appropriate way to address the information needs of key stakeholders.

As with inputs, an instance of a task may be completed without an output being in its final state. The input or output only needs to be sufficiently complete to allow successive work to begin. Similarly, there may be one or many instances of an output created as part of any given initiative. Finally, the creation of an output does not necessarily require that subsequent tasks which use that work product as an input must begin.

1.6 Techniques

Techniques provide additional information on different ways that a task may be performed or different forms the output of the task may take. A task may have none, one, or more related techniques. A technique must be related to at least one task.

The *BABOK® Guide* does not prescribe a set of analysis techniques that must be used. The techniques described in this document are those that have been demonstrated to be of value and in use by a majority of the business analysis community. Business analysts who are familiar with these techniques are therefore likely to be able to perform effectively under most circumstances that they are likely to encounter. However, these techniques are not necessarily the best possible ones to use in any given situation, nor are they necessarily able to address every situation effectively. Similarly, it is unlikely that a business analyst will be called on to demonstrate expertise with every technique defined in the *BABOK® Guide*.

A subset of the techniques in the *BABOK® Guide* can be described as being in widespread use. These techniques are in regular use by a majority of business analysts and see occasional use by the vast majority of practitioners, and it is likely that many if not most organizations will expect business analysts to have a working knowledge of these techniques. The techniques that fall into this category are:

- ▶ Acceptance and Evaluation Criteria Definition (9.1)

- ▶ Brainstorming (9.3)

- ▶ Business Rules Analysis (9.4)

- ▶ Data Dictionary and Glossary (9.5)

- ▶ Data Flow Diagrams (9.6)

- ▶ Data Modeling (9.7)

- ▶ Decision Analysis (9.8)

- ▶ Document Analysis (9.9)

- ▶ Interviews (9.14)

- ▶ Metrics and Key Performance Indicators (9.16)

- ▶ Non-functional Requirements Analysis (9.17)

- ▶ Organization Modeling (9.19)

- ▶ Problem Tracking (9.20)

- ▶ Process Modeling (9.21)

- ▶ Requirements Workshops (9.23)

- ▶ Scenarios and Use Cases (9.26)

The *BABOK® Guide* may in some cases group similar techniques, or techniques that share a single purpose, under a single heading. For example, the *Data Modeling (9.7)* technique covers class models and entity-relationship diagrams and could in principle cover concept maps, term and fact models, object role models, and other less widely-adopted analysis techniques.

Each technique in the *BABOK® Guide* is presented in the following format:

1.6.1   Purpose

Defines what the technique is used for, and the circumstances under which it is most likely to be applicable.

1.6.2   Description

Describes what the technique is and how it is used.

1.6.3   Elements

The format and structure of this section is unique to each technique. The elements section describes key concepts that are needed to understand how to use the technique.

1.6.4   Usage Considerations

Describes conditions under which the technique may be more or less effective.

1.7   Underlying Competencies

The underlying competencies are skills, knowledge and personal characteristics that support the effective performance of business analysis. The underlying competency areas relevant to business analysis include:

Analytical Thinking and Problem Solving supports effective identification of business problems, assessment of proposed solutions to those problems, and understanding of the needs of stakeholders. Analytical thinking and problem solving involves assessing a situation, understanding it as fully as possible, and making judgments about possible solutions to a problem.

Behavioral Characteristics support the development of effective working relationships with stakeholders and include qualities such as ethics, trustworthiness, and personal organization.

Business Knowledge supports understanding of the environment in which business analysis is performed and knowledge of general business principles and available solutions.

Communication Skills support business analysts in eliciting and communicating requirements among stakeholders. Communication skills address the need to listen to and understand the audience, understanding how an audience perceives the business analyst, understanding of the communications objective(s), the message itself, and the most appropriate media and format for communication.

Interaction Skills support the business analyst when working with large numbers of stakeholders, and involve both the ability to work as part of a larger team and to help that team reach decisions. While most of the work of business analysis involves identifying and describing a desired future state, the business analyst must also be able to help the organization reach agreement that the future state in question *is* desired through a combination of leadership and facilitation.

Software Applications are used to facilitate the collaborative development, recording and distribution of requirements to stakeholders. Business analysts should be skilled users of the tools used in their organization and must understand the strengths and weaknesses of each.

1.8   Other Sources of Business Analysis Information

The *BABOK® Guide* is a synthesis of information on the business analysis role drawn from a wide variety of approaches to business improvement and change. A complete listing of works referenced in the development of the *BABOK® Guide* can be found in *Appendix B: Bibliography*. Business analysts looking to expand on their understanding of business analysis may wish to consult works in these other fields, obtain training from specialists in these areas, or pursue other opportunities for education and professional development.

In particular, we have drawn on information from the following application areas for business analysis and related professional bodies of knowledge:

► Agile Development

► Business Intelligence

► Business Process Management

► Business Rules

► Decision Analysis and Game Theory

► Enterprise Architecture (including the Zachman Framework for Enterprise Architecture™ and TOGAF™)

► Governance and Compliance Frameworks, including Sarbanes-Oxley, Basel II, and others

► IT Service Management (including ITIL®)

► Lean and Six Sigma

► Organizational Change Management

► Project Management

► Quality Management

► Service Oriented Architecture

► Software Engineering (particularly Requirements Engineering)

► Software Process Improvement (including CMMI®)

► Software Quality Assurance

► Strategic Planning

► Usability and User Experience Design

The *BABOK® Guide* focuses on defining the business analysis role across a broad range of business analysis approaches and so only touches briefly on much of the information developed by practitioners working in these fields. Business analysts will find that a study of any of those areas will be rewarded with a greater understanding of the business analysis profession, ability to collaborate with other professionals, and an understanding of a number of different ways that business analysts can benefit the organizations that employ them.

Business Analysis Planning & Monitoring

The *Business Analysis Planning and Monitoring* Knowledge Area defines the tasks associated with the planning and monitoring of business analysis activities, including:

► identifying stakeholders

► defining roles and responsibilities of stakeholders in the business analysis effort

► developing estimates for business analysis tasks

► planning how the business analyst will communicate with stakeholders

► planning how requirements will be approached, traced, and prioritized

► determining the deliverables that the business analyst will produce

► defining and determining business analysis processes

► determining the metrics that will be used for monitoring business analysis work

In addition, this knowledge area describes the work involved in monitoring and reporting on work performed to ensure that the business analysis effort produces the expected outcomes. If these outcomes do not occur, the business analyst must take corrective action to meet stakeholder expectations.

Figure 2–1: *Business Analysis Planning & Monitoring* **Input/Output Diagram**

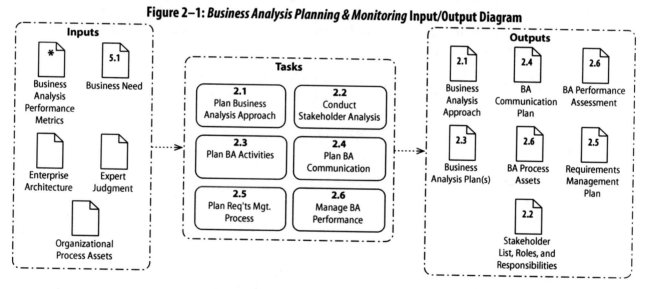

2.1 Plan Business Analysis Approach

2.1.1 Purpose

This task describes how to select an approach to performing business analysis, which stakeholders need to be involved in the decision, who will be consulted regarding and informed of the approach, and the rationale for using it.

2.1.2   Description

Business analysis approaches describe the overall process that will be followed to perform business analysis work on a given initiative, how and when tasks will be performed, the techniques that will be used, and the deliverables that should be produced.

There are multiple established ways to approach business analysis work. In software development, they range from those dictated by the waterfall approach to the use of agile techniques. Similarly, there are a number of well-known business process improvement methodologies, including Lean and Six Sigma, as well as many proprietary and in-house methodologies, customs, and practices. Elements from different approaches may be combined; however only a subset of all possible combinations will be viable for the particular organizational environment in which an initiative is being performed.

In order to plan the business analysis approach, the business analyst must understand the organizational process needs and objectives that apply to the initiative. These needs and objectives may include compatibility with other organizational processes, constraints on time-to-market, compliance with regulatory and governance frameworks, the desire to evaluate new approaches to solution development, or other business objectives. If the objectives are not known, the business analyst may be required to define the requirements that the process must meet.

In many cases, organizations will have formal or informal standards in place regarding how business analysis is done and how it fits into project and other activities. If this is the case, the business analyst reviews any existing organizational standards, including standards, guidelines, and processes relating to the current initiative. These may suggest or dictate which approach to use. Even where a standard approach exists, it must be tailored to the needs of a specific initiative. Tailoring may be governed by organizational standards that define which approaches are permitted, which elements of those processes may be tailored, general guidelines for selecting a process, and so forth.

If no standards exist, the business analyst works with the appropriate stakeholders to determine how the work will be completed. The business analyst should be capable of selecting or creating an approach and working with key stakeholders, particularly the project manager and project team, to ensure that it is suitable.

The business analysis approach is often based on or related to the project approach, but in some cases they may be independently determined (for example, an organization may use a plan-driven approach to define its business processes and then use a change-driven approach to build the supporting software applications).

2.1.3   Inputs

Business Need: The business analysis approach will be shaped by the problem or opportunity faced by the organization. It is generally necessary to consider the risks associated with it, the timeframe in which the need must be addressed, and how well the need is understood. This will help determine whether a plan-driven or change-driven approach is appropriate.

Expert Judgment: Used to determine the optimal business analysis approach. Expertise may be provided from a wide range of sources including stakeholders in the initiative, organizational Centers of Competency, consultants, or associations and industry groups.

Prior experiences of the business analyst and other stakeholders should be considered when selecting or modifying an approach.

Organizational Process Assets: Include the elements of existing business analysis approaches in use by the organization. Organizational process assets that may be useful in defining the business analysis approach include methodologies for process change or software development, tools or techniques that are in use or understood by stakeholders, corporate governance standards (such as COBIT™, Sarbanes-Oxley, and Basel II), and templates for deliverables. In addition to these general standards, the organization may have guidelines in place for tailoring the process to fit a specific initiative.

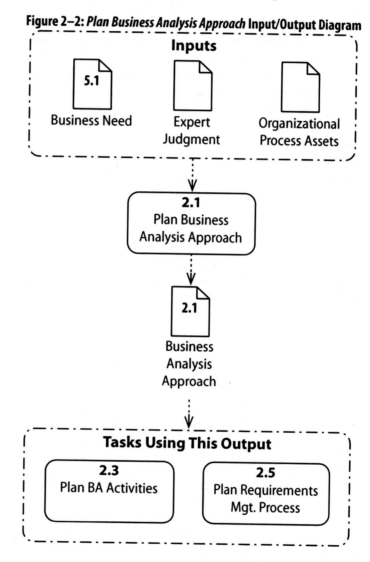

Figure 2–2: *Plan Business Analysis Approach* Input/Output Diagram

2.1.4   Elements

Almost all methodologies fit somewhere along a spectrum between plan-driven and change-driven approaches.

Plan-driven approaches focus on minimizing up-front uncertainty and ensuring that the solution is fully defined before implementation begins in order to maximize control and minimize risk. These approaches tend to be preferred in situations where requirements can effectively be defined in advance of implementation, the risk of an incorrect implementation is unacceptably high, or when managing stakeholder interactions presents significant challenges. The authority to approve requirements typically rests with selected stakeholders and the project sponsor. The project sponsor will have the final authority to approve solution requirements, but it is common for sponsors to insist that other stakeholders grant their approval before the sponsor will. Waterfall methods of software development and business process re-engineering initiatives are typical examples of plan-driven approaches.

Change-driven approaches focus on rapid delivery of business value in short iterations in return for acceptance of a higher degree of uncertainty regarding the overall delivery of the solution. These approaches tend to be preferred when taking an exploratory approach to finding the best solution or for incremental improvement of an existing solution. The authority to approve requirements usually rests with a single individual, who is an active participant in the team's daily activities—others may advise or be informed but may not withhold consent, and the approval process must be completed within a strict time limit. Agile methods of software development, as well as continuous improvement projects, are typical examples of change-driven approaches.

The performance of this task is dependent on where the selected approach falls on this spectrum. The descriptions below touch on the ends of the spectrum, and hybrid approaches may combine aspects of both. Similar considerations must be taken into account whether the business analyst is selecting or tailoring the approach.

.1   Timing of Business Analysis Work

Determine when the business analysis efforts should occur, when tasks need to be performed, and if the level of business analysis effort will need to vary over time. This includes determining whether enterprise analysis, requirements analysis, and solution assessment and validation activities will be performed primarily in specific project phases or iteratively over the course of the initiative.

Plan-driven approaches have most business analysis work occur at the beginning of the project or during one specific project phase. The exact name of the phase varies by the specific methodology, but the main focus of the phase includes such activities as eliciting, analyzing, documenting, verifying and communicating the requirements, as well as reporting on the status of the business analysis activities work for the project.

Change-driven approaches may have a business analysis effort conducted early to produce an initial list of high-level requirements (also referred to as requirements envisioning). This product backlog is then updated throughout the project as new requirements emerge. Throughout the project, these requirements will be prioritized and reprioritized based on the business need. The highest-priority requirements will be taken from the backlog for detailed requirements analysis as resources become available for implementation, and implementation will begin as soon as analysis is complete.

.2   Formality And Level Of Detail Of Business Analysis Deliverables

Determine whether requirements will be delivered as formal documentation or through informal communication with stakeholders, and the appropriate level of detail that should be contained in those documents. The expected deliverables must be defined as part of the approach. See *Chapter 4: Requirements Management and Communication* for examples of business analysis deliverables.

Plan-driven approaches typically call for a significant amount of formality and detail. Requirements are captured in a formal document or set of documents which follow standardized templates. This may be preceded by a number of requirements related documents, built with increasing levels of detail, including a high level vision and scope document that focuses on business requirements, and documents describing the requirements from the point of view of specific stakeholder groups. Relevant stakeholders must generally formally approve each of these documents before work begins on requirements at a lower level of detail. The specific content and format of the requirements documents can vary, depending on the organizational methodologies, processes, and templates.

Change-driven approaches favor defining requirements through team interaction and through gathering feedback on a working solution. Mandatory requirements documentation is often limited to a prioritized requirements list. Additional documentation may be created at the discretion of the team and generally consists of models developed to enhance the team's understanding of a specific problem. An alternative approach is to document the requirements in the form of acceptance criteria accompanied by tests. Formal documentation is often produced after the solution is implemented to facilitate knowledge transfer.

.3   Requirements Prioritization

Determine how requirements will be prioritized and how those priorities will be used to define the solution scope. Methods of prioritizing requirements are discussed in *Prioritize Requirements (6.1)*. Also see *Chapter 5: Enterprise Analysis* for information on defining the solution scope and *Chapter 4: Requirements Management and Communication* for information on managing the solution scope. Prioritization methods will also be used when performing *Allocate Requirements (7.2)*. Change-driven approaches tend to place a great deal of emphasis on effective requirements prioritization methods, due to the small scope of each iteration or release.

.4   Change Management

Changes to requirements may occur at any time. Consider the expected likelihood and frequency of change and ensure that the change management process is effective for those levels of change. Effective business analysis practices can significantly reduce the amount of change required in a stable business environment but cannot eliminate it entirely.

Plan-driven approaches seek to ensure that changes only occur when they are genuinely necessary and can be clearly justified. Each change is often handled as a "mini project," complete with requirements elicitation, estimates, design, etc. Changed requirements impact both the solution scope and the project scope and the change management process will be incorporated into the overall project management process.

Many organizations have a formal process which includes a request for change, a change log that tracks the changes that have been received, and an analysis of the impact of the change not only to the project, but also to other business and automated systems. In practice, the number and impact of change requests often increases towards the end of the project. This can be due to any combination of factors, including loosely scoped projects, lack of requirements ownership by project stakeholders, poorly performed business analysis, changing management priorities, business reorganization, regulatory change or changing business requirements.

Change-driven approaches presume that it is difficult to identify all requirements in advance of their implementation. There is generally no separate change management process distinct from the selection of requirements for a given iteration. Changes to existing solution capabilities are simply prioritized and selected for an iteration using the same criteria as new features and capabilities.

.5　　Business Analysis Planning Process

The business analyst must determine the process that will be followed to plan the execution of businesses analysis activities. In most cases, this process will be integrated into a larger project plan.

.6　　Communication With Stakeholders

Communications may be written or verbal, formal or informal. Decisions must be made at the outset of the project as to the applicability of such communications technologies such as email with regards to project decision-making and approval of deliverables.

Plan-driven approaches tend to rely on formal communication methods. Much of the communication of the actual requirements is in writing, and often uses pre-defined forms requiring signatory approvals. All project documentation is normally archived as part of the project history.

Change-driven approaches focus more on frequency of communication than on formal documentation. Official documentation is often in writing, but informal communication takes precedence over more formal written communication. Documentation frequently occurs following implementation.

.7　　Requirements Analysis and Management Tools

The business analyst must identify any requirements analysis or management tools that will be used. These tools may shape the selection of business analysis techniques, notations to be used, and the way that requirements will be packaged.

.8　　Project Complexity

The complexity of the project, the nature of the deliverables, and the overall risk to the business needs to be taken into consideration. The factors listed below, among others, increase the complexity of business analysis efforts as they increase:

► number of stakeholders

► number of business areas affected

► number of business systems affected

► amount and nature of risk

► uniqueness of requirements

► number of technical resources required

The level of requirements uncertainty is partly dependent on the domain of the project.

For example, new venture, marketing and research projects tend to have a higher requirements uncertainty, while accounting and finance projects tend to have a relatively lower level of requirements uncertainty.

Many organizations have a need for knowledge regarding a solution to be maintained over the long term, because responsibility for the solution may be outsourced, because of turnover within the project team, geographical distribution of participants, or because key personnel are on contract and will not remain available to the organization following implementation. Formal documentation may be required to address these risks.

2.1.5 Techniques

Decision Analysis (9.8): May be used to rate available methodologies against the organizational needs and objectives.

Process Modeling (9.21): Process Models can be used to define and document the business analysis approach.

Structured Walkthrough (9.30): This can be used as a means of validating a created, selected, or tailored business analysis approach.

2.1.6 Stakeholders

Customer, Domain SME, End User or **Supplier:** The approach taken may depend on their availability and involvement with the initiative.

Implementation SME: The business analysis approach taken should be compatible with the implementation lifecycle used by the implementation team.

Project Manager: The project manager must ensure that the business analysis approach is compatible with other project activities.

Tester: The business analysis approach must facilitate appropriate testing activities.

Regulator: Aspects of the approach or decisions made in the tailoring process may require approval.

Sponsor: The approach taken may depend on their availability and involvement with the initiative. The sponsor may also have needs and objectives that apply to the approach itself.

2.1.7 Output

Business Analysis Approach: This is a definition of the approach that will be taken for business analysis in a given initiative. A business analysis approach may specify team roles, deliverables, analysis techniques, the timing and frequency of stakeholder interactions, and other elements of the business analysis process. A methodology is a formalized and repeatable business analysis approach. It includes a decision about which organizational process assets will be applied and any decisions made regarding tailoring of the process for a specific situation. Documentation regarding the approach may eventually be added to the organization's repository of process assets.

2.2 Conduct Stakeholder Analysis

2.2.1 Purpose

This task covers the identification of stakeholders who may be affected by a proposed initiative or who share a common business need, identifying appropriate stakeholders for the project or project phase, and determining stakeholder influence and/or authority regarding the approval of project deliverables.

2.2.2 Description

Stakeholder analysis is performed as soon as a business need is identified and will usually be an ongoing activity as long as business analysis continues. Stakeholder analysis begins with identifying stakeholders who may be affected by the business need or a new solution. Stakeholders may be grouped into categories that reflect their involvement or interest in the initiative. The roles, responsibilities, and authority over the requirements for each stakeholder or stakeholder group must be clearly described. Stakeholder analysis also involves understanding stakeholder influence on and attitude towards the initiative, and assessing positive and negative attitudes and behaviors which may affect the outcome of the initiative and acceptance of the solution.

2.2.3 Inputs

Business Need: Identify and analyze the position of the stakeholders affected by the business need. As the understanding of that need evolves through definition of business requirements, solution scope, stakeholder requirements, and solution requirements, that additional information will be used to assist in identifying additional stakeholders or understanding how existing stakeholders may have changed their position.

Enterprise Architecture: Describes the organizational units that exist, their interactions with other organizational units, customers, and suppliers, their responsibilities within the organization, and the roles and relationships within each organizational unit.

Organizational Process Assets: These include organizational policies and procedures, forms that must be completed, suggested or prescribed methodologies, templates, and project authorization guidelines. They may be mandated or expressed in the form of guiding principles.

2.2.4 Elements

Stakeholder roles must be identified early in the project in order to help ensure timely delivery of requirements deliverables. Note that some individuals may be called on to play a variety of stakeholder roles on the same project, as well as on different roles on different projects.

.1 Identification

Understanding who the stakeholders are and the impact of proposed changes on them is vital to understanding what needs, wants, and expectations must be satisfied by a solution.

Because requirements are based on stakeholder needs, wants, and expectations, those that are uncovered either late or not at all could require a revision to requirements that changes or nullifies completed tasks or tasks already in progress, increasing

Figure 2–3: *Conduct Stakeholder Analysis* **Input/Output Diagram**

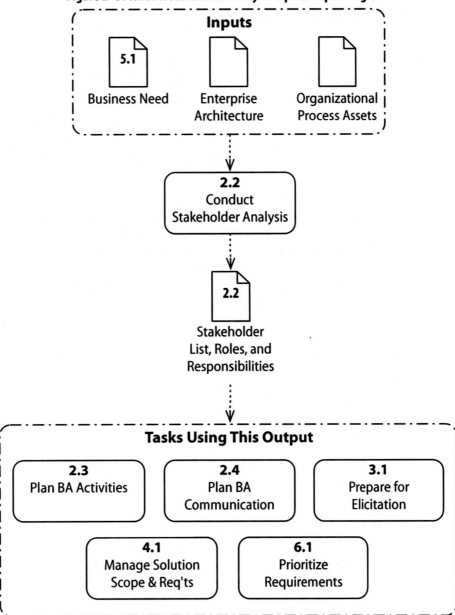

costs and decreasing stakeholder satisfaction. Change-driven approaches may better accommodate this risk, but cannot eliminate it, as late stakeholder identification can still result in alterations to the project roadmap and release content.

Who participates in which business analysis activities can vary between projects, methodologies, and organizations. For example, some organizations may encourage members of the technical team to attend requirements workshops to provide costs, technical effort estimates and information on technical impacts while others may rule that no technical discussion is permitted during these meetings.

.2   Complexity of Stakeholder Group

The complexity of interactions with a stakeholder group may be affected by factors such as:

▶ **Number and variety of direct end users** in their constituency. Different approaches, plans, reports, amount of formality, and the amount of documentation can be customized based on the number of stakeholders each subject matter expert represents. Stakeholders with fewer constituents may be able to represent their stakeholder group without much difficulty. Stakeholders representing a large number of constituents or representing those from different functional areas or divisions may need to research information or engage in requirements elicitation themselves.

▶ **Number of interfacing business processes and automated systems.** The planning for stakeholders who represent those performing complex, interfacing, or overlapping business processes is different from those whose processes are more self-contained. Since not all stakeholders can or want to attend all requirements workshops, they can be more easily persuaded if the workshop pertains to their process and the associated software application.

.3   Attitude and Influence

Assess stakeholder attitudes toward and influence over the initiative. Factors to consider include:

Attitude towards:

▶ The business goals, objectives, and solution approach:

 ▷ Do they believe that the solution will benefit the organization?

 ▷ Will the benefits affect them directly?

 ▷ Will the benefits be accrued elsewhere?

 ▷ Are the possible negative effects of the initiative on this stakeholder greater than the rewards?

 ▷ Do they believe that the project team can successfully deliver the solution?

▶ Attitude towards business analysis:

 ▷ Do they see value in defining their requirements?

 ▷ Do they present solutions and expect the requirements to be contained in that solution, and believe that this will enable them to avoid requirements definition?

▶ Attitude towards collaboration:

 ▷ Have they had success on previous collaborative efforts?

 ▷ Does the organization reward collaboration?

    ▷ Is the organization hierarchical in nature, rather than being team-based?

    ▷ Are personal agendas the norm?

► Attitude towards the sponsor:

    ▷ On cross-functional efforts, do all the SMEs support the sponsor?

    ▷ Are there SMEs who would prefer another sponsor?

► Attitude towards team members:

    ▷ Have key members of the project team (including but not limited to the business analyst) built trusting relationships or have there been prior failed projects or project phases involving those people?

Influence: Understanding the nature of influence and the influence structures and channels within an organization can prove invaluable when seeking to build relationships and work towards building trust. Understanding the influence each stakeholder may have, as well as their attitude, can help develop strategies for obtaining buy-in and collaboration. Some factors relating to influence to consider are:

► **Influence on the project.** How much influence does the stakeholder have on the project? For instance, because sponsors obtain funding, including resources, and make vital decisions, they usually exert more than end-users.

► **Influence in the organization.** There are usually formal and informal structures within organizations, and one's title or job role, while it can provide what is called authority or positional power, does not always reflect the actual importance or authority a stakeholder has.

► **Influence needed for the good of the project.** The business analyst should analyze how much influence is needed to make the project succeed compared with the amount of influence the key stakeholders, such as the project sponsor, have. For example, on a large, complex project requiring many internal and external resources, the project will need a sponsor who has effective relationships with funding groups to ensure that adequate resources are available for project work. Projects that are smaller may require sponsors with less influence. If there is a mismatch between the influence required and the amount of influence the stakeholder has or is perceived to have, develop risk plans and responses and other strategies that might be needed to obtain the required level of support.

► **Influence with other stakeholders.** Within most organizations there is an informal way influence occurs. It is best to be aware of this informal influence structure. For example, if there are stakeholders who consider themselves project champions, they can be helpful in converting those who are less enthusiastic or even outwardly hostile to the project purpose and designated outcomes.

.4   Authority Levels For Business Analysis Work

Identify which stakeholders will have authority over business analysis activities, in relation to both business analysis work and product deliverables. Stakeholders may have authority to:

► Approve the deliverables

► Inspect and approve the requirements

► Request and approve changes

► Approve the requirements process that will be used

► Review and approve the traceability structure

► Veto proposed requirements or solutions (individually or in a group)

Additional information on authority levels can be found in *Plan Requirements Management Process (2.5)*.

2.2.5   Techniques

.1   General Techniques

Acceptance and Evaluation Criteria Definition (9.1): The business analyst should, as part of the stakeholder analysis, identify which stakeholders have sufficient authority to accept or reject the solution.

Brainstorming (9.3): May assist in identifying needs and requirements that lead to possible stakeholders, or in creating a listing of possible stakeholder roles.

Interviews (9.14): Interviewees may be able to identify other stakeholders.

Organization Modeling (9.19): Assess to determine if the organizational units or people listed have any unique needs and interests that should be considered. It will describe the roles and functions in the organization and the ways in which stakeholders interact and so will help to identify stakeholders who are affected by a change.

Process Modeling (9.21): Any person involved in the execution of business processes affected by the solution will be a stakeholder. Process models can be a source for identifying additional stakeholders, since related processes may be affected. In addition, categorizing stakeholders by the systems that support their business processes can be useful when changes need to be made to those processes and systems.

Requirements Workshops (9.23): During requirements workshops, the business analyst may ask participants if they can suggest other stakeholders.

Risk Analysis (9.24): Risks to the initiative may result from stakeholder attitudes or the ability of key stakeholders to participate in the initiative.

Scenarios and Use Cases (9.26), and **User Stories (9.33):** Identified stakeholder roles may serve as a useful starting point for identifying actors and roles.

Scope Modeling (9.27): Scope models should show stakeholders that fall outside the scope of the solution but still interact with it in some way.

Survey/Questionnaire (9.31): Useful for identifying shared characteristics of a stakeholder group.

.2   RACI Matrix

The RACI matrix describes the roles of those involved in business analysis activities. It describes stakeholders as having one or more of the following responsibilities for a given task or deliverable:

► **[R]esponsible** does the work,

► **[A]ccountable** is the decision maker (only one)

► **[C]onsulted** must be consulted prior to the work and gives input

► **[I]nformed** means that they must be notified of the outcome

An example of a RACI Matrix may be seen below:

Figure 2–4: Sample RACI Matrix

Change Request Process	RACI
Executive Sponsor	A
Business Analyst	R
Project Manager	C
Developer	C
Tester	I
Trainer	I
Application Architect	C
Data Modeler	C
Database Analyst (DBA)	C
Infrastructure Analyst	C
Business Architect	R
Information Architect	C
Solution Owner	C
End User	I
Subject Matter Expert (SME)	C
Other Stakeholders	R, C, I (varies)

.3   Stakeholder Map

Stakeholder maps are visual diagrams that depict the relationship of stakeholders to the solution and to one another. There are many forms of stakeholder map, but two common ones include:

► A matrix mapping the level of stakeholder influence against the level of stakeholder interest

► An onion diagram indicating how involved the stakeholder is with the solution (which stakeholders will directly interact with the solution or participate in a business process, which are part of the larger organization, and which are outside the organization)

Stakeholder maps often include lines of communication between stakeholders.

Figure 2–5: Stakeholder Matrix

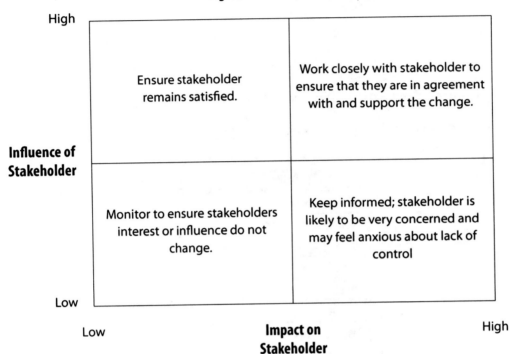

Figure 2–6: Stakeholder Onion Diagram

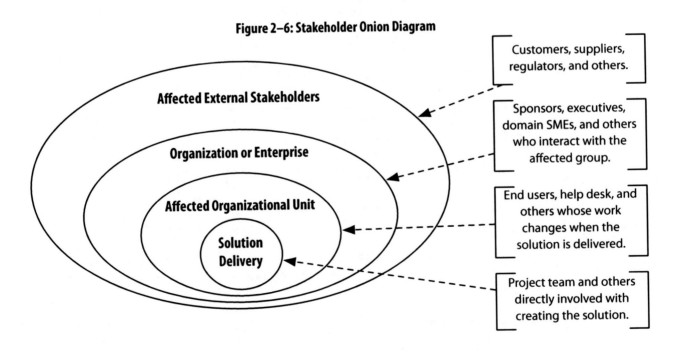

2.2.6   Stakeholders

Domain SME: May be able to recommend other business experts to assist in defining requirements.

Implementation SME: May be able to identify and recommend stakeholders.

Project Manager: May be able to identify and recommend stakeholders. In the context of a project with a designated project manager, responsibility for stakeholder identification and management must be shared with the project manager. The business analyst and project manager should collaborate on performing this task. The project manager is accountable for ensuring that the project team meets commitments made to the stakeholders, managing the assignment of stakeholders to project tasks and their involvement in the execution of the project, and ensuring that changes that impact the project scope are appropriately managed and approved. The business analyst will also assist the project manager in defining which project team members should be involved in developing, reviewing or approving business analysis deliverables.

Tester: May be able to identify and recommend stakeholders.

Regulator: May require that specific stakeholder representatives or groups be involved in the process.

Sponsor: May be able to identify domain subject matter experts to help with requirements definition.

2.2.7   Output

Stakeholder List, Roles, and Responsibilities: This may include information such as:

- ▶ List of required roles
- ▶ Names and titles of stakeholders
- ▶ Category of stakeholder
- ▶ Location of stakeholders
- ▶ Special needs
- ▶ Number of individuals in this stakeholder role
- ▶ Description of stakeholder influence and interest
- ▶ Documentation of stakeholder authority levels

2.3   Plan Business Analysis Activities

2.3.1   Purpose

Determine the activities that must be performed and the deliverables that must be produced, estimate the effort required to perform that work, and identify the management tools required to measure the progress of those activities and deliverables.

2.3.2 Description

The business analyst determines which activities are required for a given initiative, how those activities will be carried out, the work effort involved, and an estimate of how long the activities will take. This task includes activities to:

▶ Identify business analysis deliverables

▶ Determine the scope of work for the business analysis activities

▶ Determine which activities the business analyst will perform and when

▶ Develop estimates for business analysis work.

The activities that are executed and how they are executed will determine the quality and timeliness of the business analysis deliverables and ultimately of the solution. The business analysis plan(s) identify and schedule the activities and resources required to produce a clear, concise set of requirements that support development of the solution.

This planning activity will typically occur more than once on a given initiative or project, as plans frequently must be updated to address changing business conditions, issues encountered by the business analyst or other team members, lessons learned through the performance of business analysis activities, or other changing circumstances.

One way of accommodating change on a larger initiative is to plan on an incremental or rolling-wave basis. This approach to planning creates a high-level plan for the long term and detailed plans to address near-term activities, with the understanding that the long-term plans will change as more information becomes available. An alternative, used in change-driven methodologies, is to follow a well-defined, time-limited process for developing requirements and limit each iteration to the work that can be completed in the time allotted. A long-term roadmap may be used to set expectations, but the contents of the roadmap are constantly revisited as priorities change.

2.3.3 Input

Business Analysis Approach: Defines the lifecycle, deliverables, templates, and tasks that should be included. Plan-driven approaches seek to define requirements as early as possible to reduce uncertainty, while change-driven approaches encourage requirements to be defined as close to implementation as possible. These differences will lead to different deliverables and tasks being identified as well as different sequences and dependencies of tasks. The approach will also determine how the planning process is performed.

Business Analysis Performance Assessment: The business analyst must use prior experiences on this initiative or on others to determine the effort involved in performing business analysis work.

Organizational Process Assets: The organizational standards and process assets in place may mandate certain deliverables. Lessons learned from previous initiatives, as well as from currently ongoing business analysis activities, may be used in the development of business analysis plans.

Stakeholder List, Roles, and Responsibilities: Stakeholders will exhibit individual

Figure 2–7: *Plan Business Analysis Activities* Input/Output Diagram

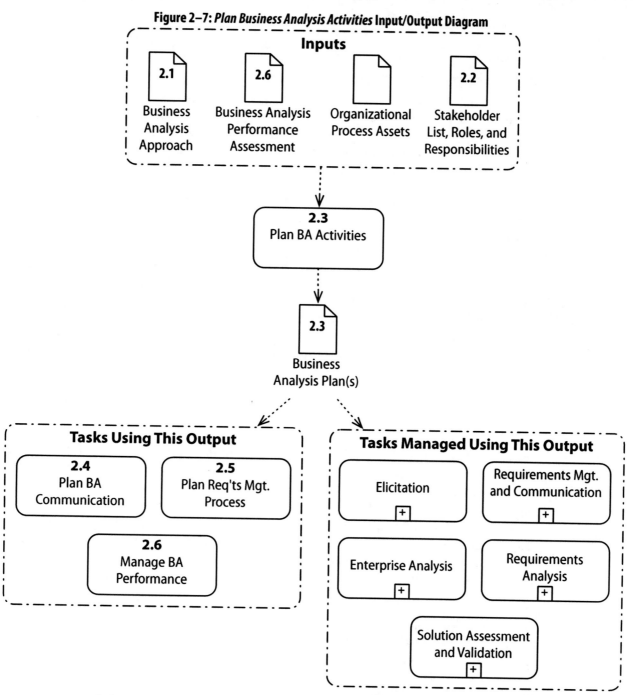

behaviors and preferences that may need to be met. For example, one key stakeholder may prefer the use of process maps, which could influence the planning of business analysis tasks related to this stakeholder. Another stakeholder may have some experience using a particular technology and be in favor of its choice for the current project, which might also influence the business analysis deliverables, tasks, and estimates. Understanding their roles and responsibilities on the project will help to determine how much those preferences will shape the plan. In addition, time will have to be set aside to work with stakeholders to elicit and analyze requirements and for those stakeholders with decision-making authority to approve requirements. The role of each stakeholder must be understood so that the appropriate activities can be scheduled and the necessary time allotted.

2.3.4   Elements

.1   Geographic Distribution of Stakeholders

The business analyst must consider the physical location of key stakeholders on the project. Some projects will have the stakeholders located in a single location while others will have some of their key stakeholders dispersed over a wide area. These latter projects may well involve increased complexity, which will have an impact on the estimate of some activities and tasks in the project. Stakeholders may be collocated or dispersed.

Collocated: All key stakeholders are located in the same local geographic area. There are no special location-related planning considerations for the business analyst involved in these projects.

Dispersed: These more complex projects have some key stakeholders located in different geographic regions or countries. The factors of distance, possible time differences and cultural and language differences increase the complexity for business analysis and will require effort to identify and account for these differences and how they will affect requirements planning and solution development/selection, testing and implementation. If stakeholders are dispersed, it may be necessary to have more teleconferences or videoconferences rather than face to face meetings.

Another common situation involves an outsourced development project where the development team is physically located many time zones away. This type of situation, for example, will be accounted for during business analysis planning and might be better served with more detailed requirements documentation and acceptance criteria or more frequent review sessions.

.2   Type of Project or Initiative

The type of project or initiative to which the business analyst is assigned may have a significant impact on the activities that need to be performed. For example, in a project to purchase a new software package, the work will be different from an effort to develop a new business process. Different kinds of business analysis initiatives include, but are not limited to:

► Feasibility studies

► Process improvement

► Organizational change

► New software development (in-house)

► Outsourced new software development

► Software maintenance or enhancement

► Software package selection

.3   Business Analysis Deliverables

A list of deliverables is useful as a basis for activity identification. Methods for identifying deliverables include, but are not limited to:

► Interviews or facilitated sessions with key stakeholders.

► Review project documentation.

► Review organizational process assets, such as methodologies and templates, which may dictate which deliverables are required,

An organization may have a standard set of deliverables, or multiple sets that are used to support different approved methodologies. The breakdown of deliverables may also be dependent on the techniques selected by the business analyst, and may include deliverables such as interview questions, meeting minutes, use case diagrams and descriptions, and as-is/to be business process models. The business analysis approach frequently mandates the use of certain techniques. Most agile methods assume that user stories will be used to document stakeholder requirements, and a Business Process Management initiative will require process modeling.

Frequently, additional techniques may be selected on an ad-hoc basis during execution of business analysis as the business analyst encounters situations for which they are most appropriate. For example, the business analyst may decide to elicit requirements using a requirements workshop, and then determine in that workshop that a particular stakeholder has additional requirements which are best identified through an interview or observing that stakeholder on the job.

Deliverables will often take the form of a requirements package, as described in *Prepare Requirements Package (4.4)*. The selection and format of requirements packages is likely to be mandated by the business analysis approach.

.4 Determine Business Analysis Activities

An important tool in defining the scope of work and in developing estimates is the work breakdown structure (WBS). The WBS decomposes the project scope into smaller and smaller pieces, creating a hierarchy of work. A WBS may break down the project into iterations, releases, or phases; break deliverables into work packages; or break activities into smaller tasks.

Work packages include at least one and usually many activities, which can be further broken into smaller and smaller tasks. This decomposition of activities and tasks creates the Activity List.

The Activity List can be created in different ways, such as by:

► Taking each deliverable, assigning the activities required to complete the deliverable, and breaking each activity into tasks

► Dividing the project into phases, iterations, increments, or releases, identifying the deliverables for each, and adding activities and tasks accordingly

► Using a previous similar project as an outline and expanding it with detailed tasks unique for the business analysis phase of the current project

The elements identified for each activity and task may include:

▶ **Unique Number** to uniquely identify each task.

▶ **Activity description** labeled with a verb and a noun, and describing the detailed tasks that comprise each activity. For example, an activity might be labeled "Update Requirements Document".

In addition, it may include other information, such as:

Assumptions: For each task, there may be factors or conditions which are considered to be true. The business analyst can document these factors, and where present estimates will be developed using these assumptions.

Dependencies: Identify logical relationships, such as which activities have to be completed before subsequent tasks can begin.

Milestones: Represent significant events in the progress of a project. Milestones are used to measure the progress of the project and compare actual progress to earlier estimates. Milestones can be used as a time to celebrate the completion or delivery of a major deliverable or section of project work. An example of a major milestone is the stakeholders' and sponsor's formal approval of a requirements document.

2.3.5 Techniques

Estimation (9.10): A variety of estimation techniques can be used to produce an overall assessment of the amount of business analysis work required. In some cases, multiple techniques may be used to validate one another. Estimates are normally developed in conjunction with the project manager and other team members, and make use of the organizational methodology and templates for developing estimates.

Functional Decomposition (9.12): Decomposition of the tasks in a project (using a work breakdown structure) or product (using a solution breakdown structure) can be used to facilitate an understanding of the work at a sufficient level of detail to enable estimation of tasks.

Risk Analysis (9.24): Identify risks that might impact the business analysis plan(s).

2.3.6 Stakeholders

All stakeholders listed here may potentially participate in the verification and validation of business analysis deliverables.

Customer, Domain SME, End User, and **Supplier:** Domain SMEs will likely be a major source of requirements and their availability is critical when planning activities. Their understanding of business analysis techniques may shape the selection of techniques or require that the business analyst devote some time to assist them in understanding how the requirements are defined. Customers and suppliers may be especially difficult to schedule effectively.

Implementation SME: The Implementation SMEs may participate in business analysis activities in order to facilitate understanding of stakeholder needs. They will need to know in what form and when deliverables will be produced as inputs into their own activity planning.

Operational Support: May use business analysis deliverables as a basis for planning operational support activities or developing appropriate documentation.

Project Manager: In a project, the business analysis plan is integrated with and a component of the overall project plan. The project manager should participate in business analysis planning and is responsible for ensuring that those plans are integrated with the work performed by other project personnel. In addition, the scope of business analysis work within a project is managed as part of the overall project scope, and changes to that scope of work (for example, as new stakeholders are identified or business requirements change) may require approval of a project scope change. The project manager will also play a key role in identifying resources to perform tasks, scheduling the activities, and developing cost estimates.

Tester: Will need to know in what form and when deliverables will be produced as inputs into their own activity planning.

Sponsor: Must participate in the approval of business analysis deliverables.

2.3.7   Output

Business Analysis Plan(s): The business analysis plan(s) may include information such as a description of the scope of work, the deliverable Work Breakdown Structure, an Activity List, and estimates for each activity and task. It should also describe when and how the plan should be changed in response to changing conditions. The level of detail associated with the plan(s) is determined by the business analysis approach and the overall methodology.

Note: All tasks in all other knowledge areas have business analysis plans as an implicit input. The plan(s) determine when and how any task is performed.

2.4   Plan Business Analysis Communication

2.4.1   Purpose

A business analysis communications plan describes the proposed structure and schedule for communications regarding business analysis activities. Record and organize the activities to provide a basis for setting expectations for business analysis work, meetings, walkthroughs, and other communications.

2.4.2   Description

Planning business analysis communications includes determining how best to receive, distribute, access, update, and escalate information from project stakeholders, and determining how best to communicate with each stakeholder.

Requirements can be presented in various formats. This task describes the work required to decide which format(s) are appropriate for a particular initiative and its stakeholders. Requirements should be presented in formats that are understandable for the reviewer; they must be clear, concise, accurate, and at the appropriate level of detail.

Considerations for the business analysis communications plan include:

▶ what needs to be communicated;

▶ what is the appropriate delivery method;

▶ who is the appropriate audience;

▶ and when the communication should occur.

Stakeholder needs and constraints relevant to communication include:

▶ Physical location/time zone of the stakeholders.

▶ Communication approach for the stakeholder.

▶ What types of communications will be required (e.g. status, anomalies, issues and their resolution, risks, meeting results, action items, etc.)

▶ What types of requirements will be elicited (business, stakeholder, solution, or transition; high level vs. detailed) and how best to elicit them (see the *Elicitation* KA for options).

▶ How best to communicate requirements conclusions/packages, including authority level (signoff authority, veto authority, or review only).

▶ Time and resource availability constraints.

2.4.3   Input

Business Analysis Approach: May include standards and templates used for communication, and expectations regarding when and how communication should occur.

Business Analysis Plan(s): Determines when work will be performed and the deliverables that will be produced, and which need to be communicated.

Organizational Process Assets: May include a defined set of templates for use in business analysis communication, including presentation formats, requirements documentation templates, and others.

Stakeholder List, Roles, and Responsibilities: Used to identify the stakeholders who will require information regarding business analysis work, determine when information needs to be provided, and how a stakeholder is expected to use that information.

Figure 2–8: *Plan Business Analysis Communication* **Input/Output Diagram**

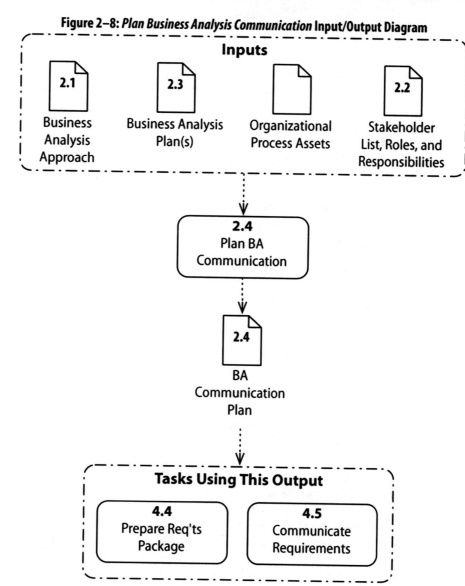

2.4.4 Elements

.1 Geography

The communications needed for a team that is collocated will be different from communications required for a project with geographically dispersed stakeholders. For example, it is more difficult to have short, daily team meetings when the participants live in vastly different time zones, when technology is not readily accessible, and where multiple, complex deliverables with complex interfaces are being developed simultaneously in different locations.

.2 Culture

Cultural diversity should also be taken into account when planning communications. Cultural considerations are important regardless of where the team members are located.

In addition to the obvious language barriers, there may be more subtle differences that should be considered in the plan, including:

▶ **Relationship to time.** Some cultures view deadlines as firm commitments, while others may view deadlines as a goal to be balanced against other concerns and interests.

▶ **Relationship to task completion.** Some cultures complete tasks because they have committed to the planned activities. Others complete tasks primarily when trust and the human relationship have been built.

▶ **Relationship to contracts.** Some cultures believe in the letter of the law, others in the spirit of the contract. This difference might surface when creating Requests for Proposal, for example.

▶ **Relationship to formal and informal authority.** Some cultures prefer a centralized power structure where decisions are made by a small group, while others prefer to involve all affected stakeholders in approving decisions.

The use of models following a standardized notation can help overcome language barriers by eliminating the need for many textual descriptions.

.3   Project Type

Different projects will necessitate different deliverables, and the extent of documentation that is needed in a requirements package will vary depending on the project. Some examples are:

A new, customized in-house software development project. In this scenario, all requirements may need to be included.

Upgrading the technology or infrastructure of a current system. In this scenario, only the technical requirements may need to be included in the package.

Change in a business process or new data for an existing application. In this scenario, the process and data requirements, business rules, functional and technical requirements will be needed.

Purchase of a software package. This type of project will likely require a Request For Proposal, and the package will need to include the business requirements, technical requirements, limited functional requirements and other vendor specifications.

Short, focused, agile style iterations of software development. These projects may not specify any or very little formal requirements documentation. Whiteboards, flip charts, and user stories may suffice. Agile focuses on creating the minimum necessary of documentation to deliver the requirements, and many agile teams will prefer to document the solution after it has been delivered.

.4   Communication Frequency

Investigates the frequency required by various stakeholders for each type of communication. Note the frequency of reporting can vary from stakeholder to stakeholder. For example, the frequency of reporting business analysis status can be biweekly for the sponsor, weekly for the Domain Subject Matter Experts and biweekly for the technical partners.

.5   Communications Formality

Planning communications requires taking into consideration the level of formality that is needed. This could vary from stakeholder to stakeholder, project phase to project phase, work within a project phase, and requirements presentation.

Communication tends to be more formal under the following circumstances:

► The project is unusually large (by organizational standards) and will be delivered in phases. The level of communications formality tends to increase as the scale of a project increases. This is because more stakeholders are typically involved and more communication is required.

► The domain involved is very complex. Note that the domain affected by the project may span departmental and divisional boundaries within the organization. For example, the domain of engineering employee recruitment could involve the engineering, human resources, payroll, marketing and benefits administration departments. These groups will all be key stakeholders for the project and its deliverables.

► The technology employed, if any, will be new, or new to the organization.

► The project is considered to be mission critical, in that it is tied directly to strategic objectives.

► The executive sponsor and/or key stakeholders require formality.

► The requirements are likely to be subject to regulatory review.

► The requirements will be presented to suppliers in an RFQ/RFI/RFP.

2.4.5   Techniques

See *Prepare Requirements Package (4.4)* and *Communicate Requirements (4.5)* for additional information. Communication techniques are described in *Communication Skills (8.4)*.

Structured Walkthrough (9.30): One of the most common approaches to requirements communication. Time to conduct each walkthrough and address the issues raised during the walkthrough must be included in the plan.

2.4.6   Stakeholders

Customer and **Supplier:** Major customers of an organization or suppliers to that organization (particularly institutional customers) may need to be informed of planned changes well in advance of implementation.

Domain SME: May be involved in review and approval. Likely to focus on matters of particular interest or on the areas on which they are an SME. Domain SMEs often have influence over the approvers, even if their approval is not formally required.

End User: May be involved in review and approval. May also have considerable influence over approvers even if their approval is not formally required.

Implementation SME: May be involved in review and approval.

Operational Support: May be involved in review and approval. Will primarily focus on the requirements to support the solution.

Project Manager: In a project, the business analysis communication plan will generally be integrated into the overall project communications plan. On small projects the plan may be very brief and may not be formally documented. On large and complex projects and projects with many stakeholders, it may be included as part of the project initiation documentation and is essential as part of the overall project communications plan.

Tester: Will primarily be involved in verification and validation of the requirements.

Regulator: Regulators may require that requirements, decisions, and other information regarding the execution of business analysis processes or the definition of the solution be retained and made available to them for review.

Sponsor: Communication needs for the sponsor are likely to focus on business requirements and high-level stakeholder and solution requirements.

2.4.7   Output

Business Analysis Communication Plan: Describes how, when and why the business analyst will work directly with stakeholders. Components can include:

▶ The stakeholder communications requirements for business analysis activities.

▶ Format, content, medium, level of detail.

▶ Responsibility for collecting, distributing, accessing, and updating information.

2.5   Plan Requirements Management Process

2.5.1   Purpose

Define the process that will be used to approve requirements for implementation and manage changes to the solution or requirements scope.

2.5.2   Description

This task determines the appropriate requirements management process for a particular initiative. It includes determining the process for requirements change, which stakeholders need to approve change, who will be consulted or informed of changes, and by extension, who does not need to be involved. The task also includes assessing the need for requirements traceability and determining which requirements attributes will be captured.

2.5.3   Input

Business Analysis Approach: The selected approach may include a definition of appropriate requirements management processes.

Business Analysis Plan(s): The business analysis plan(s) define which deliverables are to be produced and when. Deliverables cannot be managed until they are created.

Organizational Process Assets: Standard templates or processes for requirements management within the organization may exist. The business analyst must be knowledgeable about the organization's approach to requirements definition, as it will greatly influence the process steps, tasks and deliverables required or expected during the requirements planning and monitoring activities.

Figure 2–9: *Plan Requirements Management Process* **Input/Output Diagram**

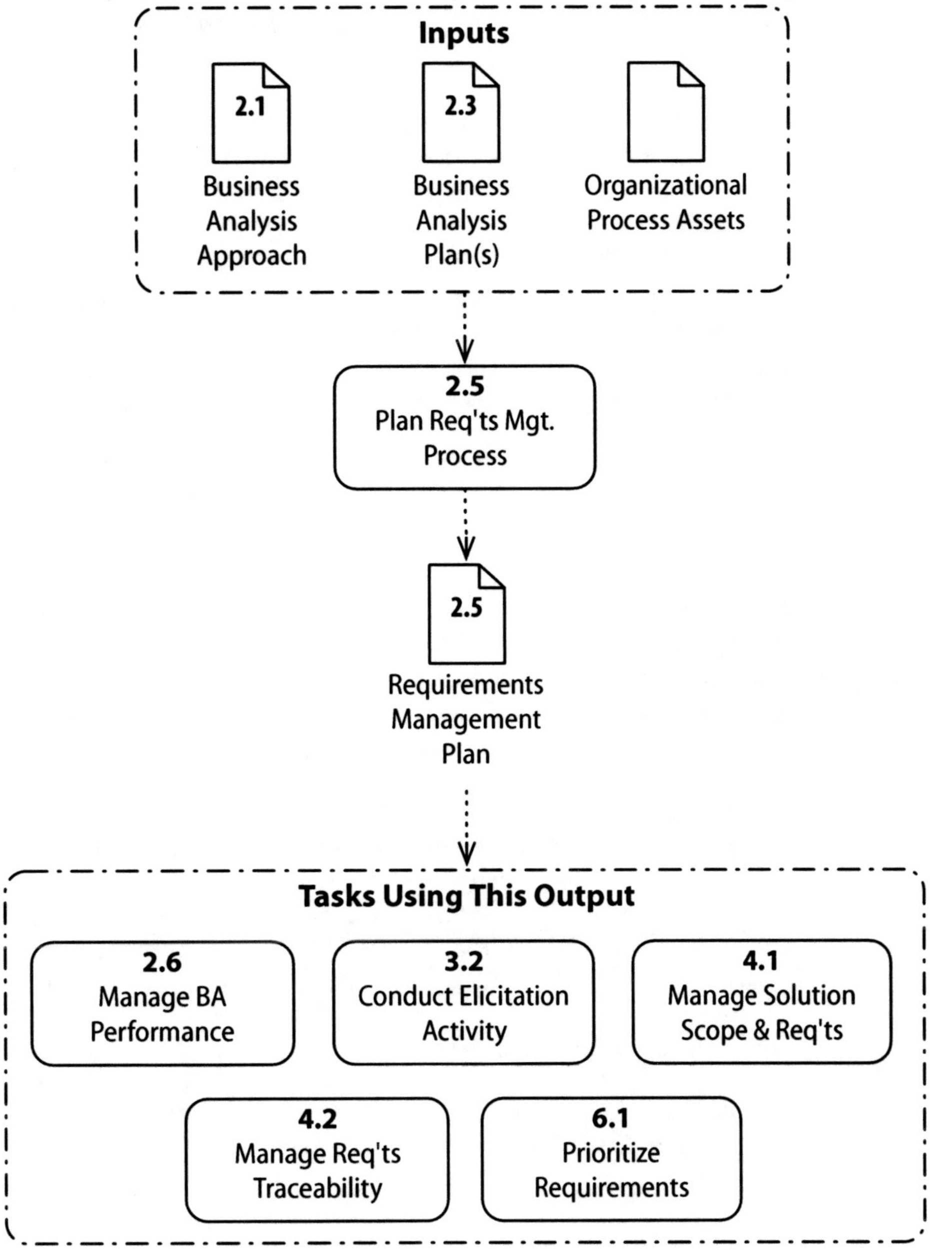

2.5.4 Elements

.1 Repository

A requirements repository is a method of storing requirements, including those under development, those under review, and approved requirements. Repositories may include whiteboards, word processing documents, diagrams and models, wikis, requirements management tools and applications, or any other method of recording information that allows requirements to be single-sourced and available to all relevant stakeholders for as long as they are needed. All approved requirements should be found in a repository (as opposed to using tools such as email, which may not reach all relevant stakeholders and may not be retained) and stakeholders need to be able to locate requirements in that repository.

The system for adding, changing and deleting requirements should be consistent and clearly understood by the team. File or component naming standards will assist with categorizing and maintaining requirements.

.2 Traceability

Determine whether and how to trace requirements based on the complexity of the domain, the number of views of requirements that will be produced, potential impacts from risk, and an understanding of the costs and benefits involved. Tracing requirements adds considerable overhead to business analysis work and must be done correctly and consistently to have value.

See *Manage Requirements Traceability (4.2)* for additional information.

.3 Select Requirements Attributes

Requirements attributes provide information about requirements, such as the source of the requirement, the importance of the requirement, and other metadata. Attributes aid in the ongoing management of the requirements throughout the project lifecycle. They need to be planned for and determined, along with the requirement themselves, but are not in themselves part of the solution definition.

Requirements attributes allow the requirements team to associate information with individual or related groups of requirements and facilitate the requirements analysis process by expressing such things as which requirements may add project risk or require additional analysis. The information documented by the attributes helps the team efficiently and effectively make tradeoffs between requirements, identify stakeholders affected by potential changes, and understand the impact of a proposed change.

Some commonly used requirements attributes include:

▶ **Absolute reference** is a unique numeric (preferred) or textual identifier. The reference is not to be altered or re-used if the requirement is moved, changed or deleted.

▶ **Author of the requirement**. If the requirement is later found to be ambiguous the author may be consulted for clarification.

► **Complexity** indicates how difficult the requirements will be to implement. This is often indicated through qualitative scales based on number of interfaces, complexity of essential processes or the number and nature of the resources required.

► **Ownership** indicates the individual or group that needs the requirement or will be the business owner after the project is released into the target environment.

► **Priority** indicates which requirements need to be implemented first. See below for further discussion on prioritizing and managing requirements.

► **Risks** associated with meeting or not meeting the requirements.

► **Source of the requirement.** Every requirement must originate from a source that has the authority to define this particular set of requirements. The source must be consulted if the requirement changes, or if more information regarding the requirement or the need that drove the requirement has to be obtained.

► **Stability** is used to indicate how mature the requirement is. This is used to determine whether the requirement is firm enough to start work on. Note that the ongoing presence of large numbers of unstable core requirements may indicate significant risk to project continuance.

► **Status** of the requirement, indicating such things as whether it is proposed, accepted, verified, postponed, cancelled, or implemented.

► **Urgency** indicates how soon the requirement is needed. It is usually only necessary to specify this separately from the priority when a deadline exists for implementation.

► Additional attributes may include information such as cost, resource assignment, and revision number, traced-from and traced-to.

.4   Requirements Prioritization Process

Requirements do not all deliver the same value to stakeholders. Requirements prioritization focuses effort on determining which requirements should be investigated first, based on the risk associated with them, the cost to deliver them, the benefits they will produce, or other factors. Timelines, dependencies, resource constraints, and other factors influence how requirements are prioritized. Planning the requirement prioritization process helps ensure that stakeholders determine and understand how requirements will be prioritized throughout and at the end of the business analysis effort.

Formality. The formality and rigor of the requirements prioritization process is determined partly by the methodology chosen, and by the characteristics of the project itself. Differences will lie in the level of detail, the amount of formal structure in the prioritization process (i.e. formal meetings versus informal conversations) and the amount of documentation needed to support the prioritization process.

Establishing The Process And Technique. The process to plan how requirements prioritization will occur needs to include which prioritization technique(s) will be used.

Plan The Participation. The business analyst, in conjunction with the project manager and sponsor should work together to determine the participants needed for the prioritization process.

Whom to invite and who does the inviting depends on organizational norms and best practices. Since sponsors are ultimately accountable for the solution's effectiveness and major project decisions, they need to be invited to participate in the discussion, even if they delegate the participation to subject matter experts. Another key stakeholder is the project manager, whose project plan is dependent on which requirements are released and when. The invitees depend on methodologies, organizational norms, and the engagement of the sponsor. When there are multiple limiting factors, invite participants accordingly.

.5 Change Management

Some considerations when planning for handling changes are:

Determine the process for requesting changes. The process can, but does not have to, set authorization levels for approving changes. For example, it may be decided that if a change is estimated to take less than a certain number of hours or dollars, the requestor and project manager can approve the change. If a predefined time or cost limit is exceeded, the sponsor has to approve it.

Determine who will authorize changes. The planning activity needs to include a designation of who can approve changes after requirements have been approved. Plan-driven methods usually have a formal Change Control Board (CCB) or Change Authority, which considers the requested change, and provides initial judgment on the merits of that request. The CCB can consist of any number of people in any number of positions. It may or may not include the sponsor, the project manager, the business analyst, subject matter experts, or other parties. Change-driven methods are more likely to allow the project team or a single product owner to have direct control over changes.

Impact Analysis. Specify who will perform the analysis of such impacts as business processes, information requirements, system and hardware interfaces, other software products, other requirements, test strategies and plans, to name a few.

Plan the wording of the request. It is important to set the expectation at the beginning of the business analysis activities that although the amount of documentation required to request changes is project and methodology dependent, the wording of the request must be clear. The requested change must be expressed in unambiguous terms. Therefore, it will be necessary to discuss the nature of the request with the requestor and other interested stakeholders.

The requirements process needs to spell out the nature of the components within a request for change. These might include:

► **Cost and time estimates of change**

    ▷ For each item, work product, or technical product affected, a brief assessment of the expected cost of change is to be estimated. As a matter of good practice, reusability will yield improvements to the change process by limiting the extent and scope of changes to other components. The goal should be to ensure responsiveness to change, not raising unlimited objections and impediments to the change process.

    ▷ The estimate will provide an integrated view of the costs, resources needed, implementation timeframe, and any dependencies.

 ► **Benefits and risks of the change**

    ▷ How the change aligns with the project and business objectives to help ensure all changes add business value.

    ▷ Since there are often unintended consequences to what seems like a favorable change, the request should include a well-structured change analysis form (written or verbal), statements of the expected risks, including both negative and positive influence on project objectives. Benefits considered may include not only financial benefits, but also the technical aspects of product features, influences on project scope, time, cost, quality, resources, and the business case.

 ► **Recommended course of action for change**

    ▷ The course of action for the change needs to be explained with the understanding of benefits and risks in the previous section. Several alternative courses can be considered, including those recommended by the requestor and by other stakeholders. By weighing the relative benefits, risks, and other criteria for each option, the decision maker, designated by the approval process, can make a choice that will best serve the needs of the project.

    ▷ The various options considered and the reasoning for the option finally selected needs to be recorded.

    ▷ The recommended course of action needs to be complete enough to permit clear coordination of the parties affected by the change. For larger changes, this course of action might be a subproject within the context of the overall project, including elements that need to be put into the overall project plan.

 ► Updates to the communications plan and the method for communication of the change to affected stakeholders.

 ► Configuration management and traceability disciplines should establish product baselines and version control practices that will clearly identify which baseline is affected by the change.

Coordinate Prioritization Of Change. The priority of the proposed change must be established relative to other competing interests within the current project phase. The requestor should provide a priority as described in the section above. Project decision makers will need to consider the priority as well any potential risk of deferring implementation until a later time.

Change-Driven Methods

Change-driven methodologies (in particular, agile software development methods) do not typically have a change control process that is separate from the requirements prioritization process. All requirements, including "new" and "changed" requirements, are recorded in the product backlog and prioritized. At the beginning of each iteration, the highest priority requirements are selected from the backlog and estimated, and these estimates are used as input to determine whether the requirement will be implemented in that iteration.

.6   Tailoring the Requirements Management Process

An organization's requirements management process may need to be tailored to meet the needs of a specific initiative or project. Factors in the tailoring process include:

► **Organizational culture.** In organizations where the culture does not support formality, but where informality jeopardizes the end product, it will be necessary to work with the stakeholders to negotiate an appropriate process.

► **Stakeholder preferences.** Some stakeholders may require more or less formality. A sponsor may, for example, want formal approval but may not want a documented process for eliciting requirements. As above, it will be necessary to recommend the most appropriate approach to handling requirements, pointing out risks and impacts as needed.

► **Complexity of project, project phase, or product (product, service, or result) being delivered.** Formal processes for configuration management and change management are more likely to be used for:

  ▷ Projects that have many interfaces, many business and/or system impacts or span a variety of functional areas.

  ▷ Products that are built with many components and subcomponents, have complex interfaces, will be used by a variety and number of stakeholders, or have other complexities.

► **Organizational maturity.** Less mature organizations tend to be less likely to want to spend time or money creating a requirements process, and there may be outright resistance to the idea of having a process to define requirements.

► **Availability of resources** needed to support the effort of creating such a process is a major consideration. Internal groups, such as a Project Management Office and external sources such as consulting firms and even vendors may be able to augment organizational resources.

2.5.5   Techniques

Decision Analysis (9.8): Can be used to assess the possible value delivered by a change and assess areas of uncertainty.

Problem Tracking (9.20): Used to track possible changes and ensure that a decision is reached.

Risk Analysis (9.24): Used to identify possible risks associated with the change management process and possible risks associated with making or choosing not to make the change.

2.5.6   Stakeholders

Domain SME: Consulted in order to determine the importance of requirements and to assess the value of change requests.

End User: Consulted in order to determine the importance of requirements and to assess the value of change requests.

Implementation SME: Consulted in order to determine the difficulty of implementing a requirement or proposed change.

Operational Support: Informed of changes to requirements to ensure that the solution can operate effectively.

Project Manager: Responsible for managing changes to the project scope and accountable for delivery of the project scope. Changes to the solution and requirements scope are almost certain to impact the project scope. Similarly, changes to the project scope may impact the solution and requirements scope. Most projects use a single change management process to handle both and describe the impacts to solution and project scope in a single change request. This will require the involvement of the project manager in this task and agreement on the person responsible for the change management process.

Tester: Informed of changes to requirements to ensure that test plans are effective.

Sponsor: Accountable for the solution scope and must approve prioritization of requirements and changes to requirements.

2.5.7   Output

Requirements Management Plan. A requirements management plan describes the:

► Approach to be taken to structure traceability.

► Definition of requirements attributes to be used.

► Requirements prioritization process.

► Requirements change process, including how changes will be requested, analyzed, approved, and implemented.

2.6   Manage Business Analysis Performance

2.6.1   Purpose

To manage the performance of business analysis activities to ensure that they are executed as effectively as possible.

2.6.2   Description

This task covers determining which metrics will be used to measure the work performed by the business analyst. It includes how to track, assess, and report on the quality of the work and take steps to correct any problems that may arise. This may feed into the development of future business analysis plans. The selected metrics are defined and described in the organizational process assets or the business analysis plans.

This task also describes how organizational process assets governing business analysis activities are managed and updated.

Figure 2–10: *Manage Business Analysis Performance* Input/Output Diagram

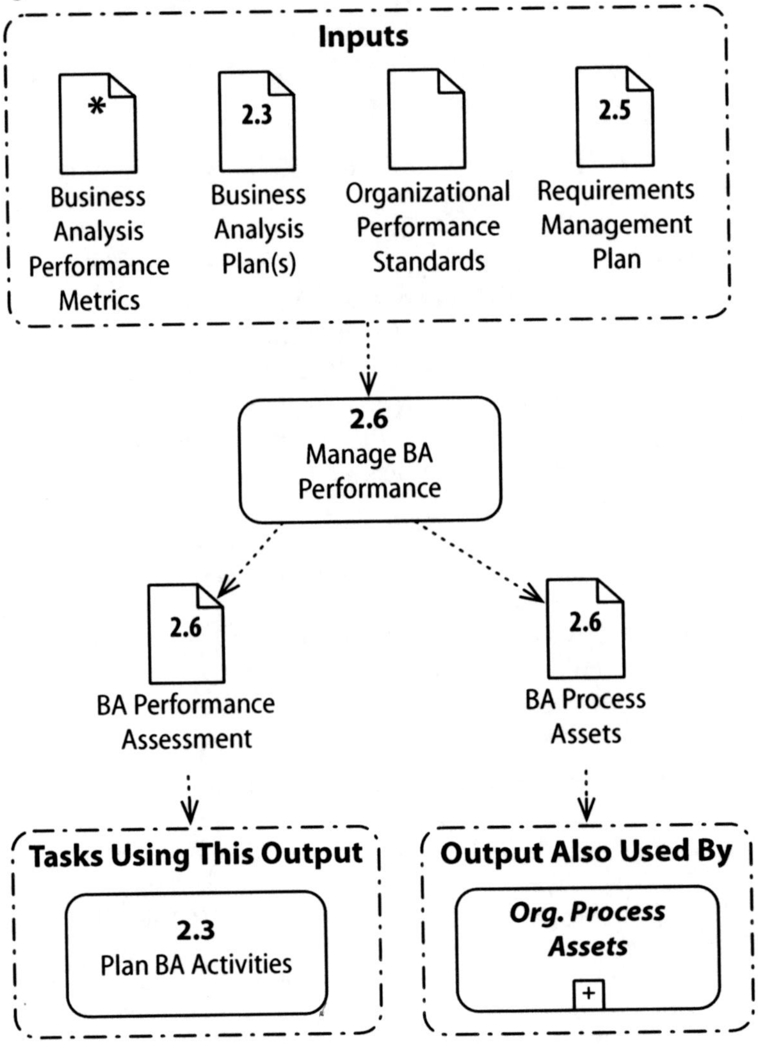

2.6.3 Input

Business Analysis Performance Metrics: Actual performance measures are captured, analyzed, and become the basis for taking corrective or preventive action. Capturing actual performance metrics is a process that occurs through the business analysis effort and is implicitly a potential output from every business analysis task.

Business Analysis Plan(s): These plans describe deliverables, activities, tasks, and estimates for all business analysis work. Conformance to these plans may be the primary metric used to judge performance.

Organizational Performance Standards: May include mandated performance metrics or expectations for business analysis work.

Requirements Management Plan: The requirements management plan may also set expectations for the frequency of changes to requirements and the work involved in managing that change.

2.6.4   Elements

.1   Performance Measures

Performance measures are used to set expectations regarding what constitutes effective business analysis work in the context of a particular organization or initiative. Performance measures may be based on deliverable due dates as specified in the business analysis plan, metrics such as the frequency of changes to requirements or the number of review cycles required, or qualitative feedback from stakeholders and peers of the business analyst. Appropriate performance measures should enable the business analyst to determine when problems are occurring that may affect the performance of business analysis or other activities, or identify opportunities for improvement.

.2   Performance Reporting

Reports can be in written format to provide for archival and tracking, or they can be informal and verbal, based on the needs of the project. Some reports may be made formally and orally as presentations to various levels of stakeholders and management.

.3   Preventive And Corrective Action

The business analyst should assess the performance measures to determine where problems in executing business analysis activities are occurring or opportunities for improving the business analysis process exist. Once this assessment is complete the business analyst should engage the necessary stakeholders to identify the correct preventative or corrective actions. Preventative or corrective action is likely to result in changes to the business analysis plan.

2.6.5   Techniques

.1   General Techniques

Interviews (9.14): Stakeholders may be interviewed to gather assessments of business analysis performance.

Lessons Learned Process (9.15): Helps identify changes to business analysis processes and deliverables that can be incorporated into future work.

Metrics and Key Performance Indicators (9.16): Can be used to determine what metrics are appropriate for assessing business analysis performance and how they may be tracked.

Problem Tracking (9.20): May be used to track issues that occur during the performance of business analysis for later resolution.

Process Modeling (9.21): Can be used to define business analysis processes and understand how to improve those processes to reduce problems from handoffs, improve cycle times, or alter how business analysis work is performed to support improvements in downstream processes.

Root Cause Analysis (9.25): Can help identify the underlying cause of failures or difficulties in accomplishing business analysis work.

Survey/Questionnaire (9.31): Can be used to gather feedback from a large number of stakeholders.

.2   Variance Analysis

The purpose of this technique is to analyze discrepancies between planned and actual performance, determine the magnitude of those discrepancies, and recommend corrective and preventive action as required. Variances can be related to planned versus actual estimates, cost, scope, product expectations, or any measures that have been established during the planning process.

When variances between the actual work and the plan are found, variance analysis measures the magnitude of the variation. Variance analysis also includes studying the causes of the variance to determine if corrective or preventive actions are required to bring the business analysis work in line with the business analysis plans.

2.6.6   Stakeholders

Domain SME and **End User:** Should be informed of the performance of business analysis activities in order to set expectations for their involvement.

Implementation SME, Operational Support, and **Tester:** Dependent on the effective performance of business analysis activities to perform their role. Should be consulted when assessing those activities.

Project Manager: The project manager is accountable for the success of a project and must be kept informed of the current status of business analysis work. If potential problems or opportunities for improvement are identified, the project manager must be consulted before changes are implemented to assess whether those changes will have an impact on the project. The project manager may also deliver reports on business analysis performance to the sponsor and other stakeholders.

Sponsor: May require reports on business analysis performance to address problems as they are identified. A manager of business analysts may also sponsor initiatives to improve the performance of business analysis activities.

2.6.7   Output

Business Analysis Performance Assessment: This includes a comparison of planned versus actual performance, understanding the root cause of variances from the plan, and other information to help understand the level of effort required to complete business analysis work.

Business Analysis Process Assets: When the analysis of the performance of the business analysis work yields less than satisfactory results, it is helpful to review not only the results themselves, but also the process that produced those results. This process analysis often results in recommendations for improvement to the business analysis process. The revised process and templates for business analysis deliverables should be analyzed and documented and lessons learned should be recorded. These may be incorporated into Organizational Process Assets.

Elicitation

Eliciting requirements is a key task in business analysis. Because the requirements serve as the foundation for the solution to the business needs it is essential that the requirements be complete, clear, correct, and consistent. Leveraging proven means to elicit requirements will help meet these quality goals. The definition of elicitation is[1]:

1. to draw forth or bring out (something latent or potential)

2. to call forth or draw out (as information or a response)

These definitions highlight the need to actively engage the stakeholders in defining requirements.

This chapter includes details for eliciting business, stakeholder, solution, or transition requirements. The business analyst should understand the commonly used techniques to elicit requirements, should be able to select appropriate technique(s) for a given situation, and be knowledgeable of the tasks needed to prepare, execute and complete each technique.

Eliciting requirements is not an isolated or compartmentalized activity. Typically, requirements are identified throughout the elicitation, analysis, verification and validation activities. For example, requirements may be elicited in interviews or requirements workshops. Later, when those requirements are used to build and verify model(s), gaps in the requirements may be discovered. This will then require eliciting details of those newly identified requirements.

To fully examine and define the requirements a combination of complementary elicitation techniques is typically used. A number of factors (the business domain, the corporate culture and environment, the skills of the analyst and the requirements deliverables that will be created) guide which techniques will be used.

Figure 3–1: Generally Accepted Elicitation Techniques and Synonyms

Elicitation Technique	Synonym
Brainstorming (9.3)	
Document Analysis (9.9)	Review existing documentation
Focus Groups (9.11)	
Interface Analysis (9.13)	External Interface Analysis
Interviews (9.14)	
Observation (9.18)	Job Shadowing
Prototyping (9.22)	Storyboarding, Navigation Flow, Paper Prototyping, Screen Flows
Requirements Workshops (9.23)	Elicitation Workshop, Facilitated Workshop
Survey/ Questionnaire (9.31)	

---

1. elicit. (2009). In Merriam-Webster Online Dictionary. Retrieved March 2, 2009, from http://www.merriam-webster.com/dictionary/elicit

Elicitation deliverables depend on the elicitation techniques used, e.g., interview notes, survey responses, glossary terms, and so forth.

It is expected that at some point while performing elicitation that sufficient material will have been elicited from the business experts to allow analysis activities to begin. The combined results of all the elicitation techniques used will serve as input to building the selected analytical models. Missing, incomplete or incorrect requirements will ideally be exposed during the analysis activities, thus requiring additional elicitation.

Note: the performance of all elicitation activities are governed by the business analysis plans (see 2.3), and business analysis performance metrics should be tracked (see 2.6).

Figure 3–2: *Elicitation* Input/Output Diagram

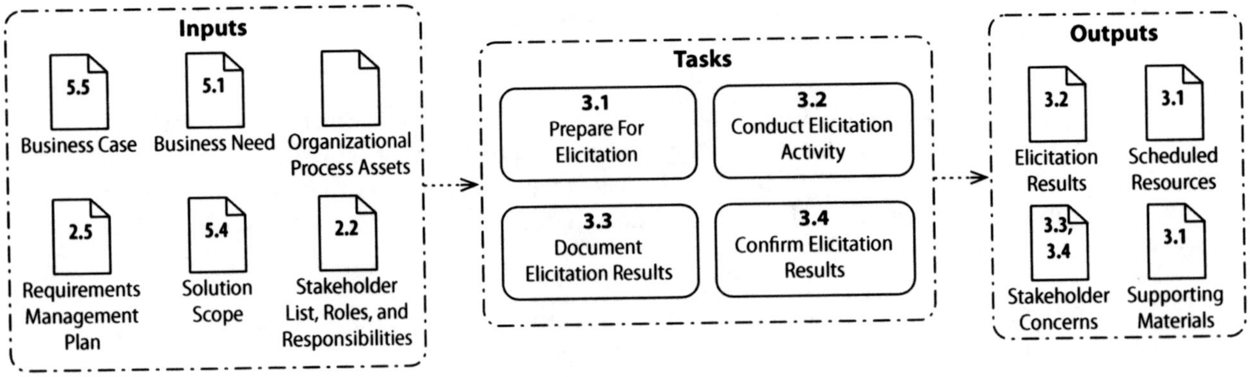

3.1   Prepare for Elicitation

3.1.1   Purpose

Ensure all needed resources are organized and scheduled for conducting the elicitation activities.

3.1.2   Description

Build a detailed schedule for a particular elicitation activity, defining the specific activities and the planned dates.

3.1.3   Input

Business Need: Required to ensure that the business analyst understands what information should be elicited from the stakeholders. This input is used when eliciting business requirements (with the exception of the business need itself).

Solution Scope and **Business Case:** Required to ensure that the business analyst understands what information should be elicited from the stakeholders. These inputs are used when eliciting stakeholder, solution, and transition requirements.

Stakeholder List, Roles, and Responsibilities: Used to identify the stakeholders who should participate in elicitation activities.

Figure 3–3: *Prepare for Elicitation* Input/Output Diagram

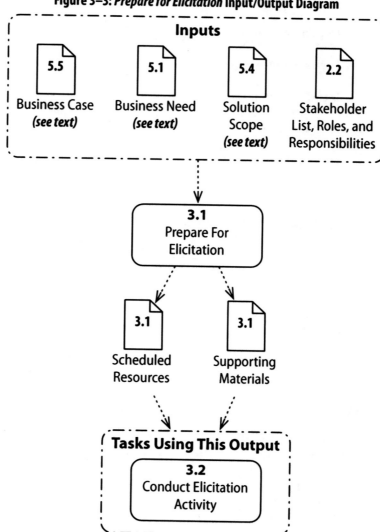

3.1.4 Elements

- Clarify the specific scope for the selected elicitation technique and gathers any necessary supporting materials.

- Schedule all resources (people, facilities, equipment).

- Notify appropriate parties of the plan.

For event-based elicitation (brainstorming, focus group, interview, observation, prototyping, requirements workshop) ground rules must be established. Agreement is reached with the stakeholders as to the form and frequency of feedback during the elicitation process as well as the mechanism for verifying and signing off on the elicited results.

3.1.5 Techniques

Additional information on the performance of this task can be found in the description of the relevant techniques.

- ► Brainstorming (9.3)

- ► Document Analysis (9.9)

- ► Focus Groups (9.11)

- ► Interface Analysis (9.13)

- ► Interviews (9.14)

- ► Observation (9.18)

- ► Prototyping (9.22)

- ► Requirements Workshops (9.23)

- ► Survey/Questionnaire (9.31)

3.1.6 Stakeholders

All Stakeholders: Depending on the requirements of the elicitation activity, any stakeholder may be a participant.

Project Manager: The project manager will assist in ensuring that the needed resources are available.

3.1.7 Output

Scheduled Resources: This includes the participants, the location in which the elicitation activity will occur, and any other resources that may be required.

Supporting Materials: Any materials required to help explain the techniques used or perform them.

3.2 Conduct Elicitation Activity

3.2.1 Purpose

Meet with stakeholder(s) to elicit information regarding their needs.

3.2.2 Description

The elicitation event takes place (brainstorming, focus groups, interviews, observation, prototyping, requirements workshops), or elicitation is performed (document analysis, interface analysis) or distributed (survey/questionnaire).

3.2.3 Input

Business Need: Required to ensure that the business analyst understands what information should be elicited from the stakeholders. This input is used when eliciting business requirements (with the exception of the business need itself).

Organizational Process Assets: May include templates or processes for these activities.

Requirements Management Plan: Determines what information needs to be recorded and tracked as an outcome of the activity. In particular, many requirements attributes must be elicited and captured while performing this task.

Scheduled Resources: The relevant stakeholders, location, and other resources must be available.

Solution Scope and **Business Case** are required to ensure that the business analyst understands what information should be elicited from the stakeholders. These inputs are used when eliciting stakeholder, solution, and transition requirements.

Supporting Materials: Whiteboards, flipcharts, documents, and other materials must be available while the activity is conducted.

Figure 3–4: *Conduct Elicitation Activity* **Input/Output Diagram**

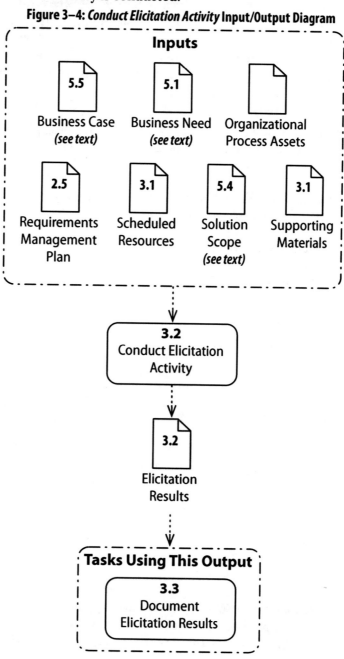

3.2.4   Elements

Tracing requirements: While eliciting the requirements it is important to guard against scope creep. Tracing requirements back to the business goals/objectives helps to validate whether a requirement should be included.

Capturing requirement attributes: While eliciting the requirements documenting requirements attributes such as the requirement's source, value and priority will aid in managing each requirement throughout its life cycle.

Metrics: Tracking the elicitation participants and the actual time spent eliciting the requirements provides a basis for future planning.

For event-based elicitation techniques, eliciting requirements is highly dependent on the knowledge of the stakeholders, their willingness to participate in defining requirements, and the group's ability to reach consensus. It is important that all defined stakeholders are heard during elicitation of requirements. It may be necessary to further clarify and possibly restate the requirements to encompass all stakeholders' perspectives.

3.2.5   Techniques

Data Dictionary and Glossary (9.5): A business glossary is an essential asset for all elicitation techniques. The glossary should contain key domain terms along with their business definitions.

General Techniques: Refer to each technique below for unique elements of conducting that particular technique.

- ▶ Brainstorming (9.3)
- ▶ Document Analysis (9.9)
- ▶ Focus Groups (9.11)
- ▶ Interface Analysis (9.13)
- ▶ Interviews (9.14)
- ▶ Observation (9.18)
- ▶ Prototyping (9.22)
- ▶ Requirements Workshops (9.23)
- ▶ Survey/Questionnaire (9.31)

3.2.6   Stakeholders

Customer, Domain SME, End User, Supplier and **Sponsor:** May participate in this task as a source of requirements.

Implementation SME, Operational Support, Project Manager, Supplier and **Tester:** May participate to improve their understanding of the stakeholder needs and to aid stakeholders in understanding the tradeoffs faced by the project team.

Regulator: May participate directly (as a source of requirements) and may also dictate that a specific process be followed or that certain records be kept.

3.2.7 Output

Elicitation Results: May include documentation appropriate to the technique and capture the information provided by the stakeholder.

3.3 Document Elicitation Results

3.3.1 Purpose

Record the information provided by stakeholders for use in analysis.

3.3.2 Description

For an elicitation event (brainstorming, focus groups, interviews, observation, prototyping, requirements workshops) a summary of the output from the event, including issues is produced.

3.3.3 Input

Elicitation Results: Includes the information provided by stakeholders that will be recorded and structured.

3.3.4 Elements

Documentation can take a number of forms, including:

► Written documents describing the outcomes, such as meeting minutes

► Visual or audio recordings

► Whiteboards (either actual or virtual) where notes are retained until they are transferred to another medium.

The technique used for elicitation, as well as the business analysis approach, will determine what kind of documentation is possible and desirable.

3.3.5 Techniques

Brainstorming (9.3): The activity generally produces the necessary documentation.

Document Analysis (9.9): A report of the findings should be produced.

Focus Groups (9.11): The results of a focus group are collated and summarized.

Interface Analysis (9.13): A report of the findings should be produced.

Interviews (9.14): Results of the interview are documented.

Observation (9.18): Results of observation are documented.

Problem Tracking (9.20): Elicitation may produce issues that need to be tracked to resolution.

Prototyping (9.22): The results of elicitation may undergo requirements analysis directly, without the need for an intermediate step to document them.

Requirements Workshops (9.23): The results of elicitation may undergo requirements analysis directly, without the need for an intermediate step to document them.

Survey/Questionnaire (9.31): The results of a survey are collated and summarized.

3.3.6 Stakeholders

Business Analyst: Other stakeholders do not need to participate in this task.

Figure 3–5: *Document Elicitation Results* **Input/Output Diagram**

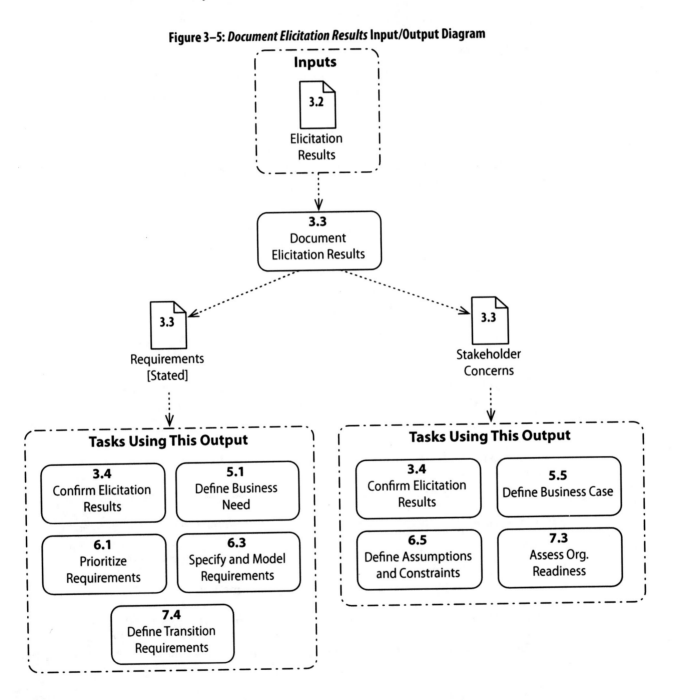

3.3.7   Output

Requirements [Stated]: Described from the perspective of the stakeholder. Stated requirements describe the stakeholder's need from the stakeholder's perspective.

Stakeholder Concerns: Includes issues identified by the stakeholder, risks, assumptions, constraints, and other relevant information.

3.4   Confirm Elicitation Results

3.4.1   Purpose

Validate that the stated requirements expressed by the stakeholder match the stakeholder's understanding of the problem and the stakeholder's needs.

3.4.2   Description

Some elicitation techniques benefit from reviewing the documented outputs with the stakeholders to ensure that the analyst's understanding conforms to the actual desires or intentions of the stakeholder.

3.4.3   Input

Requirements [Stated, Unconfirmed]: Represent the business analyst's understanding of the stakeholder's intentions.

Stakeholder Concerns [Unconfirmed]: Represent the business analyst's understanding of issues identified by the stakeholder, risks, assumptions, constraints, and other relevant information that may be used in business analysis.

3.4.4   Elements

Refer to the description of the relevant technique for unique aspects of confirming the results of the Interview and Observation techniques.

3.4.5   Techniques

▶   Interviews (9.14)

▶   Observation (9.18)

3.4.6   Stakeholders

Any stakeholder who has participated in other elicitation tasks may participate in this task.

3.4.7   Output

Requirements [Stated, Confirmed]: Identical to Requirements [Stated] for all practical purposes, including use as an input to other tasks.

Stakeholder Concerns [Confirmed]: Identical to Stakeholder Concerns for all practical purposes, including use as an input to other tasks.

Figure 3–6: *Confirm Elicitation Results* **Input/Output Diagram**

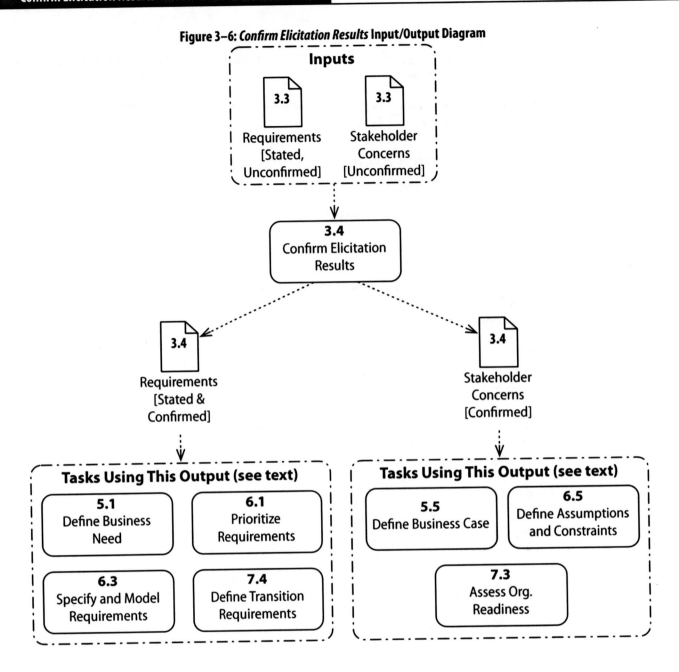

Requirements Management & Communication

The *Requirements Management and Communication* Knowledge Area describes the activities and considerations for managing and expressing requirements to a broad and diverse audience. These tasks are performed to ensure that all stakeholders have a shared understanding of the nature of a solution and to ensure that those stakeholders with approval authority are in agreement as to the requirements that the solution shall meet.

Communicating requirements helps to bring the stakeholders to a common understanding of the requirements. Because the stakeholders represent people from different backgrounds and business domains, this communication is both challenging and critical to the success of any initiative. It involves determining which sets of requirements are relevant to a particular stakeholder group and presenting those requirements in an appropriate format for that audience.

Management of requirements assists with understanding the effects of change and linking business goals and objectives to the actual solution that is constructed and delivered. Over the long term, it also ensures that the knowledge and understanding of the organization gained during business analysis is available for future use.

Note: the performance of all requirements management and communication activities are governed by the business analysis plans (see 2.3), and business analysis performance metrics should be tracked (see 2.6).

Figure 4–1: *Requirements Management and Communication* **Input/Output Diagram**

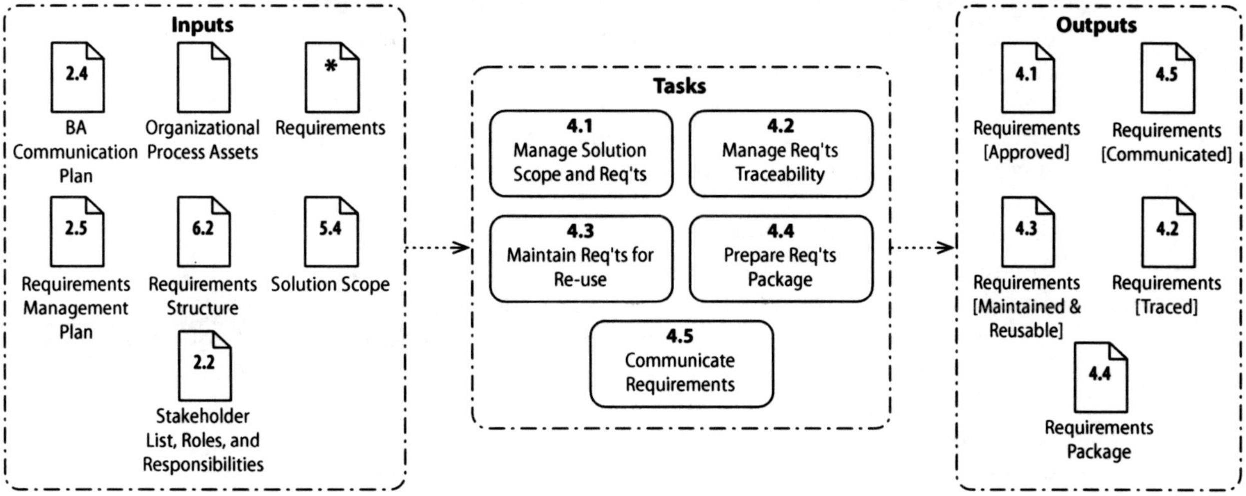

4.1 Manage Solution Scope & Requirements

4.1.1 Purpose

Obtain and maintain consensus among key stakeholders regarding the overall solution scope and the requirements that will be implemented.

4.1.2   ## Description

This task involves securing approval of requirements from those stakeholders who have the appropriate authority, and managing issues that emerge during elicitation and analysis. Approval of requirements may be sought at the end of a project phase or at a number of intermediate points in the business analysis process.

Requirements may be baselined following approval. Any changes to requirements after baselining, if changes are permitted, involves use of a change control process and subsequent approval. As requirements are refined or changed as the result of new information, changes will be tracked as well.

The solution scope is required as a basis for requirements management and is used to determine whether a proposed requirement supports the business goals and objectives. If the business need changes during the lifetime of an initiative, the solution scope must also change. Changes to the solution scope may also lead to changes in previously approved requirements, which may not support the revised scope.

Change-driven approaches typically do not use a formal change control process, as requirements are prioritized and selected for implementation at the beginning of each iteration and no changes to the requirements occur during an iteration.

4.1.3   ## Input

Requirements Management Plan: Defines the process to be followed in managing the solution scope and requirements.

Solution Scope: Requirements must support the solution scope in order to be approved, unless the solution scope is modified accordingly. The solution scope is also a requirement that can be managed in its own right. Changes to other business requirements generally do not fall within the normal change management process of a project, as they are external to the project scope.

Stakeholder List, Roles, and Responsibilities: This defines which stakeholders are involved in reviewing and approving requirements.

Stakeholder, Solution, or Transition Requirements [Communicated or Traced]: Requirements may be managed at any point in their lifecycle (stated, specified and modeled, verified, validated, etc.), although stakeholder approval is normally restricted to requirements that have been verified and validated. Requirements must be communicated to be managed, as stakeholders cannot consent to requirements if they are not aware of them. Requirements may also be managed if they can be traced to requirements that have been approved, as those requirements are a basis for determining whether other requirements fall within the scope of the solution.

4.1.4   ## Elements

.1   ### Solution Scope Management

All stakeholder and solution requirements must be assessed to ensure that they fall within the solution scope. Stakeholders will frequently identify additional needs that the solution may be capable of addressing. However, if these additional requirements are invalid (that is, they are not aligned with the approved business requirements) or

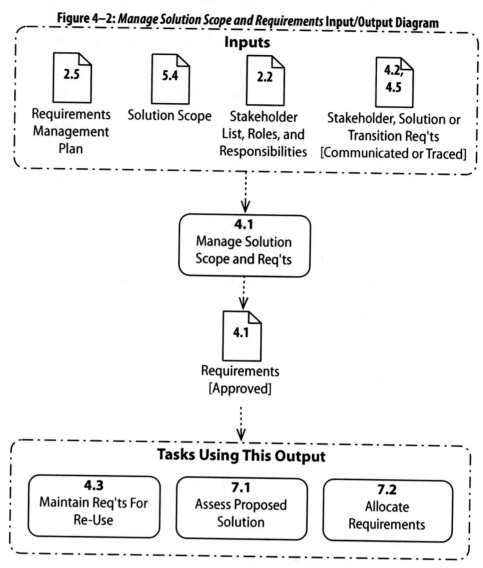

Figure 4–2: *Manage Solution Scope and Requirements* Input/Output Diagram

they do not fall within the solution scope, the business analyst must act to resolve the conflict. This may be done by amending the business requirements and solution scope or by reaching agreement that the requirement does not fall within the scope of the initiative.

.2   Conflict and Issue Management

As requirements are developed and reviewed, conflicts often arise. A conflict may result from stakeholders in different areas viewing requirements from different perspectives. It may also result from conflicting priorities. Inconsistent requirements cannot be satisfied by a single solution and so any inconsistency must be resolved.

Facilitate communication between the stakeholders who are in conflict over the requirement in order to resolve the issue. Conflicts may be resolved through formal meetings among affected stakeholders, through research, resolution by a third party, or other methods as appropriate. Conflicts that affect the requirements must be resolved before formal approval is given to those requirements.

.3   Presenting Requirements For Review

Determine how requirements will be presented to various stakeholders and whether presentations will be formal or informal. A formal presentation may be a written system requirements specification or a structured walkthrough with various levels of stakeholders, including executive summaries as well as a structured model including all of the associated diagrams, supporting text, detailed attributes, and revision information. A requirement may be presented informally in an e-mail message, a note, or verbally.

Assess the requirements, audience, and organizational process assets to determine the level of formality appropriate for business analysis communication. Generally, the more formal the communications, the more time that will be required to prepare for meetings, for reviews, for the presentation or requirements package, etc. Less formal communications may result in key stakeholders missing information or in increased ambiguity in requirements.

When presenting requirements for review and approval, there needs to be enough formality to support the methodology and ensure that the stakeholders will review, understand, and approve them.

.4   Approval

Ensure that the stakeholder(s) responsible for approving requirements understands and accepts the requirements. Stakeholder approval may be required for the result of other business analysis work, including allocation of requirements, proposed problem resolutions, and other decisions. Approval may be obtained from stakeholders individually or as a group.

A record of the decision may be kept. A decision record may include the decision made (whether or not to include the requirement or modify the scope), the reason for the decision, and the parties involved.

4.1.5   Techniques

.1   General Techniques

Problem Tracking (9.20): Allows the business analyst to manage any issues identified with requirements by stakeholders and ensure that those issues are resolved.

.2   Baselining

Once requirements are approved, they may be baselined, meaning that all future changes are recorded and tracked, and the current state may be compared to the baselined state. Subsequent changes to the requirement must follow the change control process.

As changes are approved, the requirements management plan may require that the baselined version of the requirement be maintained in addition to the changed requirement. Additional information is often maintained such as description of the change, person who made the change, and the reason for the change.

.3   Signoff

Requirements signoff formalizes agreement by stakeholders that the content and presentation of documented requirements is accurate and complete. A formal sign-off of requirements documentation may be required by organizational standards or for regulatory reasons.

Obtaining requirements signoff typically involves a face-to-face final review of requirements documentation with each stakeholder with authority to approve requirements. At the end of each review, the stakeholder is asked to formally approve the reviewed requirements document. This approval may be verbal or be recorded either physically or electronically.

If a stakeholder only has authority to sign-off on a subset of the requirements, a specific list of the requirements the stakeholder is approving, and a complementary list of the requirements the stakeholder is not approving (but to which the stakeholder explicitly has no objection) should be prepared. Under such circumstances, it is incumbent upon the business analyst to assure that each individual requirement is explicitly approved by at least one appropriate stakeholder with the authority to do so.

4.1.6   Stakeholders

Domain SME: May be involved in the review and approval of requirements, as defined by the stakeholder roles and responsibility designation.

Implementation SME: Will likely be involved in this process to ensure that the requirements can be implemented.

Project Manager: The project manager is responsible and accountable for the project scope. The project manager must be involved in assessing the solution scope in order to define the project scope, and must be involved in reviewing any changes to the solution scope for the same reason. In addition, if a proposed requirement is not accepted by key stakeholders, the project manager must manage the associated risk to the project (by altering the project scope, escalating the issue, or through other appropriate responses).

Sponsor: The business case, solution or product scope and all requirements must be reviewed and approved by the sponsor(s) according to the approval authority stated in the requirements management plan.

4.1.7   Output

Requirements [Approved]: Requirements which are agreed to by stakeholders and ready for use in subsequent business analysis or implementation efforts.

4.2   Manage Requirements Traceability

4.2.1   Purpose

Create and maintain relationships between business objectives, requirements, other team deliverables, and solution components to support business analysis or other activities.

4.2.2   Description

Requirements are related to other requirements, to solution components, and to other artifacts such as test cases. "Tracing" a requirement refers to the ability to look at a requirement and the others to which it is related. Tracing links business requirements to stakeholder and solution requirements, to other artifacts produced by the team, and to solution components.

Requirements traceability identifies and documents the lineage of each requirement, including its backward traceability (derivation), its forward traceability (allocation), and its relationship to other requirements. Traceability is used to help ensure solution conformance to requirements and to assist in scope and change management, risk management, time management, cost management, and communication management. It also is used to detect missing functionality or to identify if implemented functionality is not supported by a specific requirement.

Tracing may be performed at the individual requirement level, at the model or package level, or at the feature level as appropriate. The goal of tracing is to ensure that requirements (and ultimately, solution components) are linked back to a business objective. Tracing requirements also supports impact analysis, change management, and requirements allocation. Individual requirements almost always have inherent dependencies and interrelationships. There are several reasons for creating these relationships:

▶ **Impact Analysis.** When a requirement is changed, the business analyst can easily review all of the related requirements and software components in order to

Figure 4–3: *Manage Requirements Traceability* **Input/Output Diagram**

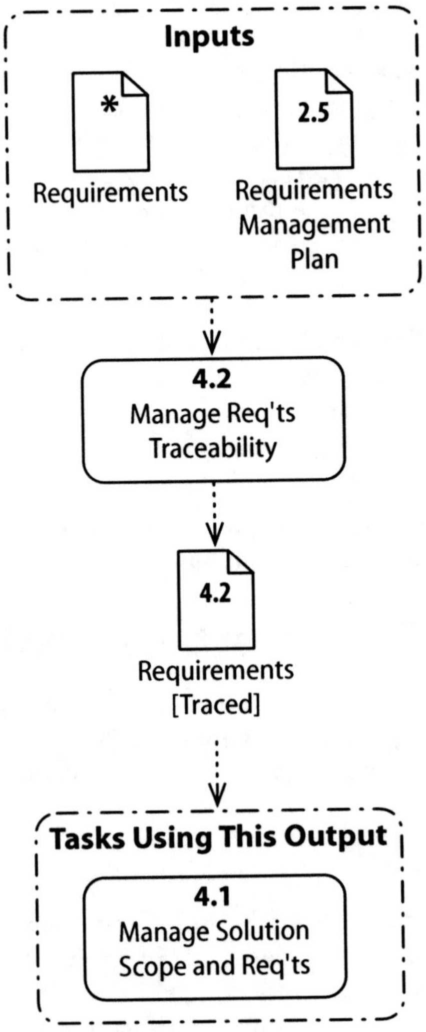

understand the "impact" of the change.

▶ **Requirements Coverage.** When business objectives are traced to detailed requirements such as business rules, data elements, and use cases it is clear how they will be accomplished. Each business objective can be reviewed to make sure that it will be addressed by the appropriate solution components. If a business objective is not tied to anything, it has not been analyzed and included in the solution. Additional information can be found in *Assess Proposed Solution (7.1)*.

▶ **Requirements Allocation.** See *Allocate Requirements (7.2)*.

4.2.3　Input

Requirements: All requirements may potentially be traced to other requirements, and all stakeholder and solution requirements must be traceable to a business requirement.

Requirements Management Plan: Defines how and whether traceability is being performed, the tools that will be used to support traceability and the processes that will be used to manage it.

4.2.4　Elements

.1　Relationships

After examining and organizing the set of requirements, record the dependencies and relationships for each of the requirements. Knowing the dependencies and relationships between requirements helps when determining the sequence in which requirements are to be addressed. Common relationships include:

▶ **Necessity:** This relationship exists when it only makes sense to implement a particular requirement if a related requirement is also implemented. This relationship may be unidirectional or bi-directional.

▶ **Effort:** This relationship exists when a requirement is easier to implement if a related requirement is also implemented.

▶ **Subset:** When the requirement is the decomposed outcome of another requirement.

▶ **Cover:** When the requirement fully includes the other requirement. This is a special case of subset, where the top-level requirement is the sum of the sub-requirements.

▶ **Value:** When including a requirement affects the desirability of a related requirement (either increasing or decreasing it). This may occur because the related requirement is only necessary if the first requirement is implemented, or because only one of the requirements should be implemented (for instance, when discussing two features that potentially meet a business requirement).

.2　Impact Analysis

Impact analysis is performed to assess or evaluate the impact of a change. Traceability is a useful tool for performing impact analysis. When a requirement changes, its relationships to other requirements or system components can be reviewed. Each related requirement or component may also require a change to support the new requirement.

These components can also be traced to their related components and those components reviewed for needed changes. Knowing the impact of a change helps business decision makers evaluate their options with facts.

.3 Configuration Management System

A specialized requirements management tool is generally needed to trace large numbers of requirements.

4.2.5 Techniques

.1 Coverage Matrix

A coverage matrix is a table or spreadsheet used to manage tracing. It is typically used when there are relatively few requirements or when tracing is limited to high-level requirements (e.g. features or models).

4.2.6 Stakeholders

Implementation SME: They must be able to link the requirements to the solution components that will implement them.

Project Manager: Traceability supports project change management.

Tester: Testers need to understand how and where requirements are implemented when creating test plans and test cases, and may trace test cases to requirements.

4.2.7 Output

Requirements [Traced]: Traced requirements have clearly defined relationships to other requirements within the solution scope such that it is relatively easy to identify the effects on other requirements of a change.

4.3 Maintain Requirements for Re-use

4.3.1 Purpose

To manage knowledge of requirements following their implementation.

4.3.2 Description

Identify requirements that are candidates for long-term usage by the organization. These may include requirements that an organization must meet on an ongoing basis, as well as requirements that are implemented as part of a solution.

To re-use requirements they must be clearly named and defined and easily available to other analysts. These requirements may be stored in a repository, and a person should be identified to manage the repository. When an existing requirement must be modified it can be accessed from the repository for re-use.

Maintenance of requirements can facilitate impact analysis of new, proposed changes to the business, reduce analysis time and effort, assist in maintenance of previously implemented solutions, and support other activities, including training, corporate governance, and standards compliance.

Figure 4–4: *Maintain Requirements for Re-Use* Input/Output Diagram

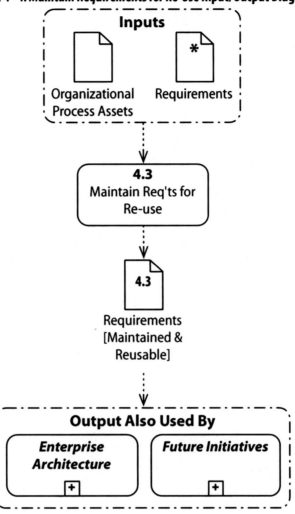

4.3.3   Input

Organizational Process Assets: These set standards regarding how and when requirements should be maintained for re-use.

Requirements: Requirements may be maintained for re-use as long as they describe information of use to the organization beyond the lifetime of an initiative. Requirements will usually be candidates for maintenance only if the describe the actual current state of an organization.

4.3.4   Elements

.1   Ongoing Requirements

Ongoing requirements are those requirements that an organizational unit is required to be able to meet on a continuous basis. These may include contractual obligations, quality standards, service level agreements, business rules, business processes, or requirements describing the work products the group produces.

.2   Satisfied Requirements

Even though a requirement has been satisfied, it is still a requirement as long as the business stakeholders need it. Maintaining these requirements helps with product enhancements and future system changes. Existing requirements may also be re-used on related business projects.

4.3.5   Techniques

None.

4.3.6   Stakeholders

Business Analyst: Re-used requirements are very likely to be used by a different business analyst than the author at some unknown future date. It may be necessary to revise and update the requirements documentation to ensure that it is self-explanatory.

Domain SME: Ongoing requirements are likely to be referenced by Domain SMEs on a regular basis to ensure that work products meet them.

Implementation SME: These requirements are likely to be used for a variety of purposes, including development of regression tests and impact analysis of enhancements.

4.3.7   Output

Requirements [Maintained and Reusable]: The output of this task are requirements that are expressed in a form that makes them suitable for long-term usage by the organization (even in the absence of the stakeholders who originally defined the requirements). They may become organizational process assets or be used in future initiatives or projects. In some cases a requirement that was not approved or implemented may be maintained for a possible future initiative.

4.4   Prepare Requirements Package

4.4.1   Purpose

To select and structure a set of requirements in an appropriate fashion to ensure that the requirements are effectively communicated to, understood by, and usable by a stakeholder group or groups.

4.4.2   Description

Requirements should be presented in formats that are understandable by the stakeholder. This task describes the work required to decide which format(s) are appropriate for a particular project and its stakeholders. They must be clear, concise, accurate, and at the appropriate level of detail. Requirements documentation should be created only to the extent needed to assure clear understanding by the team.

Requirements packages may be prepared for a number of reasons, including but not limited to early assessment of quality and planning, evaluation of possible alternatives, formal reviews and approvals, inputs to solution design, conformance to contractual and regulatory obligations, and maintenance for re-use.

The primary goal of developing a requirements package is to convey information clearly and in an understandable fashion. To help decide how to present requirements, ask the following types of questions:

► How detailed do the requirements need to be?

► What information is important to communicate? What is the appropriate level of detail to include?

► What will the particular stakeholder understand based on the type of audience they represent and on that stakeholder's preferred style of communication or learning?

► Are the requirements package presentation and format, and the requirements contained in the package, appropriate for the type of audience that needs to review it?

► How does the requirements package support the previous and subsequent phases (i.e. testing, implementation) or project activities and deliverables?

Misunderstanding of requirements will adversely affect solution implementation. It leads to re-work and cost overruns, particularly if deficiencies are uncovered late in the process.

Possible forms for requirements packages may include:

► **Formal Documentation:** Formal documentation is usually based on a template used by the organization, such as a Vision Document or Software Requirements Specification.

► **Presentation:** Delivers a high-level overview of the functionality delivered by the solution.

► **Models:** The requirements may be presented only in the form of a model, such as a process map, or captured on a whiteboard.

4.4.3   Input

Business Analysis Communication Plan: This will typically describe the stakeholder groups, their communication needs, and define whether a single requirements package or multiple requirements packages are required. The business analysis communication plan will also define the level of formality that is appropriate for the requirements.

Organizational Process Assets: May include templates that can be used to package requirements.

Requirements: The business analyst must understand which requirements will be included in the package. Requirements may be packaged at any point in their lifecycle.

Requirements Structure: A package should contain a consistent, cohesive, and coherent set of requirements.

4.4.4   Elements

.1   Work Products and Deliverables

Work Product

A *work product* is a document or collection of notes or diagrams used by the business analyst during the requirements development process. The work product may or may not become a deliverable, although during different phases of the requirements eliciting

Figure 4–5: *Prepare Requirements Package* **Input/Output Diagram**

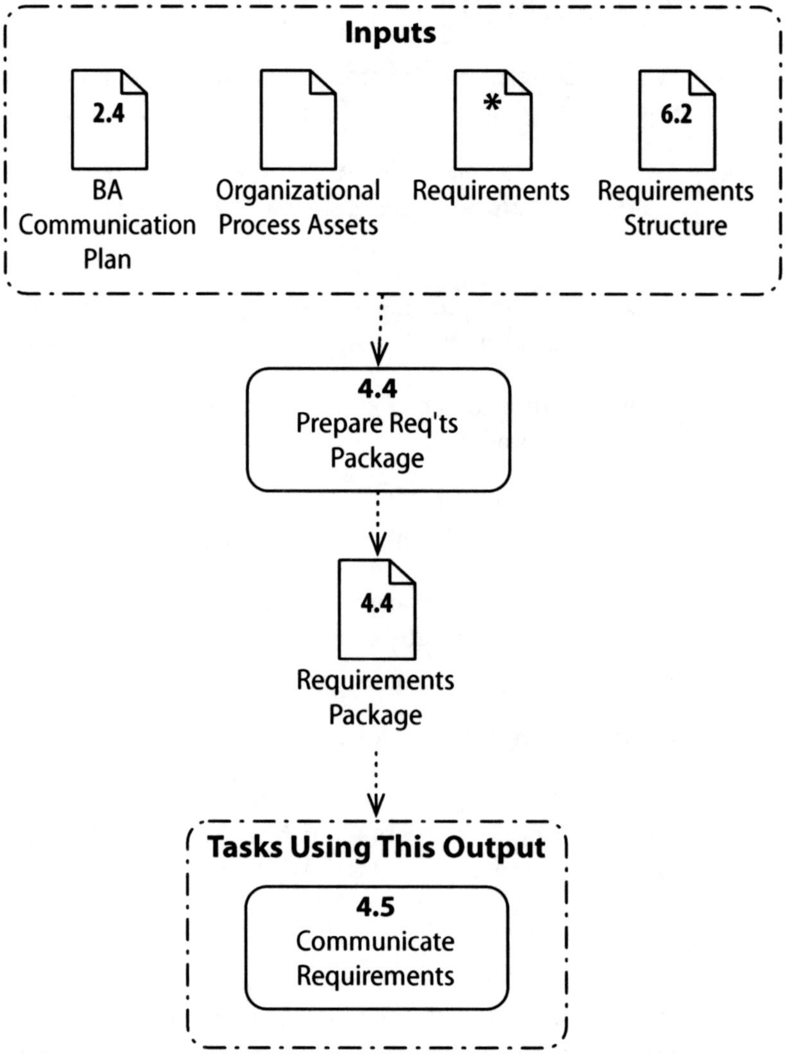

process, the business analyst may need to share this information with stakeholders in order to clarify requirements, elicit additional requirements, or assess the feasibility of the solution approach. Examples of work products might be:

► Meeting agendas and minutes

► Interview questions and notes

► Facilitation session agendas and notes

► Issues log

► Work plan, status reports

► Presentation slides used during the project

► Traceability matrices

Deliverables

A deliverable is a specific output of the business analysis process that the business analyst has agreed to produce. A requirement deliverable is used as a basis for solution design and implementation. The business analyst must understand the difference between these two concepts and use the deliverables as communication mechanisms. The business analyst will assess the needs of the audience, determine the level of detail that needs to be communicated, and ascertain which deliverables to include in each presentation package.

.2   Format

Depending on the type of requirement, the presentation technique may vary and specific formats may have been selected during development of the business analysis communication plan. There will likely be a combination of many formats in one requirements package. Consider the best way to combine and present the materials, so that they convey a cohesive, effective message to one or more audiences who will participate in the requirements review process. This may result in more than one requirements package being created for the same project.

Give careful consideration to what types of information should be included in a requirements package, and that the content may vary between different projects. The best format choice is the one that best communicates the specific content of the requirement. Each organization may have standards that the business analyst will be required to follow, and the project team will utilize the techniques appropriate for their project. Usually, each organization also has an approved suite of tools that are used for documentation.

If the package is created with the intention of obtaining formal approval, the requirements documentation must be complete in order to prepare the requirements package.

Additional Considerations for Requirements Documentation

Each requirements package may have a Table of Contents outlining what is included in the package. Grouping of the requirements into categories should be clearly identified in the Table of Contents for ease of navigation. It may also include a revision log to document changes between versions and help stakeholders verify that they have the most recent version.

4.4.5   Techniques

.1   Requirements Documentation

Requirements are frequently captured in a formal document. Many templates for requirements document exist and are in common use. While the selection of templates and documents is dependent on the business analysis approach chosen, some of the most common types of requirements documents include:

▶   Business Requirements Document (**note:** many "Business Requirements Document" templates also include stakeholder requirements)

▶   Product Roadmap

▶   Software/System Requirements Specification

► Supplementary Requirements Specification

► Vision Document

.2 Requirements for Vendor Selection

If the solution team thinks that a potential solution is available from an outside party, the business analyst may capture the requirements in the form of a Request for Information (RFI), Request for Quote (RFQ), or Request for Proposal (RFP).

While these terms are sometimes used interchangeably, they are intended to reflect differing levels of formality in the vendor selection process. The organization's purchasing agent, legal department or procurement organization is usually the owner of this process.

► An RFI is generally used when the issuing organization is open to a number of alternative solutions and is seeking information to evaluate possible options.

► An RFQ or RFP is used when the issuing organization understands the nature of the solution options available to it and is seeking vendors who can implement an option. An RFQ generally follows a less formal review and selection process than an RFP.

The solution team should carefully consider how each vendor solution will be evaluated. Often stakeholders can be impressed by a product demo when the underlying product does not truly meet the business need.

Business analysts must develop evaluation criteria based on the business requirements before looking at available products. In particular, an RFP typically includes a description of the selection criteria and process. The evaluation criteria used may be based on cost of the implementation or total cost of ownership. An objective measurement (weighting criteria) of how well the proposed solution meets the requirements may also be included.

When developing RFP questions, avoid using closed ended questions (those requiring only short answers). The goal is to stimulate the vendors to provide extensive information regarding their product and service offerings.

Most RFPs include many sections or components. Examples include:

► Business and stakeholder requirements for the particular problem/solution area

► Business strategy or business architecture description

► Technical environment constraints/limitations

► Legal, regulatory, or government requirements

The supplier may be asked to submit specific information. Examples include:

► Solution cost or total cost of ownership

► Alignment with overall business strategy

- ▶ Solution architecture, performance, quality, and support

- ▶ Solution's extensibility and ability to integrate with other applications

- ▶ Supplier's sustainability, and/or supplier's profile and reputation

4.4.6   Stakeholders

Domain SMEs and **End Users:** Need requirements that are written using familiar terminology and that are easy to understand and review. They must fully understand each requirement, since it is this group that will be most affected by the solution implemented. This group will be primarily concerned how operational processes are affected by the implementation of the project, and will be interested in ensuring that the requirements they provided to the business analyst during the requirements elicitation are achieved.

Implementation SMEs: Need to obtain an understanding of the overall requirements for the project, and will focus on requirements they will use to design the solution. External customers and suppliers will need detailed technical interface requirements to order to construct the proper network and security protocols in accordance with corporate policies.

Project Managers: Include deliverables (including specific requirements packages) in the project plan and typically track them as milestones to assess project progress. The deliverable acts as a "contract" for the project defining the agreed upon work. The deliverable becomes a project asset because it represents a project output.

Regulators: May have specific legal, contractual, or governance requirements regarding what is included in a requirements document.

Sponsors (and other managers at the executive level): Often want summaries and high-level requirements. Their primary goal is to understand that the solution will meet the return on investment expectations in accordance with their business plan, and to minimize the time required for them to make an effective decision. The project scope may suffice, including the ROI (Return on Investment) assessment, business benefits, project cost and target implementation date(s).

Testers: Focus on understanding the critical success factors of the project based on the needs of the business users. They must acquire a thorough understanding of the functional and non-functional requirements in order to build an effective testing strategy.

4.4.7   Output

Requirements Package: The result of this task is a requirements document, presentation, or package of requirements ready to be reviewed by stakeholders. A package may contain all of the project requirements or may be broken into several sub-packages.

4.5   Communicate Requirements

4.5.1   Purpose

Communicating requirements is essential for bringing stakeholders to a common understanding of requirements.

4.5.2   ## Description

Communicating requirements includes conversations, notes, documents, presentations, and discussions. Concise, appropriate, effective communication requires that the business analyst possess a significant set of skills, both soft (communication) and technical (i.e. requirements). See *Communication Skills (8.4)*.

Figure 4–6: *Communicate Requirements* Input/Output Diagram

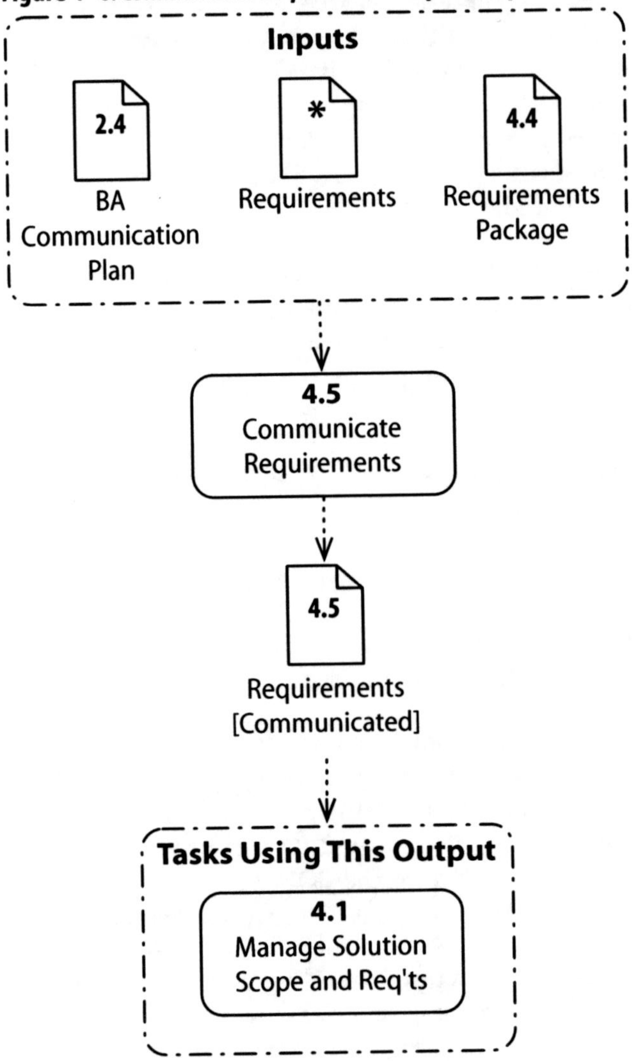

4.5.3   ## Input

Business Analysis Communication Plan: Defines what information is to be communicated, which stakeholders need to receive it, when communication should occur, and the form it should occur in.

Requirements: Any requirement may be communicated.

Requirements Package: Requirements may be communicated without being in a requirements package, but if a package has been assembled, it must be distributed, reviewed, and the contents must be communicated to stakeholders.

4.5.4   Elements

.1   General Communication

Requirements communication is performed iteratively and in conjunction with most of the tasks in the other knowledge areas.

Not all communication can or should be planned, and informal communication of requirements is likely to be needed during the performance of most business analysis tasks. In many cases, requirements communication may lead to elicitation of additional requirements.

► **Enterprise Analysis Tasks:** Business case and solution scoping information is communicated.

► **Elicitation Tasks:** Each elicitation technique requires specific communication skills. Communication of requirements may be useful during elicitation activities, as it may help stakeholders to identify other related requirements.

► **Requirements Analysis Tasks:** Requirements are refined, modified, clarified and finalized through effective communication.

► **Solution Assessment and Validation Tasks:** Assessments of the solution, allocation of requirements to solution components, organizational readiness, and transition requirements all must be communicated.

.2   Presentations

Before making any presentations of requirements to an audience, determine an appropriate format for the presentation. The formality of the presentation is driven by the objective of the communication and the audience needs. For example, the business analyst may be required to present key points using a formal presentation using presentation slides and handouts. This may be desirable when presenting to senior business representatives who are not actively involved in the detail of the project but need to understand requirements at a higher level.

A presentation may be used:

► to ensure that internal project quality standards have been adhered to

► to ensure cross-functional fit with other business process areas within the same project

► to obtain business acceptance and sign-off

► to obtain delivery team sign-off

► to obtain testing team sign-off

► as a precursor to delivery (e.g. examining solution options with a delivery team)

► to prioritize a set of requirements before proceeding to next project stage

► to make decisions regarding solution scope

Formal Presentation

Formal presentations typically disseminate information in a well-organized, structured format. Audience members may be given supporting materials before or during the presentation. Audience participation/questions may be encouraged.

Informal Presentation

An informal presentation may be used:

▶ as an informal status check of requirements (e.g. completeness, correctness, impact on other areas).

▶ to communicate requirements to the delivery team or testing team to ensure there is no ambiguity.

▶ to communicate requirements to affected business areas (those not having sign-off authority but where knowledge of changes is required).

▶ to communicate requirements to other project teams as a facilitation exercise to enhance requirement clarity. For example, by bringing business users and technical teams together, a common understanding can be reached on the relevance/ importance of individual requirements as well as the feasibility of delivering individual requirements.

4.5.5   Techniques

Requirements Workshops (9.23): Requirements may be presented as part of a requirements workshop to familiarize all parties with the existing solution scope and the current requirements.

Structured Walkthrough (9.30): A structured walkthrough often begins with a review of the requirements to be discussed.

4.5.6   Stakeholders

All.

4.5.7   Output

Communicated Requirements: Stakeholders should understand what the requirements are and their current state.

Enterprise Analysis

chapter FIVE

The *Enterprise Analysis* Knowledge Area describes the business analysis activities necessary to identify a business need, problem, or opportunity, define the nature of a solution that meets that need, and justify the investment necessary to deliver that solution. Enterprise analysis outputs provide context to requirements analysis and to solution identification for a given initiative or for long-term planning. Enterprise analysis is often the starting point for initiating a new project and is continued as changes occur and more information becomes available. It is through enterprise analysis activities that business requirements are identified and documented.

It describes the business analysis activities that take place for organizations to:

▶ Analyze the business situation in order to fully understand business problems and opportunities.

▶ Assess the capabilities of the enterprise in order to understand the change needed to meet business needs and achieve strategic goals.

▶ Determine the most feasible business solution approach.

▶ Define the solution scope and develop the business case for a proposed solution.

▶ Define and document business requirements (including the business need, required capabilities, solution scope, and business case).

Note: the performance of all enterprise analysis activities are governed by the business analysis plans (see 2.3), and business analysis performance metrics should be tracked (see 2.6).

Figure 5–1: *Enterprise Analysis* **Input/Output Diagram**

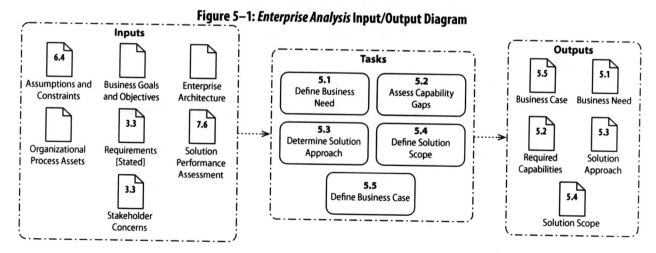

5.1   Define Business Need

5.1.1   Purpose

Identify and define why a change to organizational systems or capabilities is required.

5.1.2   ## Description

The definition of the business need is frequently the most critical step in any business analysis effort. The business need defines the problem that the business analyst is trying to find a solution for. The way the business need is defined determines which alternative solutions will be considered, which stakeholders will be consulted, and which solution approaches will be evaluated.

Figure 5–2: *Define Business Need* Input/Output Diagram

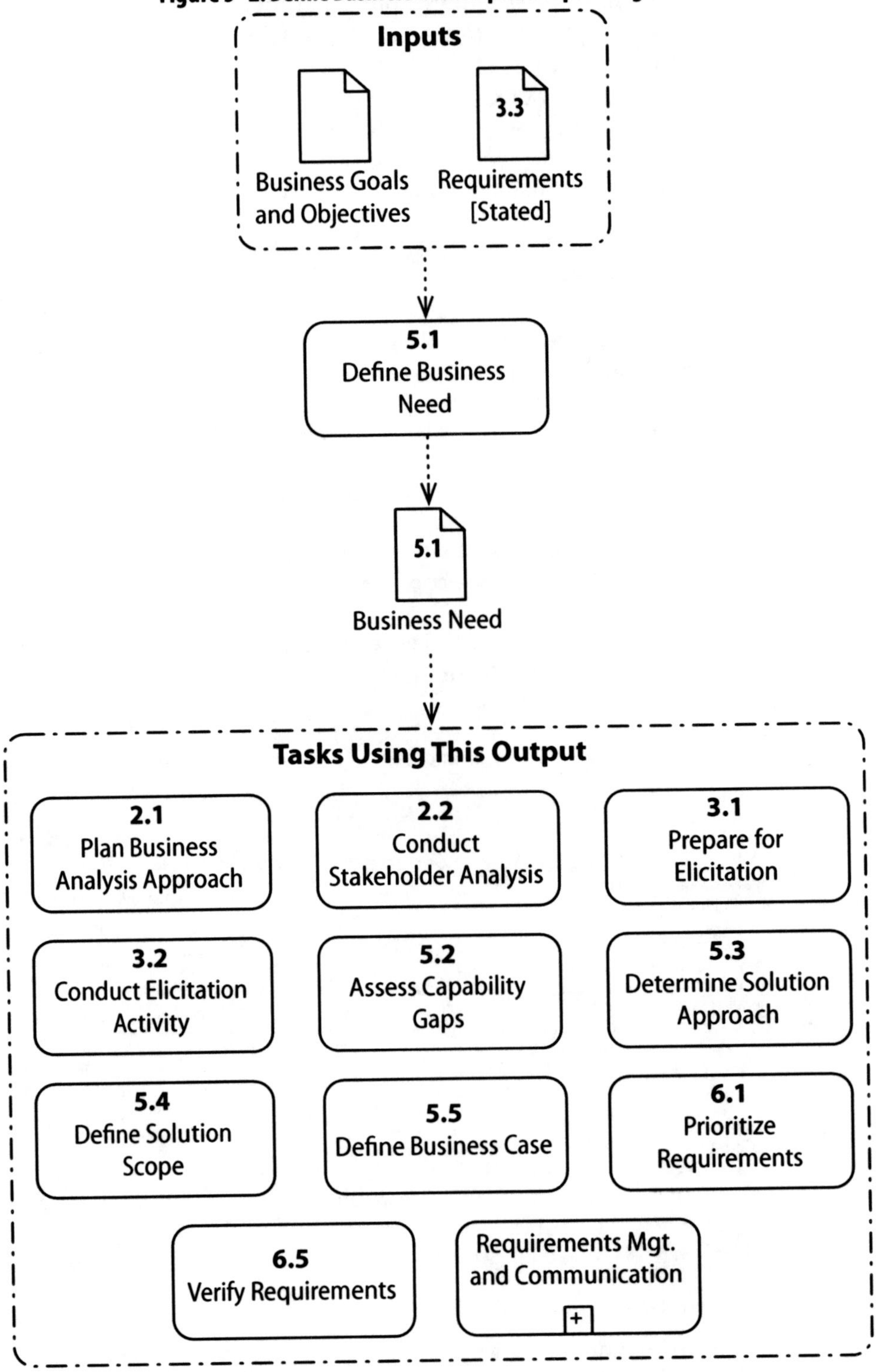

An issue encountered in the organization, such as a customer complaint, a loss of revenue, or a new market opportunity, usually triggers the evaluation of a business need. It is common for organizations to act to resolve the issue without investigating the underlying business need. The business analyst should question the assumptions and constraints that are generally buried in the statement of the issue to ensure that the correct problem is being solved and the widest possible range of alternative solutions are considered.

New business needs can be generated in several different ways:

▶ From the top down – the need to achieve a strategic goal

▶ From the bottom up – a problem with the current state of a process, function or system

▶ From middle management – a manager needs additional information to make sound decisions or must perform additional functions to meet business objectives

▶ From external drivers – driven by customer demand or business competition in the marketplace

5.1.3 Input

Business Goals and Objectives: Business goals and objectives usually have to be refined in order to define the business need. In some cases the goal or objective may be exploratory—the business need may be to understand if a methodology or business model can work.

Requirements [Stated]: Elicitation must be performed in order to assist stakeholders in defining their perceived needs. Ensure that they reflect actual business requirements, as opposed to describing solutions.

5.1.4 Elements

.1 Business Goals and Objectives

Business goals and objectives describe the ends that the organization is seeking to achieve. Goals and objectives can relate to changes that the organization wants to accomplish, or current conditions that it wants to maintain.

Goals are longer-term, ongoing, and qualitative statements of a state or condition that the organization is seeking to establish and maintain. High-level goals can be decomposed to break down the general strategy into distinct focus areas that may lead to desired results, such as increased customer satisfaction, operational excellence and/or business growth. Focus areas are usually described in brief statements. For example, a goal may be to "increase high-revenue customers" and then further refined into a goal to "increase high-revenue customers through mergers and acquisitions".

As goals are analyzed they are converted into more descriptive, granular and specific objectives, and linked to measures that make it possible to objectively assess if the objective has been achieved. A common test for assessing objectives is to ensure that they are SMART:

▶ **Specific** – describing something that has an observable outcome

▶ **Measurable** – tracking and measuring the outcome

▶ **Achievable** – testing the feasibility of the effort

▶ **Relevant** – in alignment with the organization's key vision, mission, goals

▶ **Time-bounded** – the objective has a defined timeframe that is consistent with the business need

.2　　Business Problem or Opportunity

In order to define a business need, an issue must be investigated to ensure that there is in fact an opportunity for improvement if the issue is resolved. Factors the business analyst may consider include:

▶ Adverse impacts the problem is causing within the organization and quantify those impacts (e.g., potential lost revenue, inefficiencies, dissatisfied customers, low employee morale).

▶ Expected benefits from any potential solution (e.g., increased revenue, reduced costs, increased market share).

▶ How quickly the problem could potentially be resolved or the opportunity could be taken, and the cost of doing nothing.

▶ The underlying source of the problem.

.3　　Desired Outcome

A desired outcome is not a solution. It describes the business benefits that will result from meeting the business need and the end state desired by stakeholders. Proposed solutions must be evaluated against desired outcomes to ensure that they can deliver those outcomes. Examples include:

▶ Create a new capability such as a new product or service, addressing a competitive disadvantage, or creating a new competitive advantage;

▶ Improve revenue, by increasing sales or reducing cost;

▶ Increase customer satisfaction;

▶ Increase employee satisfaction;

▶ Comply with new regulations;

▶ Improve safety;

▶ Reduce time to deliver a product or service.

Desired outcomes should address a problem or opportunity and support the business goals and objectives.

5.1.5 Techniques

Benchmarking (9.2): Understanding what competing organizations and peers are doing allows the organization to remain at a comparable level of service or identify opportunities to increase efficiency.

Brainstorming (9.3): Generate insights and options.

Business Rules Analysis (9.4): Identify changes in the policies that guide the organization towards achieving its goals and objectives.

Focus Groups (9.11): To identify and discuss problems.

Functional Decomposition (9.12): Convert business goals into achievable objectives and measures.

Root Cause Analysis (9.25): Determine the underlying source of a problem.

5.1.6 Stakeholders

Customer or **Supplier:** A business need may arise from actions taken by, or needs of, a customer or supplier. New opportunities often arise as an unmet customer need is identified.

Domain SME and **End User:** Likely to have the most direct awareness of problems or limitations that exist in current systems and the effects those have.

Implementation SME: May be aware of capabilities currently present in or easily added to existing systems that may provide new opportunities.

Regulator: May impose new regulatory or governance requirements on the organization.

Sponsor: A sponsor must be identified within the organization who is responsible for making sure that the business need is met and who can authorize action to meet it.

5.1.7 Output

Business Need: A business need describes a problem that the organization is (or is likely to) face or an opportunity that it has not taken, and the desired outcome. The business need will guide the identification and definition of possible solutions.

5.2 Assess Capability Gaps

5.2.1 Purpose

To identify new capabilities required by the enterprise to meet the business need.

5.2.2 Description

Assess the current capabilities of the enterprise and identify the gaps that prevent it from meeting business needs and achieving desired outcomes. Determine if it is possible for the organization to meet the business need using its existing structure, people, processes, and technology. If the organization can meet the business need with existing capabilities, the resulting change is likely to be relatively small.

However, if existing capabilities are inadequate, it will probably be necessary to launch a project to create that capability. Change may be needed to any component of the enterprise, including (but not limited to): business processes, functions, lines of business, organization structures, staff competencies, knowledge and skills, training, facilities, desktop tools, organization locations, data and information, application systems and/or technology infrastructure.

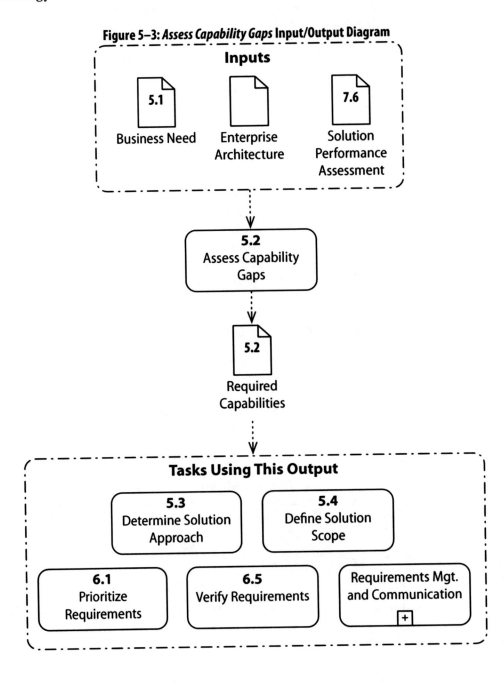

Figure 5–3: *Assess Capability Gaps* **Input/Output Diagram**

5.2.3	**Input**

Business Need: Capabilities are assessed against the business need to identify gaps.

Enterprise Architecture: The enterprise architecture defines the current capabilities of an organization.

Solution Performance Assessment: Identifies shortcomings, problems or limitations of an existing solution. In some cases, a solution may have capabilities that an organization is not using (most often, this occurs with a packaged solution or with outsourced services) which can also be assessed against a business need.

5.2.4	**Elements**

.1   Current Capability Analysis

Gather as much enterprise architecture information as is available about the current state of the areas of the enterprise affected by the business need. The goal is to understand the organization's business and how the business and technology architecture are supporting that business. If adequate information is not available, it will be necessary to develop the models and other descriptive information about the area of the enterprise that is under review. Once the current capabilities of the enterprise are fully described, they must be assessed against the desired objectives to determine whether the organization currently has the capability to meet the business need.

.2   Assessment of New Capability Requirements

If current capabilities are insufficient to meet the business need, the business analyst must identify the capabilities that need to be added. The business analyst will develop the models and other descriptive information about the future vision and describe the future state of the organization. A comparison of the current and desired future states will identify gaps in organizational capabilities that need to be filled to support the business vision, strategy, goals and objectives.

Some examples of capabilities include:

► Business processes

► Features of a software application

► Tasks that an end user may perform

► Events that a solution must be able to respond to

► Products that an organization creates

► Services that an organization delivers

► Goals that a solution will allow stakeholders to accomplish

.3   Assumptions

It will often be difficult or impossible to prove that the delivery of a new capability will meet a business need, even in cases where it appears reasonable to assume that the new capability will have the desired effect. These assumptions must be identified and clearly understood, so that appropriate decisions can be made if the assumption later proves invalid.

5.2.5　Techniques

Document Analysis (9.9): Useful to understand the current state of the enterprise, in as much as that current state is documented.

SWOT Analysis (9.32): Identify how current capabilities and limitations (Strengths and Weaknesses) match up against the influencing factors (Opportunities and Threats).

5.2.6　Stakeholders

Customer and **Supplier:** Customers and suppliers may be impacted if the business developed or changes the capabilities it has. They may also be in a position to provide or support new capabilities themselves, rather than requiring the organization to change in order to provide them.

Domain SME, End User, Implementation SME, and **Sponsor:** Will provide information on the strengths and weaknesses of current capabilities.

5.2.7　Output

Required Capabilities: An understanding of the current capabilities of the organization and the new capabilities (processes, staff, features in an application, etc.) that may be required to meet the business need.

5.3　Determine Solution Approach

5.3.1　Purpose

To determine the most viable solution approach to meet the business need in enough detail to allow for definition of solution scope and prepare the business case.

5.3.2　Description

The solution approach describes the general approach that will be taken to create or acquire the new capabilities required to meet the business need. To determine the solution approach, it is necessary to identify possible approaches, determine the means by which the solution may be delivered (including the methodology and lifecycle to be used) and assess whether the organization is capable of implementing and effectively using a solution of that nature.

Some possible approaches include:

▶ Utilize additional capabilities of existing software/hardware that already is available within the organization

▶ Purchase or lease software/hardware from a supplier

▶ Design and develop custom software

▶ Add resources to the business or make organizational changes

▶ Change the business procedures/processes

▶ Partner with other organizations, or outsource work to suppliers

Figure 5–4: *Determine Solution Approach* Input/Output Diagram

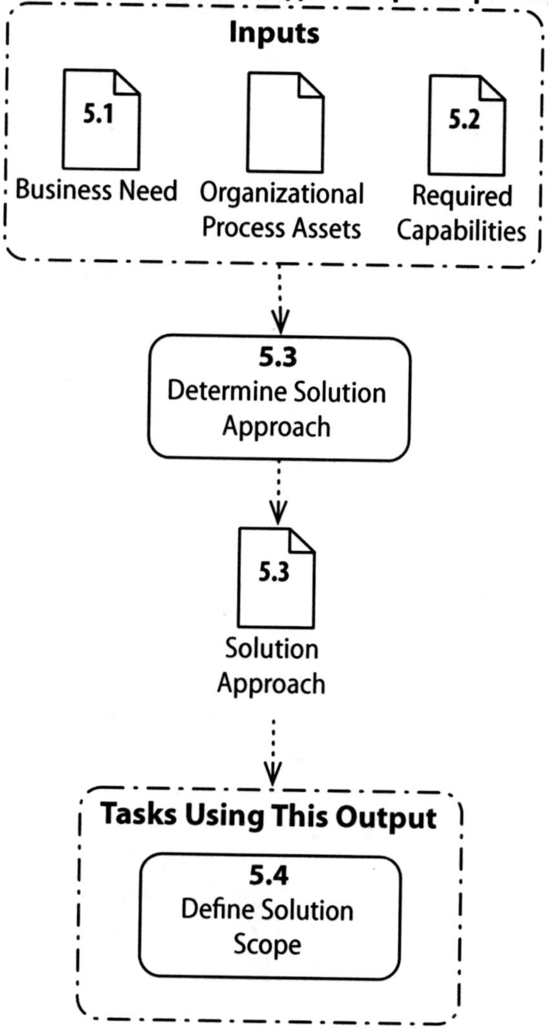

5.3.3   Input

Business Need: Possible solutions will be evaluated against the business need to ensure that it can be met by the selected approach.

Organizational Process Assets: The organization may require that specific approaches be taken to solutions of a given type (such as specific methodologies).

Required Capabilities: Identifies the new capabilities that any solution must support.

5.3.4   Elements

.1   Alternative Generation

Identify as many potential options as possible to meet the business objectives and fill identified gaps in capabilities. The list of possible alternatives should include the option of doing nothing, as well as investigating alternatives that may allow the organization to buy time.

While there is no hard and fast rule that can be used to determine when enough alternatives have been investigated, some indicators are:

► At least one of the alternative approaches is acceptable to key stakeholders;

► At least some of the approaches are distinctly different from one another;

► The effort to investigate alternatives is producing diminishing returns.

.2 Assumptions and Constraints

Assumptions that may affect the chosen solution should be identified. Certain solutions may be ruled out because they are believed not to be viable technically or for cost reasons, while other approaches may be believed to be easier to execute than they really are. Similarly, the organization may be constrained from pursuing certain solution options for contractual reasons or because they do not fit with the infrastructure of the organization. Assumptions and constraints should be questioned to ensure that they are valid.

.3 Ranking and Selection of Approaches

In order to assess an approach, record available information and analyze the operational, economic, technical, schedule-based, organizational, cultural, legal and marketing feasibility. Capture consistent information for each option to make it easier to compare them and review results to ensure accuracy and completeness.

In some cases, a particular solution approach may prove to be self-evidently superior to the alternatives. If this is not the case, solution approaches must be assessed and ranked. If there are only a few critical differences between solution options, it may be possible to make a qualitative assessment of those differences in order to make a selection. For more complex decision problems, a scoring system must be used, with sets of related requirements assigned a weighting to reflect their relative importance to the organization. Each solution is scored and the top-rated solution or solutions are then investigated in greater detail.

5.3.5 Techniques

.1 General Techniques

Benchmarking (9.2): Identify solution approaches that have proven effective in other organizations.

Brainstorming (9.3): Used as a method of generating alternatives.

Decision Analysis (9.8): Rank and select possible solution approaches.

Estimation (9.10): Develop initial cost comparisons of possible solution approaches.

SWOT Analysis (9.32): Useful method of comparing possible approaches.

.2 Feasibility Analysis

For small, relatively straightforward efforts, the solution approach can be determined by the business analyst alone or with a small team of experts examining the approaches in an informal working session. For larger change initiatives requiring significant investment, a more formal feasibility study may assist with determining the most viable solution option.

A feasibility study is a preliminary analysis of solution alternatives or options to determine whether and how each option can provide an expected business benefit to meet the business need. A feasibility study may address either a business problem to be resolved or a business opportunity to be exploited. Formal feasibility studies use reliable data and apply statistics and market research to identify and analyze potential solution options.

The feasibility analysis is an integral part of formulating a major business transformation project, e.g., re-engineering a core business process and supporting technology, establishing a new line of business, increasing market share through acquisition, or developing a new product or service. Abbreviated studies may also be conducted for change initiatives requiring lower investments.

5.3.6 Stakeholders

Customer, Domain SME, End User and **Supplier:** May be able to provide suggested approaches and identify assumptions and constraints.

Implementation SME: Will be needed to assess the feasibility of possible approaches.

Sponsor: May be the source of constraints on the solution options and will likely be required to approve the recommended approach.

5.3.7 Output

Solution Approach: A description of the approach that will be taken to implement a new set of capabilities. Solution approaches describe the types of solution components that will be delivered (new processes, a new software application, etc.) and may also describe the methodology that will be used to deliver those components.

5.4 Define Solution Scope

5.4.1 Purpose

To define which new capabilities a project or iteration will deliver.

5.4.2 Description

The purpose of this task is to conceptualize the recommended solution in enough detail to enable stakeholders to understand which new business capabilities an initiative will deliver. The solution scope will change throughout a project, based on changes in the business environment or as the project scope is changed to meet budget, time, quality, or other constraints. The solution scope includes:

▶ The scope of analysis (the organizational unit or process for which requirements are being developed) which provides the context in which the solution is implemented.

▶ The capabilities supported by solution components, such as business processes, organizational units, and software applications.

▶ The capabilities to be supported by individual releases or iterations.

▶ The enabling capabilities that are required in order for the organization to develop the capabilities required to meet the business need.

Note: This task describes how business requirements are allocated for implementation by a project. See *Allocate Requirements (7.2)* for a discussion of how stakeholder and solution requirements are allocated to solution components and releases.

Figure 5–5: *Define Solution Scope* **Input/Output Diagram**

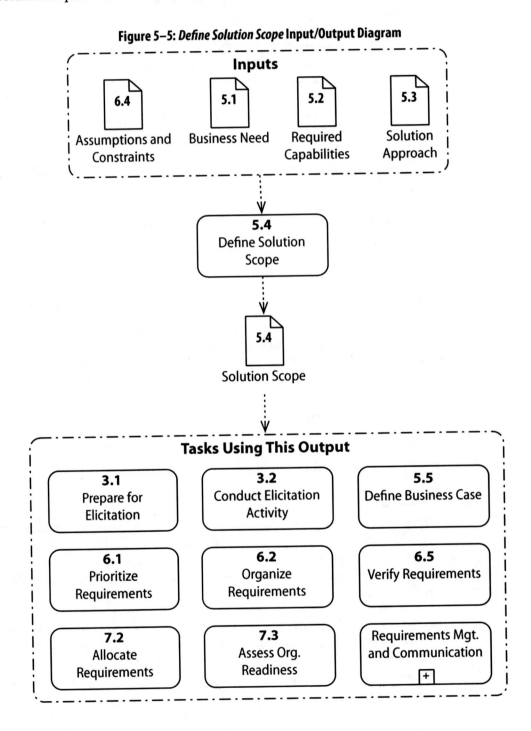

5.4.3 Input

Assumptions and Constraints: Relevant assumptions and constraints may include assumptions about how stakeholders will respond to a new product or service or about the availability of technology. Constraints may include limitations on what may be included in the solution scope. Include any schedule or funding limitations and significant standards, policies, regulations to be followed and supporting data required.

Business Need: The goals, objectives, and desired outcomes of the organization.

Required Capabilities: Describes the new capabilities required to meet the business need, which serve as the basis for the solution scope.

Solution Approach: The general approach taken to delivery of the new capabilities required by the business will be used when assessing options for the implementation of solution components.

5.4.4 Elements

.1 Solution Scope Definition

The solution is described in terms of the major features and functions that are to be included, and the interactions that the solution will have with people and systems outside of its scope. State in-scope and out-of-scope components of the solution. Describe the business units that will be involved, business processes to be improved or redesigned, process owners, and IT systems and other technology that will likely be affected.

.2 Implementation Approach

The implementation approach describes how the chosen solution approach will deliver the solution scope. For example, if the solution approach involves partitioning the proposed project into releases that will deliver useful subsets of functionality to the business, the implementation approach will describe the functionality in each release and the timeframe that it is expected to be delivered in. If the solution approach involves outsourcing key processes, the implementation approach will define which processes are candidates for outsourcing, or the process that will be used to identify those candidates. The implementation approach may break delivery down into specific releases or provide a roadmap that indicates the timeframe in which a capability can be expected.

.3 Dependencies

Define major business and technical dependencies that will impose constraints to the effort to deploy the solution, including dependencies that may exist between solution components.

5.4.5 Techniques

.1 General Techniques

Functional Decomposition (9.12): To understand the scope of work and to break the solution scope into smaller work products or deliverables.

Interface Analysis (9.13): Depict the scope of work required to integrate the new solution into the business and technical environments.

Scope Modeling (9.27): Identify appropriate boundaries for the solution scope.

User Stories (9.33): Describe stakeholders and the goals the system supports and as such can also be used to define the solution scope.

.2   Problem or Vision Statement

A problem or vision statement states the business need, identifies key stakeholders, and briefly describes the positive impact that meeting the business need will have on those stakeholders.

Figure 5–6: Example Problem Statement

The problem of	Describe the problem.
Affects	The stakeholders affected by the problem.
The impact of which is	What is the impact of the problem – on each stakeholder.
A successful solution would	List some key benefits of a successful solution

5.4.6   Stakeholders

Domain SME: Will participate in identifying the affected organizational units, modeling the scope of possible solutions, and determining the relative priorities of the required capabilities.

Implementation SME: Will participate in the allocation of capabilities to solution components and in determining the time and effort required to deliver new capabilities.

Project Manager: May assist with the development of the overall solution scope, which will be used as an input into the Project Charter. The project manager is responsible for the definition of the project scope, which is the work required to deliver the solution scope or a portion of it. The project manager will play a major role in allocating capabilities to components and will be primarily responsible for determining the time and effort required to deliver a capability.

Sponsor: Will participate in setting priorities and approving the solution scope.

5.4.7   Output

Solution Scope: Defines what must be delivered in order to meet the business need, and the effect of the proposed change initiative on the business and technology operations and infrastructure.

5.5   Define Business Case

5.5.1   Purpose

To determine if an organization can justify the investment required to deliver a proposed solution.

5.5.2   Description

The business case describes the justification for the project in terms of the value to be added to the business as a result of the deployed solution, as compared to the cost to develop and operate the solution. The business case may also include qualitative and quantitative benefits, estimates of cost and time to break even, profit expectations, and follow on opportunities. The business case may present expected cash flow consequences of the action over time, and the methods and rationale that were used for quantifying benefits and costs. This provides a framework to demonstrate how the initiative is expected to achieve business objectives. In addition, the business case lists the constraints associated with the proposed project, along with the estimated budget, and alignment with strategies established by the organization.

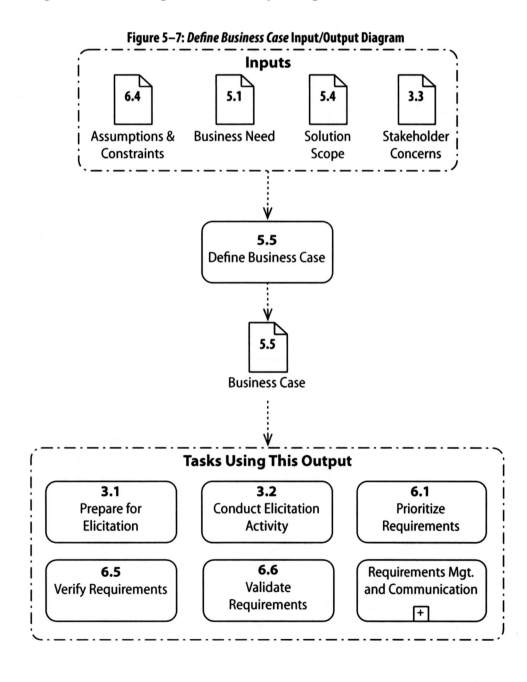

Figure 5–7: *Define Business Case* Input/Output Diagram

5.5.3   Input

Assumptions and Constraints: Include assumptions about the revenue generated or retained by the solution or non-financial improvements it will deliver.

Business Need: Defines the value that a solution will deliver to the organization and how it aligns with the business goals and objectives.

Solution Scope: Defines the capabilities that will be implemented, the methods that will be used to deliver them, and the areas of the organization that will be affected.

Stakeholder Concerns: May include risks or issues that must be accounted for in the business case.

5.5.4   Elements

.1   Benefits

Measure the benefits of the recommended solution in terms of both qualitative and quantitative gains to the enterprise. Where possible, benefits should be quantified. Benefits of a non-financial nature (such as improved staff morale, increased flexibility to respond to change, improved customer satisfaction, or reduced exposure to risk) are also important and add significant value to the organization, even if they must be assessed qualitatively. Benefit estimates should relate back to strategic goals and objectives.

.2   Costs

Estimate the total net cost of the solution. This requires estimates to be made of capital expenditures for the new investment, costs of developing and implementing the change, opportunity costs of not investing in other options, costs related to changing the work and practices of the organization, total cost of ownership to support the new solution and consequential costs borne by others.

.3   Risk Assessment

The purpose of the initial risk assessment is to determine if the proposed initiative carries more risk than the organization is willing to bear.

This initial risk assessment focuses mainly on solution feasibility risks, and is revisited throughout the project. The risk assessment should consider technical risks (whether the chosen technology and suppliers can deliver the required functionality), financial risks (whether costs may exceed levels that make the solution viable or potential benefits may disappear) and business change and organizational risks (whether the organization will make the changes necessary to benefit from the new solution).

.4   Results Measurement

The business case articulates not only the projected costs and benefits to be realized, but also how those costs and benefits will be assessed and evaluated.

5.5.5   Techniques

Decision Analysis (9.8): Cost-benefit analysis compares the costs of implementing a solution against the benefits to be gained. Financial analysis includes the use of financial models that estimate the market value of an organizational asset.

Estimation (9.10): Forecast the size of the investment required to deploy and operate the proposed solution.

Metrics and Key Performance Indicators (9.16): Assessed to support benefit management, measurement and reporting, including where realignment of internal measures or systems is needed to ensure that the behaviors we are seeking can be seen, evaluated, and realized.

Risk Analysis (9.24): Used to assess potential risks that may impact the solution and the costs and benefits associated with it.

SWOT Analysis (9.32): Demonstrate how the solution will help the organization maximize strengths and minimize weaknesses.

Vendor Assessment (9.34): If purchase or outsourcing to a third party is in consideration, an assessment of the vendor may be performed as part of the business case.

5.5.6   Stakeholders

Sponsor: Approves the business case and authorizes funding.

Domain SME: Assists in estimating business benefits expected from the new initiative.

Implementation SME: Assists in estimating cost projections for the technology needed to support the new solution.

Project Manager: Participates in developing time and cost estimates, and may develop a preliminary project plan or Work Breakdown Structure in collaboration with the project team. The project manager will use the business case as an input for a project charter.

5.5.7   Output

Business Case: Presents the information necessary to support a go/no go decision to invest and move forward with a proposed project.

Requirements Analysis

The *Requirements Analysis* Knowledge Area describes the tasks and techniques used by a business analyst to analyze stated requirements in order to define the required capabilities of a potential solution that will fulfill stakeholder needs. It covers the definition of stakeholder requirements, which describe what a solution must be capable of doing to meet the needs of one or more stakeholder groups, and solution requirements, which describe the behavior of solution components in enough detail to allow them to be constructed. The tasks in this knowledge area apply to both stakeholder and solution requirements.

In addition, requirements analysis may be performed to develop models of the current state of an organization. These domain models are useful for validating the solution scope with business and technical stakeholders, for analyzing the current state of an organization to identify opportunities for improvement, or for assisting stakeholders in understanding that current state.

Note: the performance of all requirements analysis activities are governed by the business analysis plans (see 2.3), and business analysis performance metrics should be tracked (see 2.6).

Figure 6–1: *Requirements Analysis* **Input/Output Diagram**

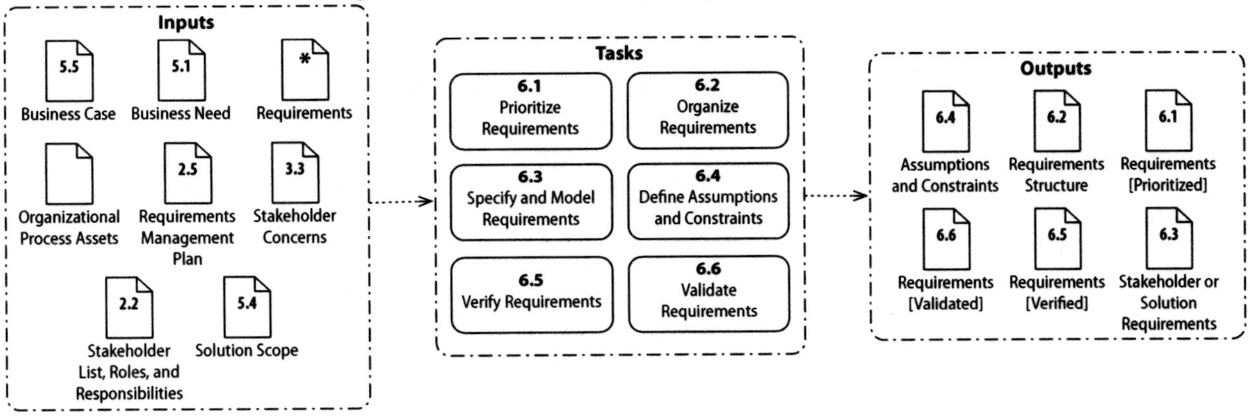

6.1   Prioritize Requirements

6.1.1   Purpose

Prioritization of requirements ensures that analysis and implementation efforts focus on the most critical requirements.

6.1.2   Description

Requirement prioritization is a decision process used to determine the relative importance of requirements. The importance of requirements may be based on their relative value, risk, difficulty of implementation, or on other criteria.

These priorities are used to determine which requirements should be targets for further analysis and to determine which requirements should be implemented first.

Figure 6–2: *Prioritize Requirements* **Input/Output Diagram**

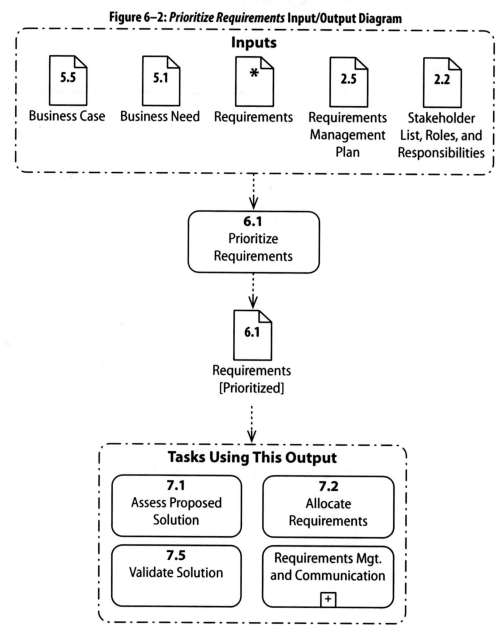

6.1.3   Input

Business Case: The business case states the key goals and measures of success for a project or organization, and priorities should be aligned with those goals and objectives.

Business Need: Serves as an alternative to the business case if no business case has been defined.

Requirements: Any requirement may be prioritized, at any point in its lifecycle. Requirements prioritization requires that requirements have been stated by stakeholders; however, the requirements may not have been fully analyzed or in their final form.

Requirements Management Plan: Defines the process that will be used to prioritize requirements.

Stakeholder List, Roles, and Responsibilities: The list of stakeholders, annotated with their levels of authority and influence, is used to determine which stakeholders need to participate in prioritization.

6.1.4   Elements

.1   Basis for Prioritization

Requirements may be prioritized using a number of different criteria, including:

Business Value: This approach prioritizes requirements based on cost-benefit analysis of their relative value to the organization. The most valuable requirements will be targeted for development first. This approach is common when enhancing an existing solution that already meets specified minimal requirements, or when delivering the solution incrementally.

Business or Technical Risk: This approach selects requirements that present the highest risk of project failure. Those requirements are investigated and implemented first to ensure that if the project fails it does so after as little expenditure as possible.

Implementation Difficulty: This approach selects requirements that are easiest to implement. This approach is often selected during a pilot of a new development process or tools or when rolling out a packaged solution, as it allows the project team to gain familiarity with those things while working on lower-risk requirements.

Likelihood of Success: This approach focuses on the requirements that are likely to produce quick and relatively certain successes. It is common when a project is controversial and early signs of progress are needed to gain support for the initiative.

Regulatory or Policy Compliance: This approach prioritizes requirements that must be implemented in order to meet regulatory or policy demands imposed on the organization, which may take precedence over other stakeholder interests.

Relationship to Other Requirements: A requirement may not be high value in and of itself, but may support other high-priority requirements and as such may be a candidate for early implementation.

Stakeholder Agreement: This approach requires the stakeholders to reach a consensus on which requirements are most useful or valuable. It is often used in combination with one or more of the other approaches described above.

Urgency: This approach prioritizes requirements based on time sensitivity.

.2   Challenges

Challenges in facilitating a requirements prioritization session include:

Non-negotiable Demands: Stakeholders attempt to avoid difficult choices, fail to recognize the necessity for making tradeoffs, or desire to rank all requirements as high priority.

Unrealistic Tradeoffs: The solution development team may intentionally or unintentionally try to influence the result of the prioritization process by overestimating the difficulty or complexity of implementing certain requirements.

6.1.5   Techniques

.1   General Techniques

Decision Analysis (9.8): Decision analysis may be used to identify high-value requirements.

Risk Analysis (9.24): Requirements that are considered risky may need to be investigated or implemented first, so that if risks cause the project to fail, the organization has invested as little as possible at that point.

.2   MoSCoW Analysis

MoSCoW analysis divides requirements into four categories: Must, Should, Could, and Won't. Category descriptions are as follows:

Must: Describes a requirement that must be satisfied in the final solution for the solution to be considered a success.

Should: Represents a high-priority item that should be included in the solution if it is possible. This is often a critical requirement but one which can be satisfied in other ways if strictly necessary.

Could: Describes a requirement which is considered desirable but not necessary. This will be included if time and resources permit.

Won't: Represents a requirement that stakeholders have agreed will not be implemented in a given release, but may be considered for the future.

.3   Timeboxing/Budgeting

Timeboxing or budgeting prioritizes requirements for investigation and implementation based on allocation of a fixed resource. It is used when the solution approach has been determined. Timeboxing prioritizes requirements based on the amount of work that the project team is capable of delivering in a set period of time. By contrast, budgeting is used when the project team has been allocated a fixed amount of money. The approach is most often used when a fixed deadline must be met or for solutions that are enhanced on a regular and frequent basis. There are a number of approaches that can be taken to determine which requirements can be included in a timeboxed iteration:

▶   **All In:** Begin with all the eligible requirements with assigned Duration or Cost. Remove the requirements in order to meet the calendar dates or budget limit.

▶   **All Out:** Begin with adding the requirement(s) with assigned duration or cost to the calendar or budget. Stop when the calendar dates are met or budget limit is reached.

▶   **Selective:** Begin by identifying high priority requirements added to the calendar or budget. Add or remove requirements in order to meet the calendar date or budget limit.

.4   Voting

Voting methods allocate a fixed amount of resources (votes, play money, or other tokens) to each participant for them to distribute among proposed features or requirements.

The requirements that receive the most resources are the ones that will be investigated or developed first.

6.1.6 Stakeholders

Domain SME: Domain subject matter experts may be invited to participate in the prioritization of requirements, to assess the relative business need, and to negotiate their importance.

Implementation SME: Implementation subject matter experts may be asked to evaluate the relative complexity or risk associated with the implementation of certain requirements.

Project Manager: The project manager is responsible for the implementation of the solution and will use the priority of requirements as an input into the project plan.

Sponsor: Since sponsors are ultimately accountable for the business solution and major project decisions, they need to be invited to participate in the discussion.

6.1.7 Output

Requirements [Prioritized]: A prioritized requirement has an attribute that describes its relative importance to stakeholders and the organization. At the completion of this task, each requirement should have an assigned priority. The priorities may apply to a requirement or to a group or related requirements.

6.2 Organize Requirements

6.2.1 Purpose

The purpose of organizing requirements is to create a set of views of the requirements for the new business solution that are comprehensive, complete, consistent, and understood from all stakeholder perspectives.

6.2.2 Description

There are two key objectives when organizing requirements.

► Understand which models are appropriate for the business domain and solution scope.

► Identify model interrelationships and dependencies. Requirements alone are not complex; it is the relationships and interdependencies among requirements that adds the element of complexity. Therefore, the organized requirements must also clearly depict the inherent relationships between requirements.

6.2.3 Input

Organizational Process Assets: Describe the structures and types of requirements information that stakeholders expect.

Requirements [Stated]: Requirements are stated in various forms as an output from elicitation activities. Stated requirements are the expressed desires of stakeholders, which must be analyzed to ensure that they reflect a genuine need.

Solution Scope: The selected requirements models must be sufficient to fully describe the solution scope from all needed perspectives.

Figure 6–3: *Organize Requirements* Input/Output Diagram

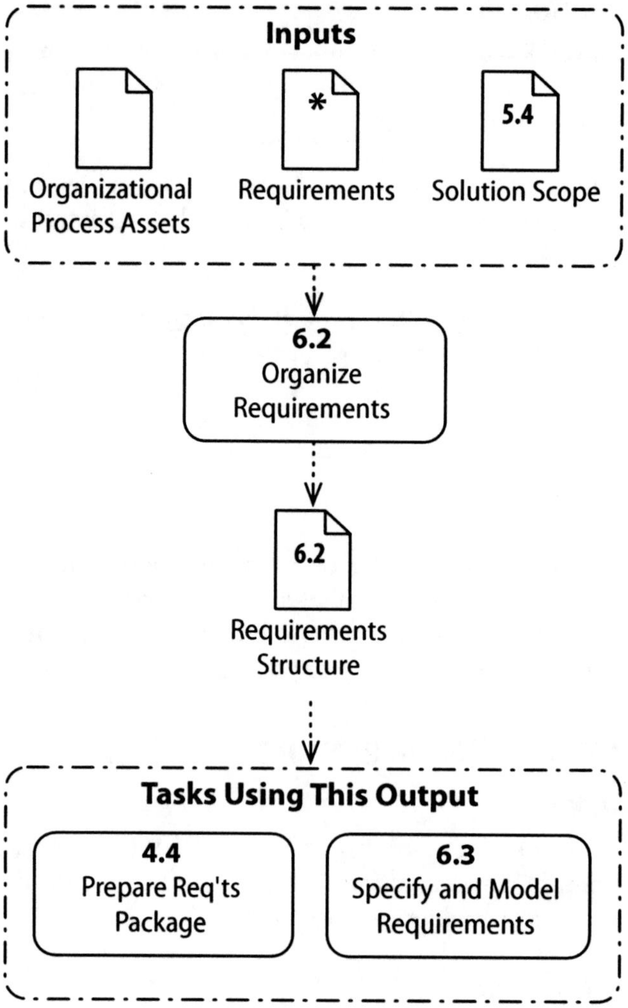

6.2.4   Elements

The following guidelines will assist in promoting consistency, repeatability and a high level of quality:

▶ Follow organizational standards that describe the types of requirements that will be used consistently on projects. If no standard exists, the business analyst must select an appropriate set of techniques.

▶ Use simple, consistent definitions for each of the types of requirements described in natural language, and using the business terminology that is prevalent in the enterprise.

▶ Document dependencies and interrelationships among requirements.

▶ Produce a consistent set of models and templates to document the requirements, as described in *Specify and Model Requirements (6.3)*.

The various levels of abstraction and models used are not mutually exclusive. It will usually be beneficial to create multiple models of and perspectives on the requirements in order to ensure understanding, although any given requirement should only appear in one model in order to avoid confusion or contradictions.

.1 Levels of Abstraction

Requirements can be articulated on a number of different levels of abstraction. Requirements are frequently described as needing to say *what* needs to be done, not *how* to do it. This formulation can be problematic, as whether something is a "what" or a "how" depends on the perspective of the audience. For instance, a decision to implement a business process management engine can be *what* we are doing (from the perspective of the project team) and *how* we are improving our process agility (from the perspective of the enterprise architecture group). When practicing business analysis, we can distinguish between what and how by understanding that our perspective on the difference between those terms needs to be aligned with the perspective of our business stakeholders.

There are a number of formal structures for levels of abstraction, including those outlined in enterprise architecture frameworks. Alternatively, the business analyst may informally designate a set of requirements as "high" or "low" level based on the level of detail included. While requirements often become less abstract as the business analyst defines business requirements, stakeholder requirements, and solution requirements, this is not mandatory—any category of requirement can be expressed at whatever level of abstraction is appropriate for the audience. Methodologies may also determine the level of abstraction used when defining requirements.

.2 Model Selection

The business analyst must determine which types of models will be required to describe the solution scope and meet the informational needs of stakeholders. These needs may vary over time.

Models abstract and simplify reality. No model can be a complete description of reality; the objective of developing a model is to simplify reality in a way that is useful. Each model represents a different view into the reality of the business domain. It is usually necessary to develop multiple models using different modeling techniques to completely analyze and document requirements.

Models do not have any inherent hierarchy—effective analysis can potentially start with any aspect of the model and reach out to encompass the others. For example, use case analysis can start with goals or events and capture process and relevant rules. Business Process Management starts by identifying processes and then derive roles, events and rules from the processes.

There are a number of general modeling concepts that are relevant to business analysis:

User Classes, Profiles, or Roles. These models categorize and describe the people who directly interact with a solution. Each role groups together people with similar needs, expectations, and goals. Each role is likely to correspond to a stakeholder and should be investigated as a source of requirements. These are usually identified by performing *Conduct Stakeholder Analysis (2.2)* and are used in a number of analysis models, particularly in *organization models (9.19), process models (9.21)*, and *use cases (9.26)*.

Concepts and Relationships. Concepts usually correspond to something in the real world; a place, a person, a thing, an organization. They define the objects, entities or facts that are relevant to the business domain and what relationships they have with other concepts. *Data models (9.7)* expand on this to also describe the attributes associated with a concept.

Events. A request to a business system or organization to do something, such as a customer placing an order, or a manager requesting a report, can be described as an event. The organization must respond to an event, and in most cases an event will trigger or affect a business process. Events can come from outside the business area, from within it, or occur at scheduled times. Events can serve as the basis for a *scope model (9.27)* and may be described in other models, including *process models (9.21)*, *state diagrams (9.29)*, and *use cases (9.26)*.

Processes. Processes are a sequence of repeatable activities executed within an organization. Processes can be simple (involving one person and a system) or complex (involving many people, departments, organizations and systems). Processes describe who and what has to be involved in fully responding to an event, or how people in the enterprise collaborate to achieve a goal. Processes are normally described in *process models (9.21)*, although useful information may also be captured in *organization models (9.19)*, *state diagrams (9.29)*, or *use cases (9.26)*.

Rules. Rules are used by the enterprise to enforce goals and guide decision-making. They determine when information associated with an entity may change, what values of information are valid, how decisions are made in a process, and what the organization's priorities are. Business rules are normally described as such, although they may also be embedded in *process models (9.21)*, *state diagrams (9.29)*, and *use cases (9.26)*.

Choose a set of modeling techniques that meet the informational needs of stakeholders and allow description of all five concepts to ensure full coverage of a business domain (assuming that full coverage is required).

6.2.5   Techniques

Business Rules Analysis (9.4): Business rules may be separated from other requirements for implementation and management in a business rules engine or similar.

Data Flow Diagrams (9.6): Shows how information flows through a system. Each function that modifies the data should be decomposed into lower levels until the system is sufficiently described.

Data Modeling (9.7): Describes the concepts and relationships relevant to the solution or business domain.

Functional Decomposition (9.12): Breaks down an organizational unit, product scope, or similar into its component parts. Each part can have its own set of requirements.

Organization Modeling (9.19): Describes the various organizational units, stakeholders, and their relationships. Requirements can be structured around the needs of each stakeholder or group.

Process Modeling (9.21): Requirements may be organized around relevant processes.

Processes themselves can embed subprocesses, and describe a hierarchy from the top level, end-to-end processes to the lowest-level individual activities.

Scenarios and Use Cases (9.26): Describe the requirements that support the individual goals of each actor, or the response to the triggering event.

Scope Modeling (9.27): Requirements may be organized based on the solution components they are related to.

User Stories (9.33): Describe the stakeholder objectives that the solution will support.

6.2.6 Stakeholders

Domain SME, End User, Implementation SME, and **Sponsor:** Affected by analysis techniques used to organize requirements since they need to verify and validate the requirements. The business analyst tailors the approach to meet the needs of key stakeholder groups, and must determine which models will be useful to each.

Project Manager: Uses the organized set of requirements to verify the scope of the solution and assess the work that needs to be done in the project.

6.2.7 Output

Requirements Structure: The output of this task is an organized structure for the requirements and a documented set of relationships between them. This structure is distinct from tracing, which links related requirements; rather, this structure is used so that the analyst and stakeholders know where a specific requirement should be found. Each model or set of requirements within the structure should have a clear implicit scope; that is, it should be clear to stakeholders what a particular model will and will not describe.

6.3 Specify and Model Requirements

6.3.1 Purpose

To analyze expressed stakeholder desires and/or the current state of the organization using a combination of textual statements, matrices, diagrams and formal models.

6.3.2 Description

Specifications and models are created to analyze the functioning of an organization and provide insight into opportunities for improvement. They also support a number of other objectives, including development and implementation of solutions, facilitating communication among stakeholders, supporting training activities and knowledge management, and ensuring compliance with contracts and regulations.

The specifics of this task are highly dependent on the techniques used for specifying and modeling requirements.

6.3.3 Input

Requirements [Stated]: Specification or modeling of requirements is performed to structure and improve our understanding of needs as expressed by stakeholders.

Requirements Structure: Defines how the requirement fits into the general requirements and which other sets of requirements may include related information.

Figure 6–4: *Specify and Model Requirements* Input/Output Diagram

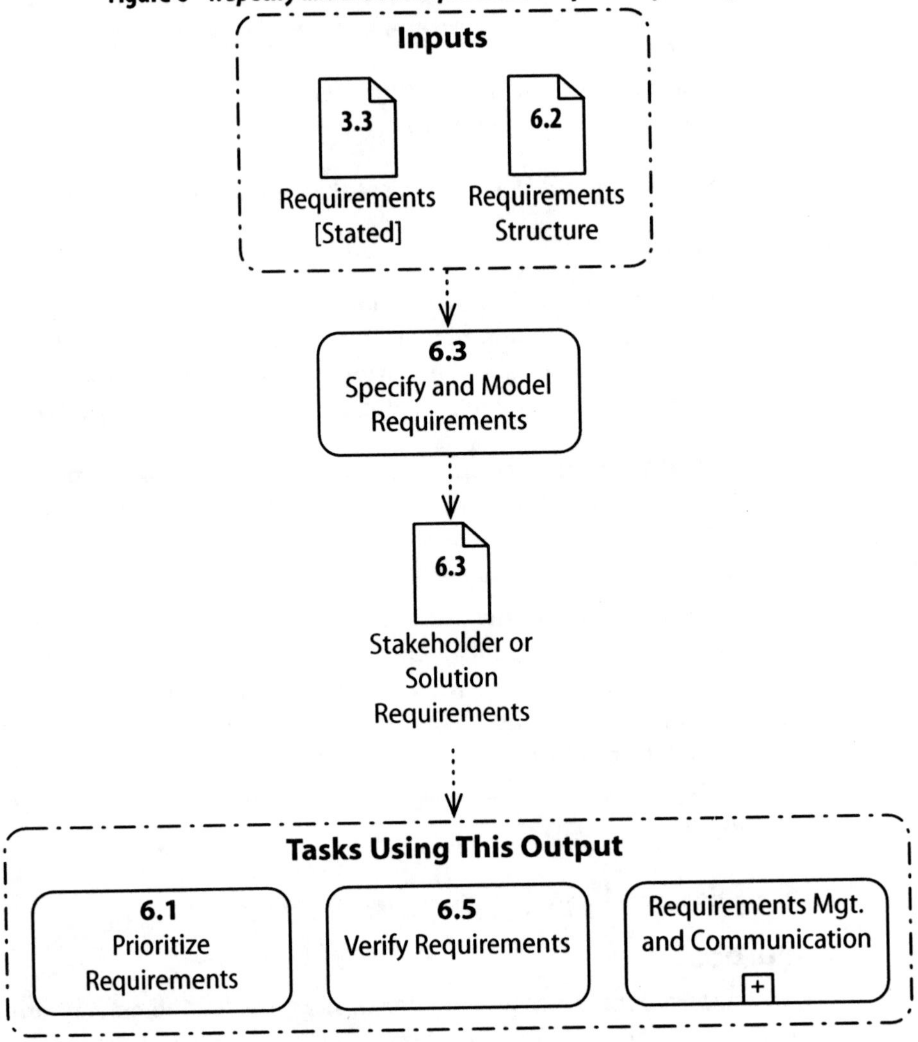

6.3.4   Elements

.1   Text

A textual requirement must describe the capabilities of the solution, any conditions that must exist for the requirement to operate, and any constraints that may prevent the solution from fulfilling the requirement. Guidelines for writing textual requirements include:

▶   Express one and only one requirement at a time.

▶   Avoid complex conditional clauses.

▶   Do not assume your reader has domain knowledge.

▶   Use terminology that is consistent.

▶   Express requirements as a verb or verb phrase.

▶ Write in the active voice, clearly describing who or what is responsible for fulfilling the requirement.

▶ Use terminology familiar to the stakeholders who must review or use the requirement.

.2   Matrix Documentation

A table is the simplest form of a matrix. A table is used when the business analyst is looking to convey a set of requirements that have a complex but uniform structure which can be broken down into elements that apply to every entry in the table.

Requirements attributes and data dictionaries are often expressed in tabular form. Matrices are often used for traceability of requirements to each other, from requirements to test cases, and for gap analysis. Matrices are also used for prioritizing requirements by mapping them against project objectives.

A more complex matrix will also express information in the rows of the table. Rather than presenting repeating information, this form of matrix is usually intended to indicate that two elements are related in some fashion (for instance, that a requirement affects a particular data element).

.3   Models

Modeling Formats

A model is any simplified representation of a complex reality that is useful for understanding that reality and making decisions regarding it. Models may be either textual or graphical, or some combination of both. Graphical models are often referred to as diagrams.

The choice of which model(s) to use for a particular set of requirements is determined by the type of information to be communicated, as well as the audience who will consume the information. Models can:

▶ Describe a situation or define a problem

▶ Define boundaries for business domains and sub-domains, and describe the components within each defined boundary

▶ Describe thought processes and action flows

▶ Categorize and create hierarchies of items

▶ Show components and their relationships

▶ Show business logic

Whether or not a diagram is used in place of or in addition to a textual description is often determined by the audience for the information, as well as the level of detail in a particular model.

Models may be used not only to document requirements in their final form, but also as a tool while performing elicitation activities.

Notations

Describe any symbol or notation used. On diagrams, this often means including a 'key' that aids in the interpretation of the symbols and/or colors used, or referring to an external standard.

Formal versus Informal Models

A formal model follows semantics and iconography that are defined in a standard to indicate the meaning of each model element. A formal model can often convey a great deal of meaning, but some of the subtleties of the model may not be properly conveyed to an audience that is unfamiliar with the specific notation.

An informal model does not have a formal semantic definition and instead connects elements in ways that are meaningful for the analyst and the audience. While the model may be less expressive, it requires no special training to interpret.

.4   Capture Requirements Attributes

As each requirement or set of requirements is specified and modeled, the relevant attributes, as selected when *Plan Requirements Management Process (2.5)* is performed, must be captured.

.5   Improvement Opportunities

Analysts should work to identify opportunities to improve the operation of the business. Some common examples of opportunities that a business analyst is likely to identify include:

Automate Or Simplify The Work People Perform: Relatively simple tasks, where decisions are made on the basis of strict or inflexible rules, are prime candidates for automation.

Improve Access To Information: Provide greater amounts of information to staff who interface directly or indirectly with customers, thus reducing the need for specialists. Decision makers may not require this level of detail, but should be made aware of where and from whom they may get it if required. Normally, decision makers need to be provided with the meaning and relevance of the data acquired and used by operational personnel.

Reduce Complexity Of Interfaces: Interfaces are needed whenever work is transferred between systems or between people. Reducing their complexity can improve understanding.

Increase Consistency Of Behavior: Different workers may handle similar cases in a very different fashion, causing customer dissatisfaction and frustration.

Eliminate Redundancy: Different stakeholder groups may have common needs that can be met with a single solution, reducing the cost of implementation.

6.3.5 Techniques

.1   General Techniques

Techniques that can be used to specify or model requirements include:

- ▶ Acceptance and Evaluation Criteria Definition (9.1)
- ▶ Business Rules Analysis (9.4)
- ▶ Data Dictionary and Glossary (9.5)
- ▶ Data Flow Diagrams (9.6)
- ▶ Data Modeling (9.7)
- ▶ Functional Decomposition (9.12)
- ▶ Interface Analysis (9.13)
- ▶ Metrics and Key Performance Indicators (9.16)
- ▶ Non-functional Requirements Analysis (9.17)
- ▶ Organization Modeling (9.19)
- ▶ Process Modeling (9.21)
- ▶ Prototyping (9.22)
- ▶ Scenarios and Use Cases (9.26)
- ▶ Sequence Diagrams (9.28)
- ▶ State Diagrams (9.29)
- ▶ User Stories (9.33)

6.3.6 Stakeholders

Any Stakeholder: The business analyst may choose to perform this task alone and then separately package and communicate the requirements to stakeholders for their review and/or approval, or invite some or all stakeholders to participate in this task (depending on which requirements are being analyzed, the business analysis approach, the preferences of the business analyst, and other factors).

6.3.7 Output

Requirements [Analyzed]: Modeled and specified requirements are produced by this task.

6.4   Define Assumptions and Constraints

6.4.1 Purpose

Identify factors other than requirements that may affect which solutions are viable.

6.4.2   Description

Assumptions are factors that are believed to be true, but have not been confirmed. Assumptions may affect all aspects of the project and pose a certain degree of risk if they do not prove to be true. The business analyst identifies and documents assumptions, attempts to confirm the accuracy of the assumptions, and identifies and manages risks related to the ability of a solution to meet the business need.

Constraints are defined as restrictions or limitations on possible solutions. The business analyst is responsible for documenting any restrictions or limitations to the solution design, construction, testing, validation and deployment. Solution constraints describe aspects of the current state, or planned future state that may not be changed. They are not requirements, since they are not implemented in any form by the project team. Constraints are provided to the project team to inform them that options they would normally be allowed to consider are not available.

Assumptions and constraints are generally documented with associated attributes (e.g., date identified, owner, impact, associated risk, and other explanatory information). They are defined and clarified as requirements are understood. In many cases, lower-level requirements may be dependent on, and therefore traced back to, the presence of an assumption or constraint and so may be affected if the assumption proves false or the constraint is changed.

6.4.3   Input

Stakeholder Concerns: Assumptions and constraints are identified through elicitation from stakeholders.

6.4.4   Elements

.1   Assumptions

An assumption is anything that is believed to be true but that has not actually been verified. Assumptions can relate to something in the present or in the future. Assumptions need to be documented, and if an assumption is found to be false it will usually impact the project in some manner. Assumptions are therefore a source of potential project risk. Assumptions may also reflect an understanding of how desired outcomes are likely to be achieved. For instance, stakeholders may believe that customers will respond in a certain way to a change in how a product is delivered, but there may be only anecdotal evidence to support that belief.

.2   Business Constraints

Business constraints describe limitations on available solutions, or an aspect of the current state that cannot be changed by the deployment of the new solution. They may reflect budgetary restrictions, time restrictions, limits on the number of resources available, restrictions based on the skills of the project team and the stakeholders, a requirement that certain stakeholders not be affected by the implementation of the solution, or any other organizational restriction. Constraints need to be carefully examined to ensure that they are accurate and justified.

.3   Technical Constraints

Technical constraints include any architecture decisions that are made that may impact the design of the solution. These may include development languages, hardware and software platforms, and application software that must be used. Technical constraints may also describe restrictions such as resource utilization, message size and timing, software size, maximum number of and size of files, records and data elements. Technical constraints include any enterprise architecture standards that must be followed.

Technical constraints may create a situation where a requirement cannot be met using the current solution approach or by a solution component and the business analyst must work with the project team to identify other ways to meet the associated business need.

Figure 6–5: *Define Assumptions and Constraints* Input/Output Diagram

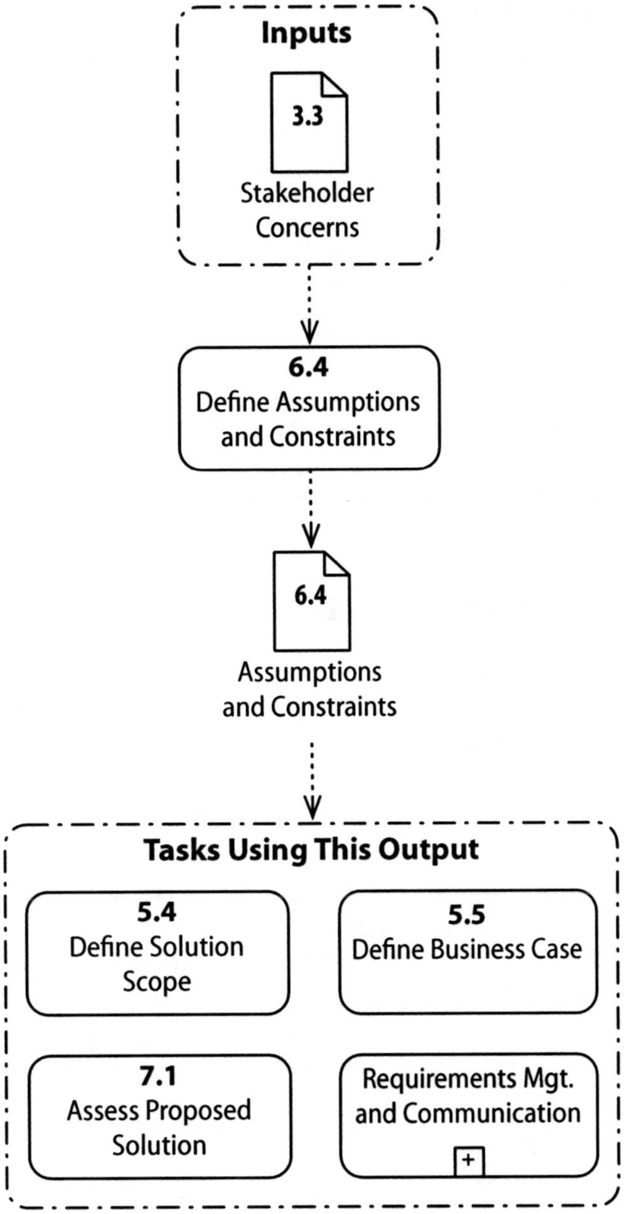

6.4.5   Techniques

Problem Tracking (9.20): Both assumptions and constraints are often identified, reviewed and managed using the ongoing planning, monitoring, and issue/risk management activities of the project team.

Risk Analysis (9.24): Assess the risk (both positive and negative) if an assumption proves invalid, or a constraint is removed.

6.4.6   Stakeholders

Implementation SME: Must take the assumptions and constraints into account when designing a solution.

Project Manager: Must assess assumptions and constraints to identify potential risks that may impact project delivery, and manage against schedule, cost and resource constraints.

All Stakeholders: The stakeholder who is responsible for defining a particular assumption or constraint should be involved in any discussion that involves changing it. Since assumptions and constraints can originate from and/or affect any stakeholder all stakeholders may be involved in the identification of assumptions or constraints.

6.4.7   Output

Assumptions and Constraints: Assumptions and constraints will limit potential solution options and will be monitored for potential changes. While they are not technically requirements, they can be managed and communicated by performing the tasks in *Chapter 4: Requirements Management and Communication.*

6.5   Verify Requirements

6.5.1   Purpose

Requirements verification ensures that requirements specifications and models meet the necessary standard of quality to allow them to be used effectively to guide further work.

6.5.2   Description

Verifying requirements ensures that the requirements have been defined correctly; that is, that they are of acceptable quality. Requirements that do not meet quality standards are defective and must be revised. Requirements verification constitutes a final check by the business analyst and key stakeholders to determine that the requirements are:

▶   ready for formal review and validation by the customers and users, and

▶   provide all the information needed for further work based on the requirements to be performed.

6.5.3   Input

Requirements [Any Except Stated]: Any requirement may be verified (including business, stakeholder, solution, and transition requirements). Verification is a quality check performed following analysis of a requirement.

Figure 6–6: *Verify Requirements* Input/Output Diagram

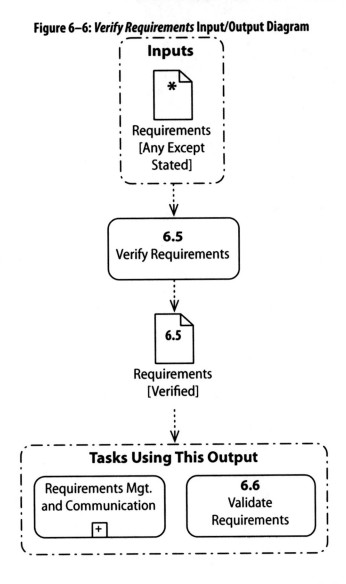

6.5.4   Elements

The business analyst verifies that requirements have been specified in well-written requirements statements.

.1   Characteristics of Requirements Quality

At a minimum, a high quality requirement exhibits the following characteristics:

Cohesive: A cohesive set of requirements relates to only one thing, whether that is a business process, business rule, organizational unit, or so forth. All requirements in a set or model should support its overall purpose and scope.

Complete: The entire set of requirements should represent all relevant requirements. Also each individual requirement should be complete. Ensure each requirement is self-contained without any missing information.

Consistent: Ensure that individual requirements do not contradict each other or describe the same requirement using different wording. In addition, the level of detail supplied for each requirement in a set or model should be the same.

Correct: Defects in requirements will lead to defects in the resulting solution.

Feasible: Each requirement must be implementable within the existing infrastructure, with the existing budget, timeline and resources available to the team (or the project must develop the capability to implement the requirement). The business analyst needs to work with the project team to make these determinations.

Modifiable: Related requirements must be grouped together in order for requirements to be modifiable. This characteristic is exhibited by a logical structuring of the requirements.

Unambiguous: Individual requirements must never be unclear. A requirement must not allow for multiple divergent valid interpretations of the requirement.

Testable: There must be a way to prove that a requirement has been fulfilled. Each requirement should be testable—that is, it must be possible to design a test that can be used to determine if a solution has met the requirement or some other means of determining whether to accept a solution that meets the requirement.

.2   Verification Activities

Verification activities are typically performed iteratively throughout the requirements analysis process. Verification activities include:

▶ Check for completeness within each requirements model. For example, data flow diagrams will have all components and data flows labeled, and all data flows will have arrows indicating direction.

▶ Compare each prepared requirements model (textual or graphical) against all other prepared requirements models. Check for elements that are mentioned in one model that are missing in the other models. Also check that the same component is referenced the same way in all models – for example, use of consistent language, e.g., 'customer' and 'client'. Resolve all discrepancies, correcting terminology, or adding/ deleting components as needed.

▶ Make sure all variations to the documented processes have been identified and documented. Pay particular attention to common branching logic – e.g. "none found", "one and only one found" or "more than one found".

▶ Make sure all triggers and outcomes have been accounted for in all variations.

▶ Make sure the terminology used in expressing the requirement is understandable to stakeholders and consistent with the use of those terms within the organization.

▶ Add examples where appropriate for clarification and to strengthen the business case.

6.5.5   Techniques

.1   General Techniques

Acceptance and Evaluation Criteria Definition (9.1): Ensure that requirements are stated clearly enough to devise a set of tests that can prove that the requirement has been met.

Problem Tracking (9.20): May be used to ensure that any problems identified during verification are resolved.

Structured Walkthrough (9.30): Used to inspect requirements documentation to identify ambiguous or unclear requirements.

.2   Checklists

Checklists are useful as a quality control technique for requirements documentation. They may include a standard set of quality elements that the business analyst or other reviewers use to validate the requirements or be specifically developed to capture issues of concern to the project. The purpose of a checklist is to ensure that items that the organization or project team has determined are important are included in the final requirements deliverable(s), or that process steps that the organization or project team has determined must be followed are addressed. Checklists may also be developed on a project basis to help ensure consistency of approach and outcomes, particularly on large projects where multiple sub-project teams are working.

6.5.6   Stakeholders

All Stakeholders: The business analyst, in conjunction with the domain and technical subject matter experts, has the primary responsibility for determining that this task has been completed. Other stakeholders may discover problematic requirements during requirements communication. Therefore, virtually all project stakeholders are involved in this task.

6.5.7   Output

Requirements [Verified]: Verified requirements are of sufficient quality to allow further work based on those requirements to be performed.

6.6   Validate Requirements

6.6.1   Purpose

The purpose of requirements validation is to ensure that all requirements support the delivery of value to the business, fulfill its goals and objectives, and meet a stakeholder need.

6.6.2   Description

Requirements validation is an ongoing process to ensure that stakeholder, solution, and transition requirements align to the business requirements.

Assessing what the outcome will be for the stakeholder when their need is satisfied can be helpful when validating requirements. Implementation of the requirements as a whole must be sufficient to achieve that desired future state for customers and users. In many cases, stakeholders will have different, conflicting needs and expectations that may be exposed through the validation process and will need to be reconciled. See *Manage Solution Scope and Requirements (4.1)*.

6.6.3   Input

Business Case: The business case describes the overall business objectives and measurements that the solution is expected to deliver. To be valid, a requirement must contribute directly or indirectly to the business case. Other business requirements, including the business need, required capabilities, and solution scope may also be used for validation.

Stakeholder, Solution, or Transition Requirements [Verified]: Requirements need to be verified for validation to be completed. If a requirement cannot be verified, it cannot be successfully implemented and so cannot meet a business need. However, validation activities may begin before requirements are completely verified.

Figure 6–6: *Validate Requirements* Input/Output Diagram

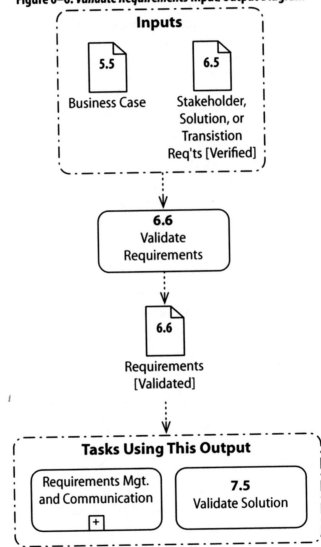

6.6.4   Elements

.1   Identify Assumptions

In many cases it may not be possible to prove that implementation of the requirement will result in the desired benefit. If an organization is launching an unprecedented product or service, it may be necessary to make assumptions about customer or stakeholder response, as there are no similar previous experiences to rely on. In other cases, it may be difficult or impossible to prove that a particular problem derives from an identified root cause. Stakeholders may have assumed that certain benefits will result from the implementation of a requirement, and these assumptions must be identified and defined so that associated risks can be managed. See *Define Assumptions and Constraints (6.4)*.

.2   Define Measurable Evaluation Criteria

While the forecasted business benefits are defined in the business case, the specific measurement criteria and evaluation process may not have been included. Following the definition of the benefits that will result from the implementation of a requirement, it is necessary to define the evaluation criteria that will be used to evaluate how successful the resulting change has been after the solution is deployed (see *Metrics and Key Performance Indicators (9.16)* for information on the selection of appropriate criteria, and *Evaluate Solution Performance (7.6)* for details on how this assessment is performed post-implementation).

.3   Determine Business Value

The business case defines the value delivered by a solution that meets the solution scope, but it is also possible to assess individual requirements or features to determine if they also deliver business value. *Specify and Model Requirements (6.3)* outlines some ways in which a requirement can deliver business value. A requirement that does not deliver direct or indirect value to a stakeholder is a strong candidate for elimination. Value does not need to be monetary. Business value can be delivered through requirements that support compliance with regulatory or other standards, alignment with internal standards or policies of the organization, or increased satisfaction for stakeholders, even if those things do not have a direct measurable financial benefit.

.4   Determine Dependencies for Benefits Realization

Not all requirements contribute directly to the end result desired by the organization and described in the business case. See *Manage Requirements Traceability (4.2)* for the types of relationships that might exist.

.5   Evaluate Alignment with Business Case and Opportunity Cost

A requirement can be of value to a stakeholder and still not be a desirable part of a solution. A requirement that is not aligned with the business case should be defined and approved in a separate business case, or considered for removal from the solution scope. Ultimately, each requirement must be traceable to the objectives in the business case, and should also minimize the opportunity cost of implementation.

At the project level, opportunity cost refers to the benefits that could have been achieved with an alternative investment rather than this one. In other words, it is the cost of what you cannot do or have because you chose to invest in this project instead of another one. This concept can also be applied to decisions made within a project. For example, if a project team spends time and energy implementing a feature in a software application, that effort cannot be applied towards additional testing, training for the users, bug fixes, or other project work. That lost work represents the opportunity cost of the decision. The opportunity cost of any decision is equal to the value of the best alternative use of those resources.

6.6.5   Techniques

Acceptance and Evaluation Criteria Definition (9.1): Acceptance criteria are the quality metrics that must be met to achieve acceptance by a stakeholder.

Metrics and Key Performance Indicators (9.16): Used to select appropriate performance measures for a solution, solution component, or requirement.

Prototyping (9.22): Prototyping of product components is used to gain user agreement with the proposed solution.

Risk Analysis (9.24): Risk analysis can be used to identify possible scenarios that would alter the value delivered by a requirement.

Structured Walkthrough (9.30): Review meetings are conducted to confirm whether the stakeholder agrees that their needs are met.

6.6.6   Stakeholders

All Stakeholders: Virtually all stakeholders are involved in or impacted by validation activities.

6.6.7   Outputs

Requirements [Validated]: Validated requirements are those that can be demonstrated to deliver value to stakeholders and are aligned with the business goals and objectives. If a requirement cannot be validated, it does not benefit the organization, does not fall within the solution scope, or both.

Solution Assessment & Validation

chapter SEVEN

The *Solution Assessment and Validation* Knowledge Area describes the tasks that are performed in order to ensure that solutions meet the business need and to facilitate their successful implementation. These activities may be performed to assess and validate business processes, organizational structures, outsourcing agreements, software applications, and any other component of the solution.

Business analysis plays a vital role in ensuring that the process of reviewing, selecting, and designing the solution is done in a way that maximizes value delivered to stakeholders. The business analyst knows the business environment and can assess how each proposed solution would affect that environment. The business analyst is responsible for ensuring that stakeholders fully understand the solution requirements and that implementation decisions are aligned with the relevant requirements.

Note: the performance of all solution assessment and validation activities are governed by the business analysis plans (see 2.3), and business analysis performance metrics should be tracked (see 2.6).

Figure 7–1: *Solution Assessment and Validation* Input/Output Diagram

Inputs	Tasks	Outputs
6.4 Assumptions and Constraints	7.1 Assess Proposed Solution	7.1 Assessment of Proposed Solution
Enterprise Architecture	7.2 Allocate Requirements	7.5 Identified Defects
* Requirements	7.3 Assess Org. Readiness	7.5 Mitigating Actions
Solution [Constructed, Deployed, or Designed]	7.4 Define Transition Requirements	7.3 Organizational Readiness Assessment
Solution Option(s)	7.5 Validate Solution	7.2 Requirements [Allocated]
Solution Performance Metrics	7.6 Evaluate Solution Performance	7.4 Transition Requirements
5.4 Solution Scope		7.6 Solution Performance Assessment
3.3 Stakeholder Concerns		7.5 Solution Validation Assessment

7.1   Assess Proposed Solution

7.1.1   Purpose

To assess proposed solutions in order to determine how closely they meet stakeholder and solution requirements.

7.1.2   Description

Solution assessment may be performed on a single solution or to compare multiple proposed solutions.

When assessing a single solution, the business analyst determines whether the solution delivers enough business value to justify its implementation. This will most often be the case when a custom solution has been created to meet a particular business need.

When assessing multiple alternative solutions, the business analyst has the additional

Figure 7–2: *Assess Proposed Solution* **Input/Output Diagram**

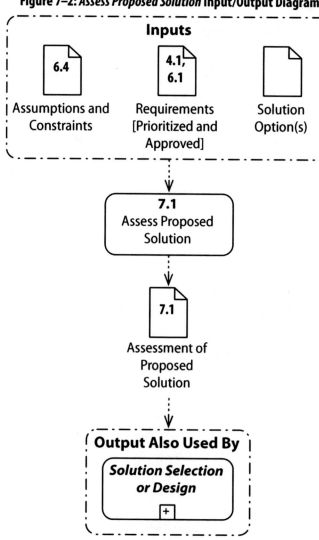

goal of attempting to determine which solution delivers the greatest business value. This requires understanding the advantages and disadvantages of each alternative.

7.1.3 Input

Assumptions and Constraints: Assumptions may lead to certain solutions being favored, while constraints may limit available solution options.

Requirements [Prioritized and Approved]: The relative priorities of requirements allow analysis to identify the choices that meet the most important requirements. Requirements must be approved in order to allow a decision to be made.

Solution Option(s): Information on each proposed solution must be available. The information should be in a form that facilitates effective comparison of the different available options.

7.1.4 Elements

.1   Ranking of Solution Options

When relatively few criteria are involved, it may be easiest focus on those criteria where substantive differences exist between solution options. Those differences then form the basis for the decision.

For more complex decision problems, a scoring system may be used, with sets of related requirements assigned a weighting to reflect their relative importance to the organization. Each solution is scored and the top-rated solution or solutions are then investigated in greater detail.

.2 Identification of Additional Potential Capabilities

Solution options will sometimes offer capabilities (whether potential or actual) to the organization above and beyond those identified in the requirements or the original business case. In many cases, these capabilities are not of immediate value to the organization but have the potential to provide future value, as the solution may support the rapid development or implementation of those capabilities if they are required (for example, a software application may have features that the organization anticipates using in the future).

7.1.5 Techniques

Acceptance and Evaluation Criteria Definition (9.1): Requirements should be expressed in the form of acceptance criteria to make them most useful when assessing proposed solutions.

Decision Analysis (9.8): Decision analysis methods directly support the assessment and ranking of solution options.

Vendor Assessment (9.34): When an option is being provided in whole or in part by a third party, the assessment of the solution should be coupled with an assessment of the vendor to ensure that all parties will be able to develop and maintain a healthy working relationship.

7.1.6 Stakeholders

Domain SME: Domain SMEs can provide feedback during the selection process or participate in assessing options.

Implementation SME: Gather information from experts with specific expertise in the solution options under consideration. Interoperability with the organization's enterprise architecture needs to be considered.

Operational Support: Provide information on technical constraints that may limit the solutions that can be implemented.

Project Manager: Will need to plan and manage the selection process.

Supplier: Will provide information on the functionality associated with a particular solution option.

Sponsor: Approves the expenditure of resources to purchase or develop a solution and approve the final recommendation.

7.1.7   Output

Assessment of Proposed Solution: Assess the value delivered by each proposed solution. If multiple options are available, a recommendation of the best solution should be made. A recommendation to terminate the initiative may be given if no solution delivers enough value to justify being implemented.

7.2   Allocate Requirements

7.2.1   Purpose

Allocate stakeholder and solution requirements among solution components and releases in order to maximize the possible business value given the options and alternatives generated by the design team.

7.2.2   Description

Requirements allocation is the process of assigning stakeholder and solution requirements to solution components and to releases. Allocation is supported by assessing the tradeoffs between alternatives in order to maximize benefits and minimize costs. The business value of a solution changes depending on how requirements are implemented

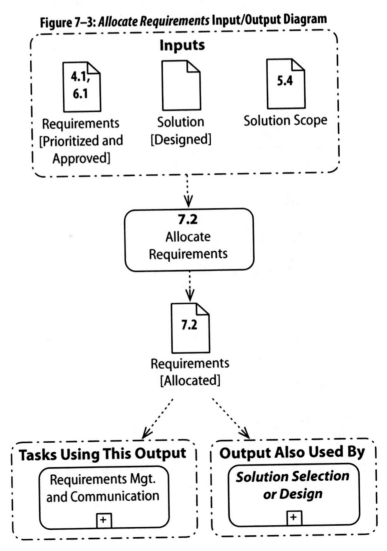

Figure 7–3: *Allocate Requirements* Input/Output Diagram

and when the solution becomes available to stakeholders, and the objective of allocation is to maximize that value.

Requirements may be allocated between organizational units, between job functions, between people and software, software application components or releases of a solution. Requirements allocation typically begins early in the project lifecycle (as soon as the solution approach can be determined) and will continue to be performed until all valid requirements are allocated. Allocation typically continues through design and construction of a solution.

7.2.3 Input

Requirements [Prioritized and Approved]: Requirements allocation may be performed with requirements in any state (e.g. stated, analyzed, verified, validated) although completion of this task requires requirements have been approved.

Solution [Designed]: The solution design must have a defined set of components, and the costs and effort associated with delivery of those components must have been estimated. Tradeoffs can then be made between the functionality allocated to each component and the cost associated with developing that component.

Solution Scope: The solution scope allocates business requirements to components and releases. The associated stakeholder and solution requirements should match that allocation, or the solution scope will have to be revised.

7.2.4 Elements

.1 Solution Components

The majority of business solutions (with the exception of minor changes or upgrades to an existing solution) will be composed of multiple components. Each component implements a subset of the requirements. The allocation of requirements to solution components will be a primary driver of the cost to implement the solution and the benefits delivered by it.

Solution components may include:

▶ Business policies and business rules

▶ Business processes to be performed and managed

▶ People who operate and maintain the solution, including their job functions and responsibilities

▶ Software applications and application components used in the solution.

▶ Structure of the organization, including interactions between the organization, its customers, and its suppliers

During solution design, it may become necessary to revisit the initial allocation of functionality between components as defined in the solution scope as the cost to implement each component becomes better understood, and to determine which allocations have the best cost/benefit ratio.

As costs and effort are understood for each solution component, the business analyst will need to assess whether the allocation represents the most effective tradeoffs between delivery options. Considerations are likely to include:

▶ **Available resources**: The suppliers will be faced with limitations regarding the amount of requirements they can implement based on the allocated resources. In some instances, the business analyst may be able to develop a business case that justifies additional investment.

▶ **Constraints on the solution**: Regulatory requirements or business decisions may require that certain requirements be handled manually or automatically, or that certain requirements must be prioritized above all others.

▶ **Dependencies between requirements**: Some capabilities may in and of themselves provide limited value to the organization, but need to be delivered in order to support other high-value requirements.

.2   Release Planning

Facilitate the decisions about which requirements will be included in each release/phase/iteration of the project. There are many factors that will guide these decisions, such as the overall project budget, the need to implement a solution or parts of the solution by a certain date, resource constraints, training schedule and ability for the business to absorb changes within a defined timeframe. Ensure all parties understand the consequences to the organization based on the planned schedule of releases and identify the solution capabilities that will deliver the greatest business value.

There may be organizational restraints or policies that must be adhered to in any implementation, including constraints such as freeze periods for implementation, general company policies, and any phased-in activities. Business analysts assist in planning the timing of the implementation within a business cycle in order to cause minimal disruption of business activities.

7.2.5   Techniques

Acceptance and Evaluation Criteria Definition (9.1): A minimal set of acceptance criteria may need to be met by a particular release.

Business Rules Analysis (9.4): Business rules can be managed and monitored by people or automated by a software application.

Decision Analysis (9.8): Can be used to estimate the value associated with different allocation decisions and optimize those decisions.

Functional Decomposition (9.12): Can be used to break down solution scope into smaller components for allocation

Process Modeling (9.21): Activities in the process model may be allocated to different roles, or outsourced to a supplier. A solution can be developed that incrementally supports some subprocesses or activities.

Scenarios and Use Cases (9.26): Alternative flows can be separated from the base use case and included in an extension to be moved into a later release.

7.2.6 Stakeholders

Customers and **Suppliers:** Will be affected by how and when requirements are implemented and may have to be consulted about, or agree to, the allocation decisions.

Domain SME: May have recommendations regarding the set of requirements to be allocated to a solution component or to a release.

End User: May require a minimal defined set of requirements to be implemented before a release can be accepted. If requirements are reallocated to a manual process, the additional workload may seriously affect their job performance and satisfaction. End users may have concerns about the frequency of change that they are prepared to accept and will need to be aware of reallocations.

Implementation SME: Will be responsible for the design and construction of some or all solution components and the estimation of the work required. Will make recommendations regarding the allocation of requirements and may take ownership of allocation if the decision regarding a particular allocation does not have any significant impact on the ability of the solution to meet business or stakeholder requirements. In particular, allocation of requirements between the individual software application components is usually the responsibility of a system architect or developer.

Operational Support: Will be affected by the allocation of requirements to components and releases and need to be aware of when and where requirements are allocated.

Project Manager: Responsible for the work being done by the project team and will need to participate in requirements allocation in order to manage the project scope and work. May need to request reallocation in order to reduce project work or seek adjustments to the scope or budget of the project.

Tester: Responsible for verifying releases and solution components and will therefore need to know how requirements have been allocated.

Sponsor: Responsible for funding of the project and therefore required to approve the allocation of requirements to components and releases based on the recommendation of the business analyst and the project team.

7.2.7 Output

Requirements [Allocated]: Allocated requirements are associated with a solution component that will implement them.

7.3 Assess Organizational Readiness

7.3.1 Purpose

Assess whether the organization is ready to make effective use of a new solution.

7.3.2 Description

An organizational readiness assessment describes the effect a new solution will have on an organization and whether the organization is prepared for the organizational change that the solution implementation will cause. Effective communication of solution impacts assists in enabling necessary organizational change management practices and identifying training requirements for solution implementation.

In order to identify impacts the business analyst should understand what changes will occur in the business area, technical infrastructure or processes and how these affect other business units or operations.

Figure 7–4: *Assess Organizational Readiness* Input/Output Diagram

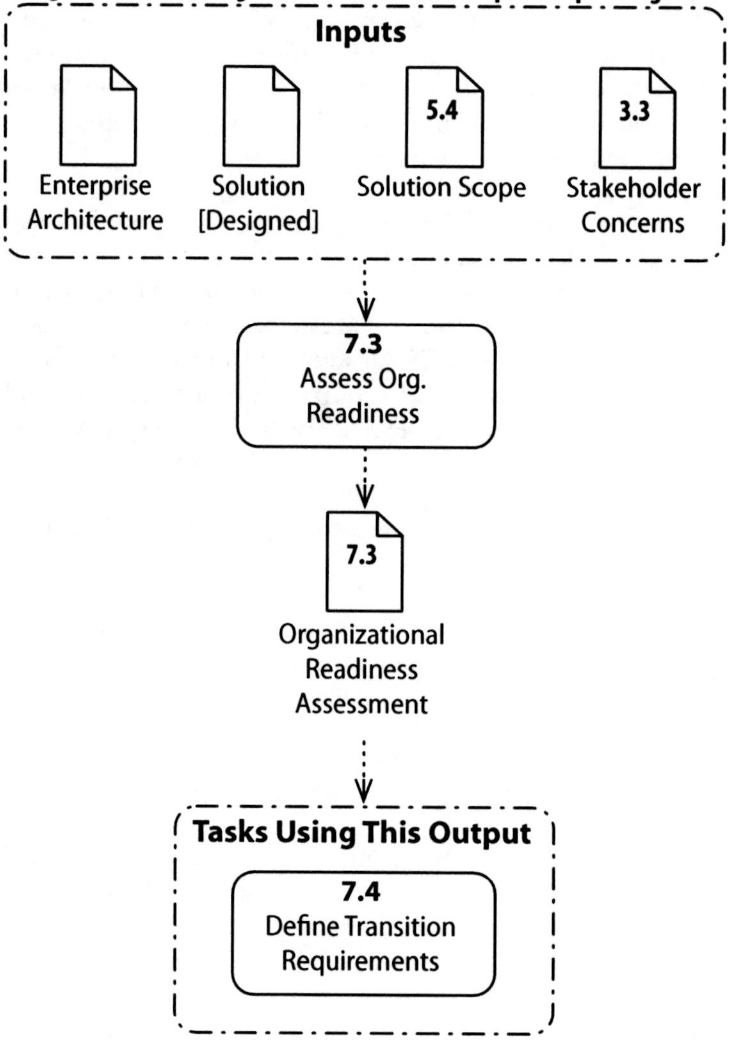

7.3.3   Input

Enterprise Architecture: Describes the current state of the enterprise, including the organizational structure, business processes, systems, information, etc.

Solution Scope: used to determine which components of the business architecture are affected.

Solution [Designed]: Used in place of the solution scope, if available.

Stakeholder Concerns: Used to assess potential problems or issues.

7.3.4   Elements

.1   Cultural Assessment

Determine whether stakeholder groups genuinely want the change to be successful. Assess the beliefs, attitudes and feelings common to key stakeholder groups and the willingness of those stakeholder groups to accept a change. Determine whether stakeholders understand the reasons that a new solution is being implemented, whether they view that solution as something that will be beneficial, and they understand the reasons why a new solution is required.

.2   Operational or Technical Assessment

Determine whether the organization is able to take advantage of the capabilities provided by the new solution, and evaluate whether stakeholders are prepared to make use of the new solution. Determine if training has been performed, whether new policies and procedures have been defined, whether IT systems required to support it are in place, and whether the solution is capable of performing at a required level.

.3   Stakeholder Impact Analysis

Understand how change will affect a particular stakeholder group. Some things that may be considered in an impact analysis include:

Functions: What processes involve the stakeholder and what applications does the stakeholder use?

Location: Are the stakeholders located in a single place or in a distributed team? If they are distributed, will the change affect their communications?

Tasks: What tasks are performed by people associated with that stakeholder group? Will the change alter how those tasks are performed, or affect the skill levels required to perform them? Will stakeholders have more or less flexibility in performing their tasks?

Concerns: What are this group's usability requirements, preferences, and their proficiency level regarding interaction with computer systems? Will their work become more or less demanding? Are any members of the group at risk of losing their jobs? Will the changes affect their work satisfaction?

7.3.5   Techniques

.1   General Techniques

Acceptance and Evaluation Criteria Definition (9.1): Acceptance criteria must reflect solution performance levels that would allow the organization to have confidence in solutions that meet those criteria.

Data Flow Diagrams (9.6) and **Process Models (9.21):** Useful for identifying the activities that are likely to change with the implementation of a new solution and the stakeholders who performed those activities.

Focus Groups (9.11), Interviews (9.14) and **Survey/Questionnaire (9.31):** Can assist with identifying stakeholder concerns or issues.

Organization Modeling (9.19): Used to identify stakeholders or stakeholder groups that may be impacted by the new solution.

Problem Tracking (9.20): Used to ensure that issues identified by the organizational readiness assessment are resolved.

Risk Analysis (9.24): Used to assess potential problems that are identified during the organizational readiness assessment, determine which possible problems are the most important to deal with, and develop a mitigation strategy.

SWOT Analysis (9.32): Used to assess strategies developed to respond to identified issues.

.2   Force Field Analysis

Force field analysis is a graphical method for depicting the forces that support and oppose a change. It involves identifying the forces that support and oppose a change, depicting them on opposite sides of a line, and then estimating the strength of each force in order to assess which set of forces are stronger. Once this analysis is complete, the next step is to look for ways to strengthen the forces that support the desired outcome or generate new forces.

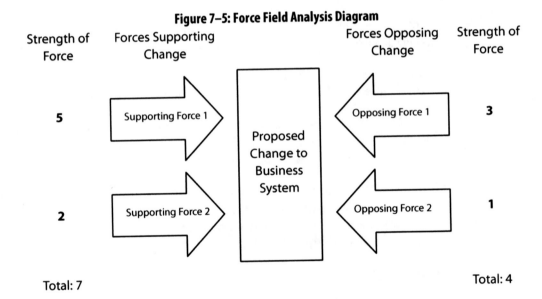

Figure 7–5: Force Field Analysis Diagram

7.3.6   Stakeholders

Domain SME: Provides information on the likely impact to stakeholders and the capabilities of the enterprise.

Implementation SME: Supplies information on the skills and capabilities necessary to successfully operate the new solution. There are a number of Implementation SMEs that can have a significant effect on the ability of an organization to implement change, including, but not limited to:

► Organizational Change Management SMEs assist organizations with communicating change to their stakeholders and creating support among those stakeholders for the change.

▶ Usability SMEs assist with the evaluation and design of software applications that are easier to understand and use.

▶ Training SMEs assist with the creation of a training plan to help stakeholders develop the skills that they need to effectively use the new solution.

Operational Support: Provides information on their ability to support the operation of the solution. Will need to understand the nature of the solution in order to be able to support it.

Project Manager: Requires the organizational readiness assessment to determine if additional project work is required for a successful implementation of the solution. An implementation plan should be created to outline the steps to be taken and the order in which they must be executed to resolve any issues identified in the organizational readiness assessment.

Sponsor: Authorizes and champions action to resolve problems identified in the organizational readiness assessment.

7.3.7 Output

Organizational Readiness Assessment: Describes whether stakeholders are prepared to accept the change associated with a solution and are able to use it effectively. May lead to revisions in solution or project scope.

7.4 Define Transition Requirements

7.4.1 Purpose

To define requirements for capabilities needed to transition from an existing solution to a new solution.

7.4.2 Description

In most cases, a solution is implemented within an enterprise in order to enhance or replace an existing solution. During the transition period (the time when both the old and new solutions are operational), the enterprise may need to operate both solutions in parallel, move information between the new and old solution, conduct training to enable stakeholders to effectively operate the new solution, and so forth. In addition to developing the solution itself, the implementation team is likely to have to develop additional capabilities to support this transition.

These capabilities are requirements, as stakeholders need to be able to make this transition successfully—but they are different in nature from other kinds of requirements, as they cannot be defined until a solution has been designed. These requirements also have a different lifespan from other types of requirements, as they remain relevant only during the transition period between solutions.

Transition requirements are elicited, analyzed, managed, and communicated by performing the same tasks as for other requirements. The difference is not in the methods for defining them, but in the inputs, the nature of transition requirements, and in that they cease to be relevant once the existing solution is eliminated.

In instances where there is no existing solution, and the new solution is adding a entirely new capability to the enterprise rather than extending and improving an existing capability, then transition requirements do not need to be analyzed.

Figure 7–6: *Define Transition Requirements* Input/Output Diagram

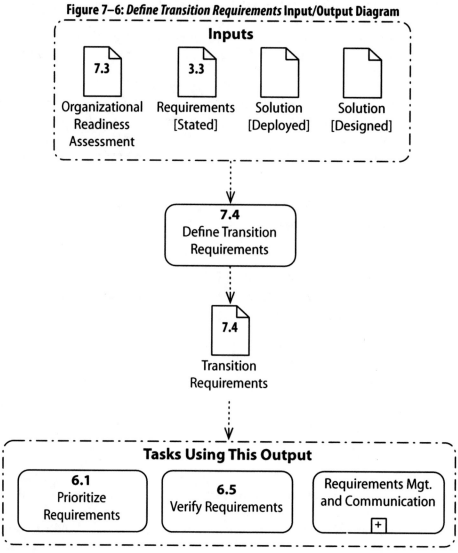

7.4.3   Input

Organizational Readiness Assessment: Used to identify areas where the organization needs to add new capabilities to manage and operate the new solution.

Requirements [Stated]: Stakeholders will identify the information and processes they need during transition.

Solution [Deployed]: The deployed (or existing) solution will be investigated to understand what needs to be transitioned to the new solution. It may be necessary to elicit a description of the capabilities of the solution and perform some analysis tasks in order to ensure that current capabilities are fully understood.

Solution [Designed]: The design for the new solution must be sufficiently defined to allow major differences to be identified.

7.4.4   Elements

Examine the solution currently in place to identify features that are implemented in a substantially different fashion in the new solution, information that needs to be transferred to the new solution, and other areas of significant change. Likely sources of transition requirements include:

.1   Data

The actual data and metadata managed by the old system needs to be evaluated to determine whether to archive the information or transfer it to the new solution. Rules for conversion of this information will need to be developed, and business rules may need to be defined to ensure that the new solution interprets the converted data correctly.

.2   Ongoing Work

It is likely that work will be ongoing in the old version of the solution at the time the new version is implemented. Options for managing this ongoing work may include finishing existing work using the current solution and starting new work in the new solution, holding the processing of new work for a period of time, or converting all work at the time of implementation.

.3   Organizational Change

The business analyst may be involved in developing a process for managing the people side of change related to the solution. Organizational change management generally refers to a process and set of tools for managing change at an organizational level. The business analyst may help to develop recommendations for changes to the organizational structure or personnel, as job functions may change significantly as the result of work being automated. New information may be made available to stakeholders, and new skills may be required to operate the solution.

7.4.5   Techniques

Business Rules Analysis (9.4): Additional business rules may be defined to assist in migrating data, or to manage work migrated from the existing solution (as it is possible that different rules may apply depending on when the work was performed).

Data Flow Diagrams (9.6), Process Modeling (9.21) and **Organization Modeling (9.19):** These may be analyzed to identify the differences between the existing and new solutions.

Data Modeling (9.7): Physical data models of the existing and new solutions will be compared to enable a mapping between the two.

7.4.6   Stakeholders

Customer: May be negatively affected during the transition based on the transfer of ongoing work, or if information is incorrectly transferred.

Domain SME: Will provide information on the existing solution and assist in verification and validation of the transition requirements.

End User: If the existing and the new solution are both in use for a period, they will need to know how to co-ordinate between them.

Implementation SME: Will be the source for many of the transition requirements.

Operational Support: May need to operate two solutions simultaneously.

Project Manager: Will need to plan for the work required to implement the transition requirements. This may affect the project scope.

Regulator: May require that records of the transition requirements and process be retained for long-term review and compliance with regulations.

Tester: Will verify that the transition has been performed correctly, including the development of test plans.

Sponsor: Will need to be informed of the potential effects of the transition on the costs and benefits of the new solution.

7.4.7   Output

Transition Requirements: Transition requirements describe capabilities that must be developed in order for an organization to successfully transition between solutions. Transition requirements are analyzed by this task and must still be verified, validated, managed and communicated.

7.5   Validate Solution

7.5.1   Purpose

Validate that a solution meets the business need and determine the most appropriate response to identified defects.

7.5.2   Description

Solution validation is required to ensure that a delivered solution meets the business needs on an ongoing basis. Problems that are identified through solution validation will be reported and prioritized for resolution. When a problem is identified with the solution (i.e. a failure to meet a stakeholder need, whether or not the requirement was correctly specified) the business analyst will be able to help the team determine the most appropriate action.

7.5.3   Input

Solution [Constructed]: Validation can only be performed against a solution that actually exists. The solution may or may not be in actual use by the enterprise.

Requirements [Prioritized and Validated]: The priorities are needed to determine which requirements are candidates for acceptance criteria. The requirements are used to determine whether outputs of the solution fall within acceptable parameters.

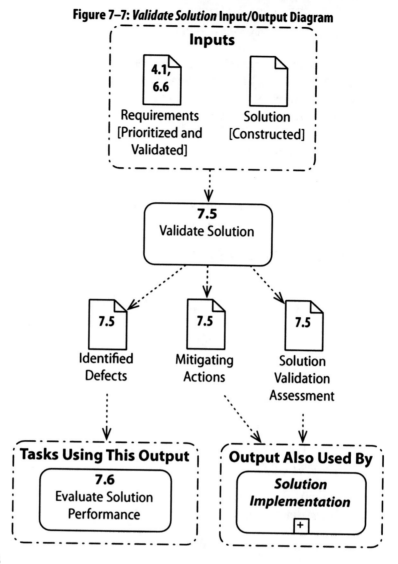

Figure 7–7: *Validate Solution* Input/Output Diagram

7.5.4   Elements

.1   Investigate Defective Solution Outputs

Identify defects in a solution or solution component by looking at cases where the outputs from the solution are below an acceptable level of quality. It is necessary to define what is considered to be a defective output. For example, a requirement might be considered to be defective if it is changed more than once before it is implemented, or if it is rejected by reviewers after the second round of reviews. When it can be determined that the solution is consistently producing defective outputs, root cause analysis should be performed in order to identify the cause of the problem.

Some solution components (software applications being the most likely example) may require an implementation SME to investigate the root cause of problems.

.2   Assess Defects and Issues

Identified defects are reviewed to assess the effect that they will have on the operation of the organization. This requires determining the severity of the defect, the probability of the occurrence of the defect, the severity of the business impact, and the capacity of the business to absorb the impact of the defects. The business analyst may be required to identify which defects must be resolved, which can be mitigated through workarounds or other approaches, and which can be accepted until resources exist to address them.

If a defect cannot be resolved in a timeframe that is acceptable from a business perspective (due to complexity, because the cause cannot be identified, because it is not a sufficiently high priority, or for any other reason), and stakeholders cannot accept the defect, the business analyst may investigate options for mitigating the effects. These may include additional quality control checks, new manual processes, removal of support for certain exception cases, or other measures.

7.5.5 Techniques

Acceptance and Evaluation Criteria Definition (9.1): Determine the set of requirements that the solution must meet in order to be considered valid.

Problem Tracking (9.20): Used to track identified defects to ensure that they are resolved.

Root Cause Analysis (9.25): Used to ensure that the underlying reason for a defect is identified, rather than simply correcting the output (which may be a symptom of a deeper underlying problem).

7.5.6 Stakeholders

Domain SME: Will provide input into the development of acceptance and evaluation criteria.

End User: May assist in the development of acceptance and evaluation criteria and participate in acceptance testing.

Implementation SME : Will support the validation process, investigate defects, correct identified defects, and participate in the defect prioritization and resolution process.

Operational Support: Will support the deployment of defect resolutions.

Project Manager: Responsible for co-ordination of work between the parties involved in the validation process.

Tester: Solution verification (that is, verifying that the solution behaves in accordance with the solution requirements) is the responsibility of the tester. Testers will develop and execute tests to identify defects which may need to be assessed and validated by the business analyst. Test plans may be reviewed to ensure that the planned set of test activities will be sufficient to assure the organization that the solution is in conformance with the requirements.

Regulator: May review the results of acceptance testing and require that records be kept regarding the process and outcomes.

Sponsor: The sponsor (or designate) must accept the solution.

7.5.7 Output

Identified Defects: Known problems that exist in a solution.

Mitigating Actions: Steps that can be taken, or processes that can be followed, to reduce or eliminate the effect an identified defect has on a stakeholder or stakeholder group.

Solution Validation Assessment: An assessment of whether the solution is able to meet the business need at an acceptable level of quality.

7.6   Evaluate Solution Performance

7.6.1   Purpose

Evaluate functioning solutions to understand the value they deliver and identify opportunities for improvement.

7.6.2   Description

Solution evaluation involves investigating how a solution is actually used after it is deployed, and assessing the effect it has had, both positive and negative. It may also be referred to as post-implementation assessment when performed immediately following the completion of a project.

Solutions may be adapted and modified directly by end users, including use of manual workarounds, recording of additional information, and adoption of informal policies and procedures in order to resolve problems that have occurred or to allow new uses of the solution. In order to properly evaluate the solution, it is also necessary to understand when, where and why this has occurred and assess the benefit that these changes have brought to the organization.

7.6.3   Input

Business Requirements: The performance of the solution will be measured against the business requirements. Without clear business requirements it is impossible to assess the solution's performance effectively, since there are no defined goals that it is supposed to meet.

Identified Defects: Any known defects must be considered in assessing the quality of a solution.

Solution Performance Metrics: These represent the criteria by which the performance of the solution is to be assessed. They may be quantitative (measures of time, volume, revenue, errors found, or other information for which hard numbers are available) or qualitative (user or customer satisfaction, recommendations, or other measures which summarize the opinions of stakeholders).

Solution [Deployed]: This task cannot be performed until the solution is in use.

7.6.4   Elements

.1   Understand Value Delivered By Solution

Gather the actual metrics that describe the performance of the solution. Applications may automatically report on some or all of the defined metrics, but where they do not, it will be necessary to gather qualitative and quantitative performance information. Significant over or under-performance against targets may be investigated to identify a root cause or determine an appropriate response.

Figure 7–8: *Evaluate Solution Performance* **Input/Output Diagram**

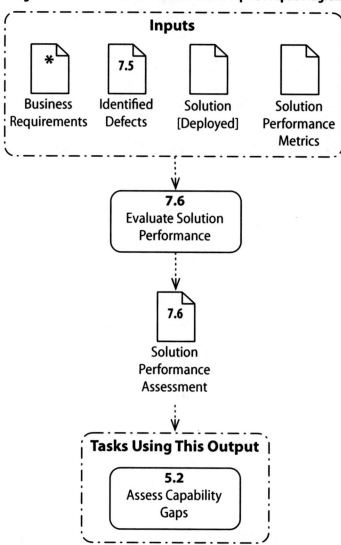

If the root cause for under-performance is a factor that is potentially under the control of the enterprise, addressing it may become a business need.

Significant over-performance may indicate that resources devoted to the solution can be used elsewhere, or that the value of the solution to the business was underestimated. It is likely that there are lessons that can be learned and applied elsewhere.

.2　Validate Solution Metrics

In some cases, the performance of a solution will be considered excellent, based on the defined performance metrics for that solution, but the business goals and objectives that those metrics are supposed to be aligned with are not being met. An analysis effort to identify and define more appropriate metrics, including modification of the solution to collect and report on those metrics, may be required.

.3　Solution Replacement or Elimination

Eventually, it will be necessary to consider the replacement of a solution or solution component. This may occur because an IT system or other technology component has reached the end of its useful life, services are being insourced or outsourced, the solution is not fulfilling the business goals set for it, or for any number of other reasons. Issues that may influence the replacement or elimination decision may include:

▶ **Ongoing Cost versus Initial Investment:** It is common for the existing solution to have increasing costs over time, while alternatives have a higher investment cost up front but lower maintenance costs.

▶ **Opportunity Cost:** Opportunity cost represents the potential value that could be realized by pursuing alternative courses of action. Replacement of an existing solution is unlikely to produce high initial returns on investment (as it will likely replicate existing capabilities, at least initially, rather than create many new ones). As the effort to develop a replacement will pull resources away from other initiatives the organization may be considering, the potential benefits from those initiatives need to be considered to determine if they are greater than the benefit of replacement (this is generally not a consideration when considering elimination).

▶ **Necessity:** Most solution components have a limited lifespan (due to obsolescence, changing market conditions, and other causes). After a certain point in the lifecycle it will become impossible to maintain the existing component.

▶ **Sunk Cost:** Sunk cost describes the money and effort already committed to an initiative. The psychological impact of sunk costs may make it difficult for stakeholders to objectively assess the rationale for replacement or elimination, as they may feel reluctant to "waste" the effort or money already invested. As this investment cannot be recovered, it is effectively irrelevant when considering future action. Decisions should be based on the future investment required and the future benefits that can be gained.

7.6.5   Techniques

Decision Analysis (9.8): A cost/benefit analysis is typically used to determine the financial impact of the solution on the organization. While critical, it is important to ensure that non-financial costs (including opportunity cost) and benefits are evaluated.

Focus Groups (9.11): Useful to gain a detailed qualitative understanding of the value of a solution to a group of stakeholders. It can be used to uncover new information beyond the scope of previously defined metrics.

Observation (9.18): May reveal uses or problems that are not being reported.

Survey/Questionnaire (9.31): Enables gathering quantitative and qualitative information from large numbers of stakeholders. If a survey is properly designed, and is responded to by a statistically significant and representative sample of the stakeholder population, it can accurately reflect the opinions of the entire population. Surveys are not especially effective at eliciting unexpected information.

7.6.6   Stakeholders

Customer, Domain SME, and **Supplier:** May provide recommendations for improvements.

End User: responsible for the day-to-day operation of the solution and a major source of information on problems or defects.

Operational Support: Will be involved in monitoring the performance and effectiveness of a solution or its components.

Regulator: May have requirements regarding the performance of a solution that must be met on an ongoing basis.

Sponsor: The person responsible for the operation of the solution from a business perspective will be responsible for deciding if the solution evaluation warrants the initiation of a change initiative.

7.6.7 Output

Solution Performance Assessment: Describes how the solution is performing in relation to business goals and objectives.

Underlying Competencies

The *Underlying Competencies* Knowledge Area provides a description of the behaviors, characteristics, knowledge and personal qualities that support the practice of business analysis.

The underlying competencies are, of course, not unique to the business analysis profession. They are described here to ensure readers are aware of the range of fundamental skills required, and provide a basis for them to investigate further into the skills and knowledge that will enable them to be accomplished and adaptable business analysts.

8.1 Analytical Thinking and Problem Solving

8.1.1 Creative Thinking

.1 Purpose

Business analysts must be effective in generating new ideas for approaches to problem solving and in generating alternative solutions.

.2 Definition

Creative thinking involves generating new ideas and concepts, as well as finding new associations between or new applications of existing ideas and concepts. These concepts should be innovative and appropriate to the situation. In addition to identifying and proposing alternatives, the business analyst can be effective in promoting creative thinking in others by asking questions and challenging assumptions.

.3 Effectiveness Measures

Measures of successful creative thinking include:

► The successful generation and productive consideration of new ideas.

► Application of new ideas to resolve existing problems.

► Willingness of stakeholders to accept new approaches.

8.1.2 Decision Making

.1 Purpose

Business analysts must be effective in understanding the criteria involved in making a decision, in making decisions, and in assisting others to make better decisions.

.2 Definition

A decision is required whenever it becomes necessary to select an alternative or approach from two or more options. Decision analysis includes gathering information relevant to a decision, breaking down the information relevant to a decision, making comparisons and tradeoffs between similar and dissimilar options, and identifying the option that is most desirable. Business analysts must be aware of the traps that can impede successful decision-making, including the tendency to accept the initial framing of a problem, the sunk cost fallacy, and the tendency to place greater weight on evidence that confirms existing impressions.

.3   Effectiveness Measures

Measures of successful decision making include:

- ▶ Confidence of the participants in the decision-analysis process that a decision is correct.

- ▶ New information or alternatives that cause a decision to be revisited are genuinely new and not simply overlooked.

- ▶ Decisions are effective in addressing the underlying problem.

- ▶ The impact of uncertainty and new information when making decisions can be effectively assessed.

8.1.3   Learning

.1   Purpose

Business analysts must be effective at learning about business domains and how they function, and then translate that learning into an understanding of how to benefit an organization.

.2   Definition

Learning is the process of gaining knowledge or skills. Learning about a domain passes through a set of stages, from initial acquisition and learning of raw facts, through comprehension of their meaning, to applying the knowledge in day-to-day work, and finally analysis, synthesis, and evaluation. A business analyst must be able to describe their level of understanding of the business domain and be capable of applying that level of understanding to determine which analysis activities need to be performed in a given situation. Once learning about a domain has reached the point where analysis is complete, the business analyst must be able to synthesize the information to identify opportunities to create new solutions and evaluate those solutions to ensure that they are effective.

.3   Effectiveness Measures

Measures of successful learning include:

- ▶ Agreement by stakeholders that analysis models effectively and completely describe the domain.

- ▶ Identification of related problems or issues from multiple areas in the domain.

- ▶ Rapid absorption of new information or new domains.

8.1.4   Problem Solving

.1   Purpose

Business analysts must be effective at defining and solving problems in order to ensure that the real, underlying problem is understood and that solutions actually address that problem.

.2 Definition

Defining a problem involves ensuring that the nature of the problem is clearly understood by all parties and that underlying issues are visible. Conflicts between the goals and objectives of the stakeholders need to be articulated and addressed. Underlying assumptions must be identified and tested. The objectives that will be met once the problem is solved need to be clearly specified and alternative solutions should be developed. Alternatives are measured against the objectives to determine which possible solution is best and identify the tradeoffs that may exist between solutions. The business analyst should be aware of a number of problem solving techniques that may be applied.

.3 Effectiveness Measures

Measures of successful problem-solving include:

▶ Confidence of the participants in the problem-solving process that a selected solution is correct.

▶ New solution options can be evaluated effectively using the problem solving framework.

▶ Selected solutions meet the defined objectives and solve the underlying problem.

▶ The problem-solving process avoids making decisions based on preconceived notions, organizational politics, or other traps that may cause a sub-optimal solution to be selected.

8.1.5   Systems Thinking

.1 Purpose

Business analysts must be effective at understanding how the people, processes and technology within an organization interact in relationships and patterns to create a system as a whole.

.2 Definition

Systems theory and systems thinking suggest that the system as a whole will have properties, behaviors and characteristics that emerge from the interaction of the components of the system, and which are not predictable from an understanding of the components alone. In the context of systems theory, the term "system" is much broader than an IT system—it also includes the people involved, the interactions between them, the external forces affecting their behavior, and all other relevant elements and factors.

.3 Effectiveness Measures

Measures of effective use of systems thinking include:

▶ Understanding of how a change to a component affects the system as a whole.

▶ Identification of reinforcing and compensating feedback loops.

▶ Understanding of how systems adapt to external pressures and changes.

8.2 Behavioral Characteristics

8.2.1 Ethics

.1 Purpose

A business analyst must be able to behave ethically in order to earn the trust and respect of stakeholders, and be able to recognize when a proposed solution or requirement may present ethical difficulties.

.2 Definition

Ethics requires an understanding of moral and immoral behavior, the standards that should govern one's behavior, and the willingness to act to ensure that one's behavior is moral or meets those standards. Business analysts need to consider the impact that a proposed solution will have on all stakeholder groups and work to ensure that those groups are treated fairly. Fair treatment does not require that the outcome be beneficial to a particular stakeholder group, but it does require that the affected stakeholders understand the reasons for the decision, that they are not deceived about the outcome, and that decisions which are made are made in the best interest of the organization. The business analyst should be able to identify when an ethical dilemma occurs and understand how such dilemmas may be resolved.

.3 Effectiveness Measures

Measures of ethical behavior include:

▶ Decisions are made with due consideration to the interests of all stakeholders.

▶ Reasons for a decision are clearly articulated and understood.

▶ Prompt and full disclosure of potential conflicts of interest.

▶ Honesty regarding one's abilities, the performance of one's work, and accepting responsibility for failures or errors.

8.2.2 Personal Organization

.1 Purpose

Personal organization skills assist the business analyst in effectively managing tasks and information.

.2 Description

Personal organization involves the ability to readily find files or information, timeliness, management of outstanding tasks, and appropriate handling of priorities. Information should be stored or filed in a way that enables the business analyst to retrieve it at a later date. Effective time management requires effective prioritization, elimination of procrastination, and clarity of goals and expectations. Standard techniques such as action plans, to-do lists and setting priorities are among the common approaches to effective time management.

.3 Effectiveness Measures

Measures of personal organization include:

► The ability of the business analyst to find information.

► Regular on-time completion of tasks.

► Efficiency in the completion of work.

► The ability to easily identify all outstanding work and the status of each work item.

8.2.3   Trustworthiness

.1   Purpose

Earning the trust of key stakeholders is necessary to ensure that the business analyst is able to elicit requirements around sensitive issues and to ensure that recommendations are evaluated properly.

.2   Definition

A trustworthy business analyst must constantly demonstrate to stakeholders that they deserve the stakeholder's confidence and are concerned with that stakeholder's best interests. Stakeholders must trust the business analyst to behave ethically and to perform business analysis work effectively, in order to offset the inherent distrust based upon the possible effects of change to vested interests in the status quo, or simple fear of change. Trustworthiness requires that the business analyst engage with the stakeholder's needs, not the stakeholder's desires, and that the business analyst must honestly address issues when they occur.

.3   Effectiveness Measures

Measures of trustworthiness include:

► Stakeholders involving the business analyst in decision-making.

► Stakeholder acceptance of the business analyst's recommendations.

► Willingness of stakeholders to discuss difficult or controversial topics with the business analyst.

► Willingness of stakeholders to support or defend the business analyst when problems occur.

8.3   Business Knowledge

8.3.1   Business Principles and Practices

.1   Purpose

Business analysts require an understanding of fundamental business principles and best practices, in order to ensure that they are incorporated into and supported by solutions.

.2   Definition

Business principles are those characteristics that are common to all organizations with a similar purpose and structure, whether or not they are in the same industry. Almost all organizations need certain functions or capabilities in order to operate. Business areas within and across industries often have a common set of business processes and associated systems. Common functional areas include:

► Human Resources

► Finance

► Information Technology

► Supply Chain Management

While these areas have common processes, they can also vary widely based on the industry and size of an organization (e.g. Human Resources will be guided by different regulatory and cultural influences, but there are universal commonalities in roles such as finding, retaining, counseling, compensating, and removing staff). Other areas, such as production, tend to have fundamentally different demands between different industries (e.g. agriculture and software). Understanding how other organizations have solved similar challenges can be useful when identifying possible solutions.

.3   Effectiveness Measures

Measures of knowledge of business practices and principles may include:

► Understanding of business environments, operations, process and practices relating to:

   ▷ Common business management and decision making concepts, principles activities and practices.

   ▷ Typical organization structures, job functions and work activities.

   ▷ Complex business functions and operations.

► Understanding of relevant regulatory, compliance, and governance frameworks.

► Understanding of auditing and security issues.

8.3.2   Industry Knowledge

.1   Purpose

Business analysts should have an understanding of the industry that their organization is in so that they may understand new challenges that may be posed by competitive moves, and which solutions have proven effective elsewhere.

.2   Definition

Industry knowledge is the understanding of the competitive forces that shape an industry. It requires that the business analyst understand the various customer segments that the industry services and the demographic or other characteristics common to that segment. An understanding of major trends impacting the industry will help shape business requirements. Competitors will be making changes to their product lineup and business operations in response to these changes, and the business analyst may need to recommend changes to an ongoing change initiative in order to respond to a competitor's action.

.3   Effectiveness Measures

Measures of effective industry knowledge may include:

- ► Understanding of industry related material and keeps abreast of what is taking place in the industry .

- ► The ability to identify key trends shaping the industry.

- ► Knowledge of major competitors and partners for the organization.

- ► Knowledge of major customer segments.

- ► Knowledge of common products and product types.

- ► Knowledge of sources of information about the industry, including relevant trade organizations or journals.

- ► Understanding of industry-specific resource and process documents.

- ► Understanding of industry standard processes and methodologies.

- ► Understanding of the industry regulatory environment.

8.3.3   Organization Knowledge

.1   Purpose

Business analysis is significantly assisted by an understanding of the organization for which it is being performed.

.2   Definition

Organization knowledge is an understanding of the business architecture of the organization that is being analyzed. It includes an understanding of the business models that the organization (that is, how the organization generates profits or otherwise accomplishes its goals), the organizational structure that is in place, the relationships that exist between business units, and the persons who occupy key stakeholder positions. Understanding of an organization requires understanding of the informal lines of communication and authority that usually exist in parallel with the formal ones, and the internal politics that govern or influence decision-making.

.3   Effectiveness Measures

Measures of a business analyst's organizational knowledge may include:

- ► Understanding of terminology or jargon used in the organization.

- ► Understanding of the products or services offered by the organization.

- ► Ability to identify subject matter experts in the organization.

- ► Organizational relationships and politics.

8.3.4 Solution Knowledge

.1 Purpose

Business analysts can use their understanding of existing solutions in order to identify the most effective means of implementing a change.

.2 Definition

Business analysts frequently work on projects that involve enhancing an existing solution, or purchasing a commercially available solution, rather than developing entirely new custom solutions. In these circumstances, it is likely that the method of implementation chosen will make a significant difference in the time and effort required. A business analyst who is familiar with the workings of a solution may be able to more easily identify and recommend changes that can be implemented easily while still providing concrete benefits. Familiarity with the range of commercially available solutions or suppliers can assist with the identification of possible alternatives.

.3 Effectiveness Measures

Measures of useful solution knowledge can include:

► Reduced time or cost to implement a required change.

► Shortened time on requirements analysis and/or solution design.

► Understanding when a larger change is justified based on business benefit.

► Understanding how additional capabilities present, but not currently used, in a solution can be deployed to provide business value.

8.4 Communication Skills

8.4.1 Oral Communications

.1 Purpose

Oral communication skills enable business analysts to effectively express ideas in ways that are appropriate to the target audience.

.2 Definition

Oral communication skills are used to verbally express ideas, information, or other matters. Oral communications are a rich channel that allows for the efficient transfer of information, including emotional and other non-verbal cues. Effective oral communication skills include both the ability to make oneself understood and the active listening skills that ensure that the statements of others are accurately understood. The business analyst must have an understanding of tone and how it can positively or negatively influence the listener. Oral communication is most effective when the information being communicated will be used in the short term.

.3 Effectiveness Measures

Effective oral communication skills can be demonstrated through:

► Effectively paraphrasing statements to ensure understanding.

► Effectively facilitating sessions, ensuring success through preparedness and co-ordination.

► Developing and delivering powerful presentations by positioning content and objectives appropriately (i.e. positive vs. negative tone).

► Can communicate the criticality or urgency of a situation in a calm, rational manner with proposed solutions.

8.4.2 Teaching

.1 Purpose

Teaching skills are required to ensure that business analysts can effectively communicate issues and requirements and to ensure that the information communicated is understood and retained.

.2 Definition

Teaching requires an understanding of how people learn and the ability to use this understanding to effectively facilitate the learning experience. Effective communication of requirements requires teaching skills, as it frequently requires that the business analyst educate implementation SMEs about the context that a solution will be implemented in. A business analyst must be aware of different learning styles, including:

► visual learners (who learn best through the presentation of visual guides and models).

► auditory learners (who learn best through oral communication and written language).

► kinesthetic learners (who learn most effectively through doing).

The business analyst should understand how different learning styles may determine the form of requirements communication. The business analyst may also teach the use of analysis techniques to stakeholders in order to allow them to participate more fully and directly in the analysis process. Effective teaching also requires an understanding of methods that may be used to confirm that the student has learned and can apply what they have learned.

.3 Effectiveness Measures

Effective teaching skills can be demonstrated through:

► Verifying that learners have acquired information that has been imparted to them.

► Ability of learners to use new skills or demonstrate new knowledge.

8.4.3 Written Communications

.1 Purpose

Written communication skills are necessary for business analysts to document elicitation results, requirements, and other information for which medium-to-long term records are required.

.2   Definition

Written communication involves the use of symbols to communicate information. It includes the ability to write effectively for various contexts and audiences. Written communication is required when information will be used at a time or place that is remote from the time and place it was created. Effective written communication requires that the business analyst have a broad vocabulary, strong grasp of grammar and style, and an understanding of which idioms and terms will be readily understood by the audience. Written communications are capable of recording a great deal of information, but it is frequently challenging to ensure that the written text is correctly understood.

.3   Effectiveness Measures

Effective written communication skills can be demonstrated through:

▶   Ability to adjust the style of writing for the needs of the audience.

▶   Proper use of grammar and style.

▶   Appropriate choice of words.

▶   Ability of the reader to paraphrase and describe the content of the written communication.

8.5   Interaction Skills

8.5.1   Facilitation and Negotiation

.1   Purpose

Business analysts facilitate interactions between stakeholders in order to help them resolve disagreements regarding the priority and nature of requirements.

.2   Definition

Facilitation is the skill of moderating discussions among a group to enable all participants to effectively articulate their views on a topic under discussion, and to further ensure that participants in the discussion are able to recognize and appreciate the differing viewpoints that are articulated. In many cases, an effectively facilitated discussion will help participants to recognize that they have differing views on a topic under discussion. The business analyst may be required to support negotiation between parties on how best to resolve those differences. The business analyst must be able to identify the underlying interests of the parties, distinguish those interests from their stated positions, and help the parties to identify solutions that satisfy those underlying interests.

.3   Effectiveness Measures

Effective facilitation and negotiation skills are demonstrated through:

▶   Ensuring that participants in a discussion correctly understand one another's positions.

▶   Use of meeting management skills and tools (including agendas and the use of meeting minutes to keep discussions focused and organized.

▶   Preventing discussions from being sidetracked onto irrelevant topics.

- ▶ Identifying common areas of agreement.

- ▶ Effective use of different negotiation styles.

- ▶ Ability to identify important issues.

- ▶ Understanding and considering all parties' interests, motivations and objectives.

- ▶ Encouraging stakeholders to reach win/win outcomes on a regular basis.

- ▶ Understanding of political implications in conflicts and negotiates in a politically sensitive manner.

- ▶ Understanding the impact of time and timing on negotiations.

8.5.2 Leadership and Influencing

.1 Purpose

Business analysts need to be able to be effective in formal and informal leadership roles, in order to guide others investigating requirements and to help encourage stakeholder support for a necessary change.

.2 Definition

The business analyst's responsibility for defining and communicating requirements will place him or her in a key leadership role in any group or project team, whether or not there are people formally reporting to the business analyst.

Leadership involves motivating people to act in ways that enable them to work together to achieve shared goals and objectives. The business analyst must understand the individual needs and capabilities of each team member and stakeholder and how those can be most effectively channeled in order to reach the shared objectives. Effective leadership therefore requires that the business analyst be able to develop a vision of a desired future state that people can be motivated to work towards and the interpersonal skills necessary to encourage them to do so.

.3 Effectiveness Measures

Effective leadership and influencing skills are demonstrated though:

- ▶ Reduced resistance to necessary changes.

- ▶ Team members and stakeholders demonstrating a willingness to set aside personal objectives when necessary.

- ▶ Articulation of a clear and inspiring vision of a desired future state.

8.5.3 Teamwork

.1 Purpose

Business analysts must be able to work closely with other team members to effectively support their work so that solutions can be effectively implemented.

.2   Definition

Business analysts customarily work as part of a team with other business analysts, project managers, other stakeholders and implementation SMEs. Relationships within the team are an important part of the success of any project or organization.

There are a number of team development models that attempt to explain how teams form and function. These models outline how the team progresses and what is normal at various stages of the team lifecycle. Recognizing the stage of the team's progress can lower the stress of team relationship development by allowing members to recognize behaviors as normal, expected, and a stage to be worked through. Communications and trust can also be enhanced through understanding and awareness of facets such as the process of setting of rules for the team, team decision-making, formal and informal team leadership and management roles.

Team conflict is quite common. If handled well, the resolution of conflict can actually benefit the team. The basic types of conflict are emotional and cognitive. Emotional conflict stems from personal interactions, while cognitive conflicts are based upon disagreements on matters of substantive value or impact on the project or organization. Resolution of cognitive conflict requires the team to focus on examining the premises, assumptions, observations and expectations of the team members. Working through such problems can have the beneficial effect of strengthening the foundation of the analysis and the solution. Many conflict situations encompass both emotional and cognitive elements.

.3   Effectiveness Measures

Effective teamwork skills are demonstrated though:

▶   Fostering a collaborative working environment.

▶   Effective resolution of conflict.

▶   Developing trust among team members.

▶   Support among the team for shared high standards of achievement.

▶   Team members have a shared sense of ownership of the team goals.

8.6   Software Applications

8.6.1   General-Purpose Applications

.1   Purpose

Business analysts use office productivity applications to document and track requirements.

.2   Definition

These applications generally consist of three components in a suite of tools: word processing, spreadsheets, and presentation software. The documents produced by these tools are the primary way in which information is stored and distributed in many organizations, and business analysts need to be proficient with their use even where more specialized tools are available. They have the advantage of being low-cost or even free, and almost every stakeholder will have access to them.

Word processors are commonly used to develop and maintain requirements documents. They allow a great deal of control over the formatting and presentation of a document. Standard requirements documentation templates are widely available for word processors. Most word processing tools have a limited capability to track changes and record comments, and are not designed for collaborative authoring.

Spreadsheets are often used to maintain lists (such as atomic requirements, features, actions, issues, or defects). Spreadsheets are the tool of choice for the capture and rudimentary algorithmic manipulation of numeric data. They can also be used to support decision analysis and are very effective at summarizing complex scenarios. Spreadsheets also support limited change tracking, and can be shared among multiple users in much the same way as a word processing document.

Presentation software is commonly used to support training or to introduce topics for discussion among stakeholders. While some of these applications can be used in a very limited way to capture requirements or simulate a low-fidelity prototype, their primary purpose is to support the structuring and delivery of verbal information.

Collaboration and knowledge management tools are used to support the capturing of knowledge distributed throughout an organization and make it as widely available as possible. They enable documents to be made available to an entire team and facilitate collaboration on those documents, enable multiple users to work on a document simultaneously, and generally support commenting on or discussion about the documents or their content as well. These tools may take the form of document repositories (which integrate with office productivity software), wikis (which allow easy creation and linking of web pages), discussion forums, or other web-based tools. They can vary widely in cost.

Communication tools, such as email and instant messaging applications, are used as needed to communicate with stakeholders who are remotely located, who cannot respond to queries immediately, or who may need a longer-term record of a discussion. They are generally available to almost all stakeholders and are very easy to use. However, they are generally not effective for long-term storage or retention of information. Their primary use is to facilitate communication over time or distance.

.3 Effectiveness Measures

Measures of skill with general-purpose applications include:

▶ Ability to apply an understanding of one tool to other similar tools.

▶ Able to identify major tools in the marketplace and describe how they are used in any given situation.

▶ Understands and is able to use most of the major features of the tool.

▶ Able to use the tools to complete requirements-related activities more rapidly than is possible without them.

▶ Able to track changes to the requirements made through the tools.

8.6.2   Specialized Applications

.1   Purpose

Business analysts use modeling tools to support the development of formal models, and in some cases, their validation and implementation as well.

.2   Definition

Diagramming tools are designed to support the rapid drawing and documentation of a model, typically by providing a set of templates for a particular notation which are used to develop diagrams based on it. They generally do not enforce or verify compliance with the notation standard, or do so in a limited fashion. They are generally low-cost and relatively easy to use, and the resulting diagrams can be integrated into a word processing document.

Modeling tools facilitate the conversion of the model into an executable form, either by use of a proprietary engine for executing the model or by generating application code which can be enhanced by a developer. The tool will verify compliance with the notation. Some modeling tools support the creation of executable models, such as business process management systems (which allow for the creation of executable process models) and business rules management systems (which allow for the enforcement of captured business rules). They are medium to high cost and often require some specialized training to use.

Requirements management tools are used to support change control, traceability, and configuration management of requirements and requirements artifacts. Some tools are also capable of linking requirements to software code. They are designed to ensure that a reason is recorded for any changes to the requirements and to help to rapidly identify any impacts from those changes. They are medium to high-cost and often require specialist training. They are most commonly used by large and/or geographically dispersed teams.

.3   Effectiveness Measures

Measures of skill with specialized applications include:

► Ability to apply an understanding of one tool to other similar tools.

► Able to identify major tools in the marketplace and describe how they are used in any given situation.

► Understands and is able to use most of the major features of the tool.

► Able to use the tools to complete requirements-related activities more rapidly than is possible without them.

► Able to track changes to the requirements made through the tools.

Techniques

chapter NINE

The *Techniques* Chapter provides a high-level overview of the techniques referenced in the Knowledge Areas of the *BABOK® Guide*. Techniques alter the way a business analysis task is performed or describe a specific form the output of a task may take.

The techniques listed here are only a subset of the techniques used by practitioners of business analysis. The ones listed here are applicable to enough different situations and business domains, and have been adopted by enough business analysis practitioners, that a skilled generalist should reasonably be expected to be familiar with the existence and purpose of the technique. Business analysts who specialize in a particular methodology or business domain may need to understand a smaller set of techniques in greater depth, or may need to develop expertise in techniques not described here.

In a number of cases, we have grouped a set of conceptually similar techniques into a single entry. This was done to indicate that any one of the variant techniques that are listed in that entry (or even variants that are not specifically mentioned) may be usable for that purpose. While there are certainly important theoretical and practical differences between these variants, most practitioners will find that expertise in a single variant is sufficient in any particular environment.

9.1 Acceptance and Evaluation Criteria Definition

9.1.1 Purpose

To define the requirements that must be met in order for a solution to be considered acceptable to key stakeholders.

9.1.2 Description

Determine which requirements can most effectively be used as acceptance or evaluation criteria.

► Acceptance criteria describe the minimal set of requirements that must be met in order for a particular solution to be worth implementing.

► Evaluation criteria are the set of requirements that will be used to choose between multiple solutions.

Either acceptance and evaluation criteria may be used to determine if a solution or solution component can be shown to objectively meet a requirement. Acceptance criteria are typically used when only one possible solution is being evaluated and are generally expressed as a pass or fail. Evaluation criteria are used to compare multiple solutions or solution components and allow for a range of possible scores.

9.1.3 Elements

.1 Testability

Acceptance and evaluation criteria, even more so than other requirements, must be expressed in a testable form. This may require breaking them down into an atomic form such that test cases can be written to verify the solution against the criteria.

.2   Determine Ranking and Scoring

Ranking is the process of determining the order of importance for all requirements, as described in *Prioritize Requirements (6.1)*. The MoSCoW technique is useful for this purpose. A "Must Have" criterion is one that will remove a proposed solution from consideration if not met. Lower levels of priority will receive lower rankings.

Scoring is the process of determining how well a solution meets a requirement. A scale should be established for scoring each requirement and multiple possible scoring levels defined.

In both cases, stakeholders must agree not only on the criteria, but how the solution will be rated against them.

9.1.4   Usage Considerations

.1   Advantages

▶   Agile methodologies may require that all requirements be expressed in the form of testable acceptance criteria.

▶   Acceptance criteria are also necessary when the requirements express contractual obligations.

.2   Disadvantages

▶   Acceptance and evaluation criteria may express contractual obligations and as such may be difficult to change for legal or political reasons.

9.2   Benchmarking

9.2.1   Purpose

Benchmark studies are performed to compare the strengths and weaknesses of an organization against its peers and competitors.

9.2.2   Description

Benchmark studies are conducted to compare organizational practices against the best-in-class practices that exist within competitor enterprises in government or industry. The objective of benchmark studies is to determine how companies achieve their superior performance levels and use that information to design projects to improve operations of the enterprise. Benchmarking is usually focused on strategies, operations and processes.

9.2.3   Elements

Benchmarking requires that the business analyst:

▶   Identify the area to be studied

▶   Identify organizations that are leaders in the sector

▶   Conduct a survey of selected organizations to understand their practices

▶   Arrange for visits to best-in-class organizations

▶ Develop a project proposal to implement the best practices

9.2.4 Usage Considerations

.1 Advantages

Benchmarking provides organizations with information about new and different methods, ideas, and tools to improve organizational performance.

.2 Disadvantages

Benchmarking is time consuming. In addition, organizations may not have the expertise to conduct the analysis and acquire or interpret useful competitive information.

Because it involves assessing solutions that have been shown to work elsewhere, with the goal of reproducing them, benchmarking cannot produce innovative solutions or solutions that will produce a sustainable competitive advantage.

9.3 Brainstorming

9.3.1 Purpose

Brainstorming is an excellent way to foster creative thinking about a problem. The aim of brainstorming is to produce numerous new ideas, and to derive from them themes for further analysis.

9.3.2 Description

Brainstorming is a technique intended to produce a broad or diverse set of options. Brainstorms help answer specific questions such as (but not limited to):

▶ What options are available to resolve the issue at hand?

▶ What factors are constraining the group from moving ahead with an approach or option?

▶ What could be causing a delay in activity 'A'?

▶ What can the group do to solve problem 'B'?

Brainstorming works by focusing on a topic or problem, and then coming up with many possible solutions to it. This technique is best applied in a group as it draws on the experience and creativity of all members of the group. In the absence of a group, one could brainstorm on one's own to spark new ideas. To heighten creativity, participants are encouraged to use new ways of looking at things and free associate in any direction. Facilitated properly, brainstorming can be fun, engaging and productive.

9.3.3 Elements

.1 Preparation

▶ Develop a clear and concise definition of the area of interest.

▶ Determine a time limit for the group to generate ideas; the larger the group, the more time required.

► Identify facilitator and participants in session. Aim for participants (ideally 6 to 8) who represent a range of background and experience with the topic.

► Set expectations with participants and get their buy in to the process.

► Establish criteria for evaluating and rating the ideas.

.2   Session

► Share new ideas without any discussion, criticism or evaluation.

► Visibly record all ideas.

► Encourage participants to be creative, share exaggerated ideas, and build on the ideas of others.

► Don't limit the number of ideas as the goal is to elicit as many as possible within the time period.

.3   Wrap-up

► Once the time limit is reached, using the pre-determined evaluation criteria, discuss and evaluate the ideas.

► Create a condensed list of ideas, combine ideas where appropriate, and eliminate duplicates.

► Rate the ideas. Distribute the final list of ideas to appropriate parties.

9.3.4   Usage Considerations

.1   Advantages

► Ability to elicit many ideas in a short time period.

► Non-judgmental environment enables creative thinking.

► Can be useful during a workshop to reduce tension between participants

.2   Disadvantages

► Dependent on participants' creativity and willingness to participate. Organizational and interpersonal politics may also limit participation.

► Group participants must agree to avoid debating the ideas raised during brainstorming.

9.4   Business Rules Analysis

9.4.1   Purpose

To define the rules that govern decisions in an organization and that define, constrain, or enable organizational operations.

9.4.2   Description

Policies and rules direct and constrain the organization and operation of an organization. A business policy is a non-actionable directive that supports a business goal. A business rule is a specific, actionable, testable directive that is under the control of an organization and that supports a business policy. Particularly complex rules, or rules with a number of interrelated dependencies, may be expressed as a decision table or decision tree, as described in *Decision Analysis (9.8)*.

A number of basic principles guide the business analyst when stating and managing business rules. The business rules should be:

▶ Stated in appropriate terminology to enable domain SMEs to validate the rules.

▶ Documented independently of how they will be enforced.

▶ Stated at the atomic level and in declarative format.

▶ Separated from processes that the rule supports or constrains.

▶ Maintained in a manner that enables the organization to monitor and adapt the rules as the business policies change.

9.4.3   Elements

Business rules require a defined glossary of terms and an understanding of the relationships between them, known as a "term and fact model" (see *Data Dictionary and Glossary (9.5)* and *Data Modeling (9.7)* for further information). In order to insure that they are independent of any implementation, rules should not depend on any other information, or include assumptions about how they will be enforced.

.1   Operative Rules

Operative rules are rules that the organization chooses to enforce as a matter of policy. They are intended to guide the actions of people working within the organization. They may oblige people to take certain actions, prevent people from taking actions, or prescribe the conditions under which an action may be taken. By definition, it must be possible for people to violate an operative rule, even if there are no circumstances under which the organization would approve of them doing so. An example of an operative rule is:

An order must not be placed when the billing address provided by the customer does not match the address on file with the credit card provider.

Because it is possible to violate an operative rule, further analysis may be conducted to determine what kinds of sanctions should be imposed when a rule is violated, allow a rule to be overridden (before or after the fact) or the circumstances when an exception to a rule is appropriate. These may lead to the definition of additional rules.

.2   Structural Rules

Structural rules are intended to help determine when something is or is not true, or when things fall into a specific category. They are expressed as rules because they describe categorizations that may change over time. Because they structure the knowledge of the organization, rather than the behavior of persons, they cannot be violated (but they can be misapplied). An example of a structural rule is:

An order must have one and only one associated payment method.

Structural rules may also describe how information may be inferred or calculated based on other data available to the business. A calculation may be the result of the application of many individual rules. Inference rules can also be used to evaluate decisions during a process. For example:

An order's local jurisdiction tax amount is calculated as (sum of the prices of all the order's taxable ordered items) × local jurisdiction tax rate amount.

9.4.4   Usage Considerations

.1   Strengths

Clearly defining and structuring rules allows organizations to make changes to policy without altering processes. The impact of changes to business rules can be assessed more easily when they are documented separately from the processes they detail or the means used to enforce the rules.

.2   Weaknesses

Organizations may produce lengthy lists of business rules. Business rules can contradict one another or produce unanticipated results when combined. It may also be important to question existing business rules for continuing relevance to current and projected modes of organizational operations and structure.

9.5   Data Dictionary and Glossary

9.5.1   Purpose

A data dictionary or glossary defines key terms and data relevant to a business domain.

9.5.2   Description

Data dictionaries or glossaries are used to formally identify and define all terminology used by the organization or organizational unit. For example, an organizational unit may differentiate between a client and a customer, where a client is a party with whom the business has an enforceable professional service agreement, whereas a customer may have a much more casual, transaction based relationship with the business. In a healthcare organization, such as a hospital, the term patient may be used, along with its unique definition, rather than either client or customer.

9.5.3   Elements

.1   Glossary

A glossary documents terms unique to the domain. It is created in order to ensure that all stakeholders understood what is meant when certain words are used. A glossary consists of a term relevant to the domain and a unique definition for each, as well as cross-referencing aliases.

.2   Data Dictionary

Data dictionaries include standard definitions of data elements, their meanings, and allowable values. A data dictionary contains definitions of each primitive data element and indicates how those elements combine into composite data elements.

Primitive Data Elements

The following information must be recorded about each data element in the data dictionary:

▶ **Name:** a unique name for the data element, which will be referenced by the composite data elements.

▶ **Aliases:** alternate names for the data element used by various stakeholders.

▶ **Values/Meanings:** a list of acceptable values for the data element. This may be expressed as an enumerated list or as a description of allowed formats for the data (including information such as the number of characters). If the values are abbreviated this will include an explanation of the meaning.

▶ **Description:** the definition of the data element in the context of the solution.

Composite Data Elements

Composite data is assembled from primitive data elements. Composite structures include:

▶ **Sequences:** show primitive data elements in order. The primitive elements must always occur in the specified order.

▶ **Repetitions:** show that one or more primitive data elements occur multiple times in the composite element.

▶ **Optional Elements:** may or may not occur in a particular instance of the data element.

9.5.4 Usage Considerations

A data dictionary or glossary is useful for ensuring that all stakeholders are in agreement on the format and content of relevant information. Capturing these definitions in a single model ensures that these terms will be used consistently.

9.6 Data Flow Diagrams

9.6.1 Purpose

To show how information is input, processed, stored, and output from a system.

9.6.2 Description

The Data Flow Diagram (DFD) provides a visual representation of how information is moved through a system. It shows the:

▶ External Entities that provide data to, or receive data from, a system

▶ The Processes of the system that transform data

▶ The Data Stores in which data is collected for some period of time

▶ The Data Flows by which data moves between External Entities, Processes and Data Stores

9.6.3   Elements

.1   External Entities

An external entity is a source or a destination of data. It is represented as a labeled rectangle.

.2   Data Store

A data store represents a location where data is not moving or transforming, but is being stored passively for future use. Data stores are represented as a label between two parallel lines or a labeled rectangle with a square.

.3   Data Process

A data process is a process that transforms the data in some way, either combining the data, reordering the data, converting the data, filtering the data or other such activities. An asterisk within the process is used to identify data processes that have further decomposition models. Data Processes are represented as a labeled circle or a rectangle with curved corners. Standard labeling is to use a Verb-object structure.

.4   Data Flow

A data flow identifies where data is being moved between a data process and an external entity, a data store or another data process. The label should be a noun phrase that identifies data being moved. It can be further specified into result flows, control flows and update flows. Data flows are represented by a single or forked line with an arrow. Lines must be labeled with a descriptor of the data being moved.

9.6.4   Usage Considerations

Data Flow Diagrams are used as part of a structured analysis approach. They are used to get an understanding of the range of data within the domain. They are typically used after a context diagram has been completed and as a prerequisite or concurrent activity to data modeling.

.1   Strengths

▶ May be used as a discovery technique for processes and data, or as a technique for verification of a *Functional Decomposition (9.12)* or *Data Model (9.7)* that have already been completed.

▶ Most users find these diagrams quite easy to understand.

▶ Generally considered a useful analysis deliverable to developers in a structured programming environment.

.2   Weaknesses

DFDs cannot easily show who is responsible for performing the work. They cannot show alternative paths through the same process.

Figure 9–1: Data Flow Diagram (Gane-Sarson Notation)

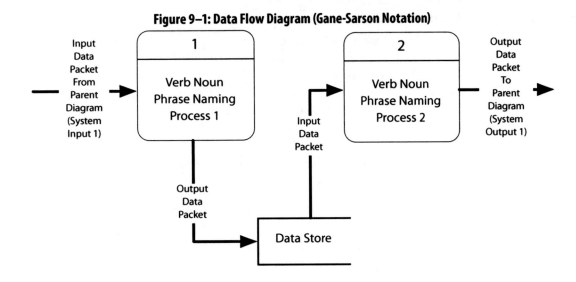

Figure 9–2: Data Flow Diagram (Yourdon Notation)

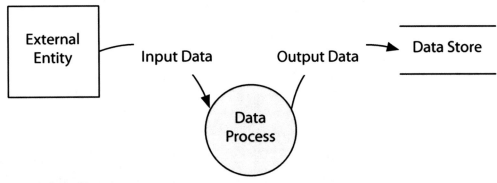

9.7 Data Modeling

9.7.1 Purpose

The purpose of a data model is to describe the concepts relevant to a domain, the relationships between those concepts, and information associated with them.

9.7.2 Description

A data model usually takes the form of a diagram supported by textual descriptions. It visually represents the types of people, places, things and concepts that are important to the business, attributes associated with them, and the significant business relationships among them. Data models are often supported by a *Data Dictionary and Glossary (9.5)* and by *Business Rules Analysis (9.4)*.

The two most widely used types of data model are the entity-relationship diagram (ERD) and the class diagram, although other modeling notations remain in use. The notation used is often determined by the technology platform of the organization. ERDs are generally preferred when the model will be used as the basis for a relational database, while class diagrams are preferred for supporting object-oriented development. Business analysts who may have to use those models should understand the unique characteristics of each type of data model—they serve similar purposes but have some important conceptual differences that emerge in practice.

9.7.3 Elements

Logical data models describe the information relevant to an organization. High-level logical data models may focus solely on describing the entities, attributes and relationships of most importance. Detailed logical data models communicate comprehensive descriptions of all entities, attributes and relationships. Physical data models describe how data is stored and managed in a software application.

.1 Concept

A concept is something of significance to the domain being described, about which the organization needs data.

Each type of concept should have a unique identifier (a type of attribute) that differentiates between actual instances of the concept. Concepts are referred to as entities in ERDs and as classes in class diagrams.

.2 Attributes

An attribute defines a particular piece of information associated with a concept—how much information can be captured in it, allowable values, and the type of information it

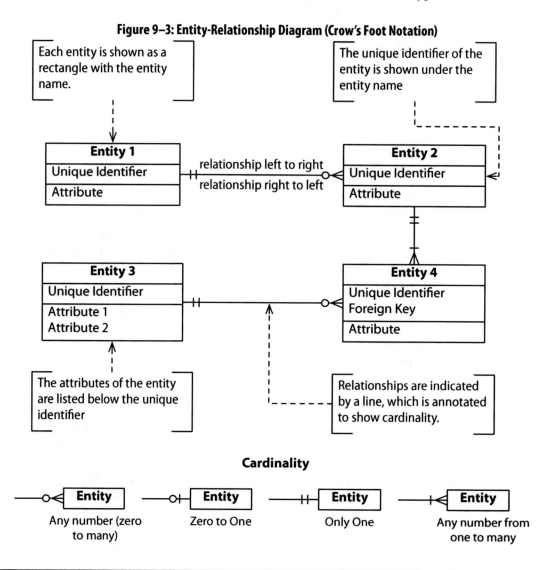

Figure 9–3: Entity-Relationship Diagram (Crow's Foot Notation)

A Guide to the *Business Analysis Body of Knowledge*®

represents.

Name: a unique name for the attribute. Other names used by stakeholders may be captured as aliases.

Values/Meanings: a list of acceptable values for the attribute. This may be expressed as an enumerated list or as a description of allowed formats for the data (including information such as the number of characters). If the values are abbreviated this will include an explanation of the meaning.

Description: the definition of the attribute in the context of the solution.

.3   Relationship

Relationships are significant business associations between concepts. The example shows the relationships between Business Analyst and Requirement as an annotated line. The labels explain the nature of the relationship from the perspective of each entity.

Relationships define how information is used in the operation of the business, and indicate the important linkages that need to be managed and maintained in the solution. Relationships may also indicate the "cardinality" or "multiplicity" of the relationship (i.e. the number of relationships allowed or required).

.4   Metadata

Metadata is defined as "data about data". Metadata describes the context, use, and validity of business information and is generally used to determine when and why

Figure 9–4: Class Diagram (UML)

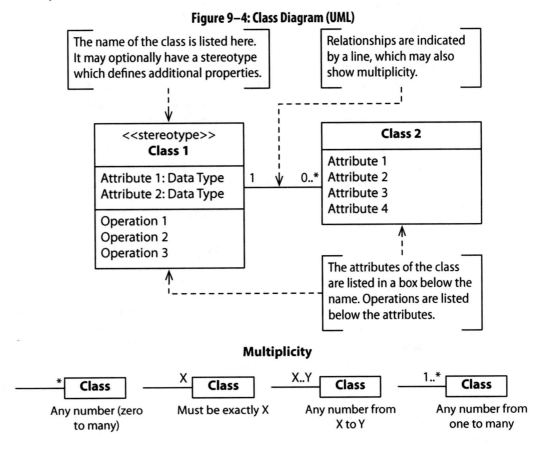

information stored in a system was changed.

9.7.4   Usage Considerations

.1   Advantages

Data models offer the flexibility of different levels of description. They provide a consistent modeling approach that supports the transition through planning, analysis, design and implementation.

Because they have a strong basis in mathematical concepts, data models are supported by rigorous rules for correctness and completeness. This encourages accuracy in the development of the models.

.2   Disadvantages

Data models can be complex, and they deal with concepts that may be unfamiliar to people without a background in Information Technology. If not properly presented, they can be difficult for users to understand and relate to. Terms and definitions may vary in use in different organizational units or domains.

9.8   Decision Analysis

9.8.1   Purpose

To support decision-making when dealing with complex, difficult, or uncertain situations.

9.8.2   Description

Decision analysis is an approach to decision-making that examines and models the possible consequences of different decisions. Decision analysis assists in making an optimal decision under conditions of uncertainty. Uncertainty may exist because of unknown factors that are relevant to the decision problem, because there are too many possible interrelated factors to consider, because of conflicting perspectives on a situation, or because of tradeoffs between the different available options.

Effective decision analysis requires that the analyst understand:

► The values, goals and objectives that are relevant to the decision problem;

► The nature of the decision that must be made;

► The areas of uncertainty that affect the decision;

► And the consequences of each possible decision.

The tasks in the *Enterprise Analysis* Knowledge Area describe much of what is required to effectively structure a decision problem. This technique describes the particular tools used to analyze outcomes, uncertainty and tradeoffs. Decision analysis can involve the use of very complex models and specialized software applications.

9.8.3   Elements

.1   Outcomes

Decision analysis generally requires that the business analyst use some form of mathematical model to assess possible outcomes.

Financial Analysis

Financial models estimate the market value of an organizational asset, for example, estimating the value of a new business solution or acquisition.

Commonly used financial valuation techniques include:

► **Discounted Cash Flow:** future value on a specific data

► **Net Present Value:** future view of costs and benefits converted to today's value

► **Internal Rate of Return:** the interest rate (or discount) when the net present value is equal to zero

► **Average Rate of Return:** estimate of rate of return on an investment

► **Pay Back Period:** the amount of time it takes for an investment to pay for itself

► **Cost-Benefit Analysis:** quantification of costs and benefits for a proposed new solution

Non-Financial Outcomes

Not all decision outcomes can be expressed in financial terms. However, effective decision analysis still requires that outcomes be directly comparable. In some cases, there will be a metric that is applicable (defects per thousand, percentage uptime, customer satisfaction rating). When there is not, a relative scoring of possible outcomes will have to be determined.

.2   Uncertainty

Uncertainty becomes relevant to a decision problem when it is impossible to know which outcome will occur. This may be due to missing information, or because the outcome depends on how others respond. A common method of dealing with uncertainty in decision problems is to calculate the expected value of outcomes. This involves estimating the percentage chance of each outcome occurring and them multiplying the numeric value associated with that outcome by that percentage.

A decision tree is a method of assessing the preferred outcome where multiple sources of uncertainty may exist.

.3   Trade-offs

Trade-offs become relevant whenever a decision problem involves multiple, possibly conflicting, objectives. Because more than one objective is relevant, it is not sufficient to simply find the maximum value for one variable (such as the financial benefit for the organization). When making tradeoffs, effective methods include:

► **Elimination of dominated alternatives.** A dominated alternative is any option that is clearly inferior to some other option. If an option is equal to or worse than some other option when rated against the objectives, the other option can be said to dominate it. In some cases, an option may also be dominated if it only offers very small advantages but has significant disadvantages.

► **Ranking objectives on a similar scale.** One method of converting rankings to a similar scale is proportional scoring. Using this method, the best outcome is assigned a rating of 100, the worst a rating of 0, and all other outcomes are given a rating based on where they fall between those two scores. If the outcomes are then assigned weights based on their relative importance, a score can be assigned to each outcome and the best alternative assigned using a decision tree.

Figure 9–5: Decision Tree

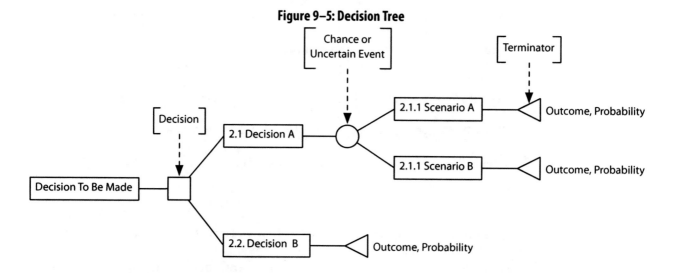

9.8.4   Usage Considerations

.1   Advantages

► Decision analysis provides an effective technique to determine the expected value of an alternative scenario to the organization.

► Using consistent financial justification techniques in all business cases provides decision makers with quantitative measures upon which to make project investment decisions.

► Decision analysis may force stakeholders to honestly assess the importance they place on different alternatives.

.2   Disadvantages

► Decision analysis requires specialized knowledge and skills, including mathematical knowledge, an understanding of probability, and similar concepts.

► The results of decision analysis may be treated as more certain than they actually are, if decision-makers do not understand the limitations of the model and the assumptions behind it.

> ▶ Decision-makers may be reluctant to revisit decisions, even when more information is available on areas of uncertainty that might change the optimal decision.

9.9   Document Analysis

9.9.1   Purpose

Document analysis is a means to elicit requirements by studying available documentation on existing and comparable solutions and identifying relevant information.

9.9.2   Description

Document analysis may include analysis of business plans, market studies, contracts, requests for proposal, statements of work, memos, existing guidelines, procedures, training guides, competing product literature, published comparative product reviews, problem reports, customer suggestion logs, and existing system specifications, among others. Identifying and consulting all likely sources of requirements will result in improved requirements coverage, assuming the documentation is up to date.

Document analysis is used if the objective is to gather details of existing solutions, including business rules, entities, and attributes that need to be included in a new solution or need to be updated for the current solution. This technique also applies in situations where the subject matter experts for the existing solutions are no longer with the organization, or are not going to be available throughout the duration of the elicitation process.

9.9.3   Elements

.1   Preparation

Evaluate which existing system and business documentation is relevant, available and appropriate for study.

.2   Document Review

▶ Study the material and identify relevant business details.

▶ Document business details as well as questions for follow-up with subject matter experts.

.3   Wrap-up

▶ Review and confirm the selected details with subject matter experts.

▶ Organize information into requirements format.

▶ Obtain answers to follow-up questions.

9.9.4   Usage Considerations

.1   Advantages

▶ Not starting from a blank page.

▶ Leveraging existing materials to discover and/or confirm requirements.

▶ A means to cross-check requirements from other elicitation techniques such as interviews, job shadowing, surveys or focus groups.

.2   Disadvantages

▶ Limited to "as-is" perspective.

▶ Existing documentation may not be up-to-date or valid.

▶ Can be a time-consuming and even tedious process to locate the relevant information.

9.10   Estimation

9.10.1   Purpose

Estimating techniques forecast the cost and effort involved in pursuing a course of action.

9.10.2   Description

Estimation techniques are used to develop a better understanding of the possible range of costs and effort associated with any initiative. Estimation is used when it is impossible to determine exact costs. Estimation cannot and does not eliminate uncertainty; rather, the purpose of estimation is to get a reasonable assessment of likely costs or effort required.

The less information that is available to the estimator, the greater the range of uncertainty will be. Estimates should be revisited as more information becomes available. Many estimation techniques rely on historic performance records from the organization to calibrate them against actual performance. Estimates should include an assessment of the range of uncertainty associated with that estimate.

9.10.3   Elements

.1   Analogous Estimation

Use of a similar project as the basis for developing estimates for the current project. It is used when little is known. Analogous estimating is often used to develop a rough order of magnitude (ROM) estimate, and is also known as "top-down" estimating. This is usually done at the beginning of the project or project phase and more detailed estimates follow as more is known.

.2   Parametric Estimation

The use of parameters, multiplied by the number of hours. For parametric estimating to be usable, enough history has to be available to be used as a basis of comparison. With this type of estimating, the business analyst has done enough work to determine which parameters can be used and how many there will be. For example, the business analyst has determined that there will be ten use cases developed. The business analyst also has history that indicates for each use case the total hours that will be spent, in this case will be 20 hours. Using this technique, the business analyst can multiply 10 x 20 to get a total, or 200 hours.

A number of well-defined methods for parametric estimation exist for software development, such as COCOMO II, Function Point Counting, Use Case Points, and Story Points.

.3   Bottom-up Estimation

Using this technique the business analyst has collected the deliverables, activities, tasks, and estimates from all the involved stakeholders and rolls them up to get a total for all the activities and tasks. Because it is normally easier to estimate smaller items than larger items, bottom-up estimating can produce the most accurate and defensible estimates.

.4   Rolling Wave

This is a technique involving refinement of estimates. Estimate the details for activities in the current iteration or increment and provide an analogous estimate for the entire scope of work. As the end of the iteration approaches, estimates for the next iteration can be made and the initial estimate for all activities is refined.

.5   Three-point Estimation

Uses scenarios for:

► The most optimistic estimate, or best-case scenario

► The most pessimistic estimate, or worst-case scenario

► The most likely estimate

Note that the most likely estimate is not an average of best and worst case scenarios. It requires in depth knowledge of the situation. Under the right circumstances, the best-case scenario may also be the most likely.

.6   Historic Analysis

Uses history as a basis for estimating. It is similar to analogous estimation, but is used not only for the top-down estimate, but for the detailed tasks as well. Historic estimates require prior project records, whether maintained formally in a project repository or informally in individual project documentation.

.7   Expert Judgment

Estimating relies on the expertise of those who have performed the work in the past. These experts can be internal or external to the project team or to the organization.

.8   Delphi Estimation

This technique uses a combination of expert judgment and history. There are several variations on this process, but they all include individual estimates, sharing the estimates with experts, and having several rounds until consensus is reached. An average of the three estimates is used. Sometimes the average is weighted by taking the optimistic, pessimistic and four times the most likely, dividing by six to get the average.

9.10.4   Usage Considerations

.1   Advantages

Estimates can help stakeholders make better decisions based on an improved understanding of the likely outcomes from an initiative.

.2   Disadvantages

Stakeholders frequently treat estimates as commitments, and expect that once an estimate is given the solution team will meet the time and cost estimate.

Estimates are often consciously or unconsciously altered to match the desires of influential stakeholders, because the estimators or others are concerned that higher estimates would cause a project to be rejected or be seen as demonstrating a lack of commitment.

9.11   Focus Groups

9.11.1   Purpose

A focus group is a means to elicit ideas and attitudes about a specific product, service or opportunity in an interactive group environment. The participants share their impressions, preferences and needs, guided by a moderator.

9.11.2   Description

A focus group is composed of pre-qualified individuals whose objective is to discuss and comment on a topic. This is an opportunity for individuals to share their own perspectives and discuss them in a group setting. This could lead participants to re-evaluate their own perspectives in light of others' experiences. A trained moderator manages the administrative pre-work, facilitates the session and produces the report. Observers may record or monitor the focus group but to not participate.

As this elicitation technique is considered a form of qualitative research, the session results are analyzed and reported as themes and perspectives, rather than numerical findings. The report may also include selected quotations to support the themes.

A traditional focus group gathers in the same physical room. An online focus group allows members to be located remotely while participating via network connection. Each approach has pros and cons in terms of logistics and expenses.

A focus group can be utilized during any life-cycle state: exploratory, under development, ready to launch, or in production. If the group's topic is a product under development, the group's ideas are analyzed in relationship to the stated requirements. This may result in updating existing requirements or uncovering new requirements. If the topic is a completed product that is ready to be launched, the group's report could influence how to position the product in the market. If the topic is a product in production, the group's report may provide direction on the revisions to the next release of requirements. A focus group may also serve as a means to assess customer satisfaction with a product or service.

The work of a focus group may be similar to that done in a brainstorming session. One difference is that a focus group is typically more structured. Another difference is that a brainstorming session's goal is to actively seek broad, creative, even exaggerated ideas.

9.11.3   Elements

.1   Preparation

Recruit Participants

A focus group typically has 6-12 attendees. It may be necessary to invite additional individuals in order to allow for those who do not attend the session due to scheduling conflicts, emergencies or for other reasons. If many people need to participate, it may be necessary to run more than one focus group.

The topic of the focus group will influence who should be recruited. If the topic is a new product, it is likely that existing users (experts and novices) should be included. There are pros and cons that should be considered when using homogeneous vs. heterogeneous composition.

▶ Homogeneous – individuals with similar characteristics. Caution: Differing perspectives will not be shared. Possible solution: conduct separate sessions for different homogeneous groups to collect differing perspectives.

▶ Heterogeneous – individuals with diverse backgrounds and/or perspectives. Caution: Individuals may self-censor if not comfortable with others' backgrounds or opinions, resulting in a lower quality of data collected.

Assign The Moderator And Recorder

The moderator should be experienced in facilitating groups. Typical skills include the ability to:

▶ promote discussion

▶ ask open questions (those requiring or promoting an extended response)

▶ facilitate interactions between group members

▶ engage all members

▶ keep session focused

▶ remain neutral

▶ be adaptable and flexible

Create Discussion Guide

The discussion guide includes goals/objectives of the session and five to six open questions.

Reserve Site And Services

Select the location for the session. Arrange for technical support to transcribe the session and, if used, audio/video taping equipment.

.2   Run The Focus Group Session

The moderator guides the group's discussion, follows a pre-planned script of specific issues, and ensures the objectives are met. However, the group discussion should appear free-flowing and relatively unstructured for the participants. A session is typically 1 to 2 hours in length. A recorder captures the group's comments.

.3   Produce Report

The moderator analyzes and documents the participants' agreements and disagreements and synthesizes them into themes.

9.11.4   Usage Considerations

.1   Advantages

▶ Ability to elicit data from a group of people in a single session saves time and cost as compared to conducting individual interviews with the same number of people.

▶ Effective for learning people's attitudes, experiences and desires.

▶ Active discussion and the ability to ask others questions creates an environment where participants can consider their personal view in relation to other perspectives.

.2   Disadvantages

▶ In the group setting, participants may be concerned about issues of trust, or may be unwilling to discuss sensitive or personal topics.

▶ Data collected (what people say) may not be consistent with how people actually behave.

▶ If the group is too homogeneous their responses may not represent the complete set of requirements.

▶ A skilled moderator is needed to manage group interactions and discussions.

▶ It may be difficult to schedule the group for the same date and time.

▶ If the goal of the focus group is to elicit ideas on a new or changing product, a focus group is not an effective way to evaluate usability.

9.12   Functional Decomposition

9.12.1   Purpose

To decompose processes, functional areas, or deliverables into their component parts and allow each part to be analyzed independently.

9.12.2   Description

Functional decomposition involves breaking down a large problem into smaller functions or deliverables. The primary goal of functional decomposition is to ensure that the problem is separated into sub-problems that are as independent as possible, so that work can be assigned to different groups. This provides the ability to scale and manage larger projects.

Figure 9–6: Functional Decomposition Diagram

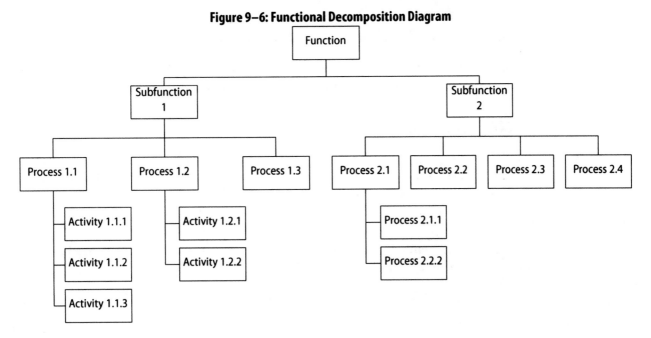

9.12.3 Elements

Functional decomposition identifies the high-level functions of an organization or solution and then breaks those functions into smaller pieces, such as sub-processes and activities, features, and so forth.

When decomposing an organizational function, models start with a top-level function, typically corresponding with an organizational unit and continue to drill down into sub-functions, representing the processes carried out by that unit, and beneath those sub-processes and individual activities (the names for each level are conventions only, and do not imply that decomposition must halt after the fourth level is reached). These can be represented by a hierarchical diagram, a tree diagram, or by numbering each sub-function. Each function is wholly comprised of the sub-functions beneath it. The process of functional decomposition continues until a sub-function cannot be broken down into two or more lower level functions.

A similar process can be carried out for the work involved in a project. This decomposition (known as a Work Breakdown Structure or WBS) breaks the project scope down phases, work packages and deliverables. Decomposition can also be performed to describe a product or process.

9.12.4 Usage Considerations

.1 Advantages

▶ Creates a conceptual model of the work that needs to be completed to deliver the new business solution.

▶ Provides all stakeholders with a consistent view of the scope of the effort.

▶ Assists estimating in that estimates can be made for smaller, and therefore more readily understandable, subsets of the whole.

.2   Disadvantages

▶   There is no way to be certain that all components have been captured.

▶   Decomposing a problem without fully understanding the relationship between pieces of the problem may create an inappropriate structure that impedes analysis.

9.13   Interface Analysis

9.13.1   Purpose

To identify interfaces between solutions and/or solution components and define requirements that describe how they will interact.

9.13.2   Description

An interface is a connection between two components. Most software applications require one or more interfaces. Interface types include:

▶   User interfaces, including human users directly interacting with the system, as well as reports provided to the user

▶   Interfaces to and from external applications

▶   Interfaces to and from external hardware devices

Interface analysis helps to clarify the boundaries of the interfacing applications. It distinguishes which application provides specific functionality along with the input and output data needs. By clearly and carefully separating the requirements for each application while defining the shared interface requirements, a basis for successful interoperability is established.

Identifying what interfaces are necessary to support an application sets the stage for eliciting a wide variety of requirements. Early identification of interfaces uncovers and confirms the interfacing stakeholders and provides a framework for subsequent analysis of the detailed requirements for each interface. Interface analysis is certainly necessary for a software solution or solution component but can also be useful for a non-software solution, such as when defining requirements for deliverables that will be produced by third parties.

9.13.3   Elements

.1   Prepare for Interface Identification

Review current documentation for any indications of interface requirements. For example, a Context Diagram, as described in *Scope Modeling (9.27)* can provide an effective visualization of the interfaces to and from external parties.

.2   Conduct Interface Identification

For each stakeholder or system that interacts with the system, identify what interfaces are needed.

For each interface:

▶   Describe the purpose of the interface.

▶ Evaluate which type of interface may be appropriate: user interface, system-to-system interface, and/or external hardware device interfaces.

▶ Elicit high-level details about the interface, depending on its type:

For an interface where the user directly engages the application, see *Prototyping*.

For a application-to-application interface or an interface with an external hardware device, outline the content and name the related events.

.3   Define Interfaces

Requirements for an interface are primarily focused on describing the inputs and outputs from that interface, any validation rules that govern those inputs and outputs, and events that might trigger interactions. There may be a large number of possible interaction types that may each need to be specified.

9.13.4   Usage Considerations

.1   Advantages

Early identification of interfaces provides an early, high-level view of interoperability for planning:

▶ Impact on delivery date. Knowing what interfaces are needed, as well as their anticipated complexity and testing needs enables more accurate project planning and potential savings in time and cost.

▶ Collaboration with other systems or projects. If the interface is to an existing system, product or device and the interface already exists, it may not be changed easily. If the interface is new, then the ownership, development and testing of the interface needs to be addressed for both applications. In case, eliciting and analyzing the interface requirements will likely require negotiation and cooperation between those responsible for both applications.

▶ Specification of the interfaces should prevent difficulties in integrating multiple components.

.2   Disadvantages

Does not provide insight into other aspects of the solution since the analysis does not assess the internal components.

9.14   Interviews

9.14.1   Purpose

An interview is a systematic approach designed to elicit information from a person or group of people in an informal or formal setting by talking to an interviewee, asking relevant questions and documenting the responses.

9.14.2   Description

In an interview, the interviewer formally or informally directs questions to a stakeholder in order to obtain answers that will be used to create formal requirements. One-on-one interviews are typically most common. In a group interview (with more than one interviewee in attendance) the interviewer must be careful to elicit responses from all attendees.

For the purpose of eliciting requirements, interviews are of two basic types:

▶ **Structured Interview:** where the interviewer has a pre-defined set of questions and is looking for answers.

▶ **Unstructured Interview:** where, without any pre-defined questions, the interviewer and the interviewee discuss topics of interest in an open-ended way.

Successful interviewing depends on several factors including, but not limited to:

▶ Level of understanding of the domain by the interviewer.

▶ Experience of the interviewer in conducting interviews.

▶ Skill of the interviewer in documenting the discussions.

▶ Readiness of interviewee to provide the relevant information.

▶ Degree of clarity in interviewee's mind about what the business requires of the target system.

▶ Rapport of the interviewer with the interviewee.

9.14.3   Elements

.1   Prepare For The Interview

Define the interview's focus or goal before proceeding.

Identify Potential Interviewees

The business analyst considers the following questions when identifying who should be interviewed:

▶ Who holds the most authentic and the most current information on the subject of interest?

▶ What is their stake in the initiative?

▶ What is the relative importance of information held by one person relative to that held by another person? This information is helpful when analyzing conflicting comments across interviews.

Design the Interview

The interviewer may need to custom design the interview for each identified interviewee. The interviewee's ability to participate and the desired outcome of an interview govern the design of an interview. In addition, these factors are also considered:

▶ The format for the interview, structured vs. unstructured. If a structured interview, the type of questions:

> **Closed-ended questions:** Questions that are used to elicit a single response such as: yes, no, or a specific number. Example: How many hours does it take for the claim process to be completed?

> **Open-ended questions:** Questions that are used to elicit a dialog or series of steps and cannot be answered in a yes or no fashion but need explaining. Example: What does a claim processor do on receipt of a claim form?

- **Organization of the questions:** use a logical order or an order of priority/significance. Examples of order would be general questions to specific questions, start to finish, detail to summary, etc. The actual organization is based on factors such as the interviewee's level of knowledge and the subject of the interview. The goal is to follow a logical order rather than jump around when asking questions.

- **Location of participants:** An interview can be conducted in-person or via telephone, web conference, or other remote communication methods.

- The interview time and site are convenient to the interviewee.

- Determine if a scribe is needed and if so, include that person in the scheduling process. Determine if the interview needs to be recorded. If so, discuss the recording's purpose and usage with the interviewee.

Contact Potential Interviewees

The interviewer contacts the selected interviewees and explains to them why their assistance is needed. The purpose is to explain the objective of the interview to the potential interviewee.

.2 Conduct The Interview

- **Opening the interview.** The interviewer states the purpose of the interview, addresses any initial concerns raised by the interviewee, and explains that notes will be taken and shared with the interviewee after the interview.

- **During the interview**

  > The interviewer maintains focus on the established goals and pre-defined questions.

  > All concerns raised by the interviewee are addressed during the interview or documented for follow-up after the interview or in a subsequent interview.

  > The interviewer practices active listening to confirm what has been understood from the information offered at various times during the interview.

- **Closing the interview.** The interviewer asks the interviewee for areas that may have been overlooked in the session. Lastly, the interviewer summarizes the session, reminds the interviewee of the upcoming review process and thanks the interviewee for their time.

.3 Post Interview Follow-Up And Confirmation

After the interview is complete, the interviewer organizes the information and sends the notes to the interviewee for review. Documenting the discussion for review allows the interviewee to see all of the information in context. This review may point out items that are incorrect or missing because the interviewer (or scribe) missed documenting them, or because the interviewer (or scribe) documented them incorrectly, or because the interviewee missed discussing them. This review is not intended to address whether or not the requirements are valid nor whether they will ultimately be approved for inclusion into the deliverables but solely to determine if the interview has been adequately documented.

9.14.4 Usage Considerations

.1 Advantages

▶ Encourages participation and establishes rapport with the stakeholder.

▶ Simple, direct technique that can be used in varying situations.

▶ Allows the interviewer and participant to have full discussions and explanations of the questions and answers.

▶ Enables observations of non-verbal behavior.

▶ The interviewer can ask follow-up and probing questions to confirm their own understanding.

▶ Maintains focus through the use of clear objectives for the interview that are agreed upon by all participants and can be met in the time allotted.

▶ Allows interviewees to express opinions in private that they may be reluctant to express in public.

.2 Disadvantages

▶ Interviews are not an ideal means of reaching consensus across a group of stakeholders.

▶ Requires considerable commitment and involvement of the participants.

▶ Training is required to conduct effective interviews. In particular, unstructured interviews require special skills including facilitation/virtual facilitation and active listening.

▶ Depth of follow-on questions may be dependent on the interviewer's knowledge of the business domain.

▶ Transcription and analysis of interview data can be complex and expensive.

▶ Based on the level of clarity provided during the interview, the resulting documentation may be subject to interviewer's interpretation.

▶ There is a risk of unintentionally leading the interviewee.

9.15   Lessons Learned Process

9.15.1   Purpose

The purpose of the lessons learned process is to compile and document successes, opportunities for improvement, failures, and recommendations for improving the performance of future projects or project phases.

9.15.2   Description

Lessons learned sessions can include any format or venue that works for the key stakeholders identified as participants in these sessions.

9.15.3   Elements

Sessions can include a review of:

► Business analysis activities

► Business analysis deliverables

► The final product

► The business analysis process

► Automation and technology used or not used

► Managerial concerns or issues

► How organizational process assets helped or hindered the business analysis and requirements processes

► Performance against plan

► Variances

  ▷ Root causes for the variances

  ▷ Whether the variances were routine or significant anomalies

► Corrective and/or preventive action recommended, approved or rejected, and taken.

Lessons learned sessions may take place in formal, facilitated meetings with set agendas and meeting roles, formal or informal working sessions, or informal get-togethers, any of which may or may not include a celebration.

9.15.4   Usage Considerations

.1   Advantages

► Useful for identifying opportunities for process improvement.

► Can help build team morale after a difficult period.

.2   Disadvantages

▶   All participants must be prepared to avoid any urge to assign blame during these sessions or honest discussion may not occur.

▶   Participants may be reluctant to document and discuss problems

▶   May risk becoming a "gripe" session and improvement opportunities may be neglected.

9.16   Metrics and Key Performance Indicators

9.16.1   Purpose

The purpose of metrics and key performance indicators are to measure the performance of solutions, solution components, and other matters of interest to stakeholders.

9.16.2   Description

A metric is a quantifiable level of an indicator that an organization uses to measure progress. An indicator identifies a specific numerical measurement that represents the degree of progress toward achieving a goal, objective, output, activity or further input. A Key Performance Indicator is one that measures progress towards a strategic goal or objective. Reporting is the process of informing stakeholders of metrics of indicators in specified formats at specified intervals.

Metrics and reporting are key components of monitoring and evaluation. Monitoring is a continuous process of collecting data to determine how well a solution has been implemented compared to expected results. Evaluation is the systematic and objective assessment of a solution to determine its status and efficacy in meeting objectives over time, and to identify ways to improve the solution to better meet objectives. The top priorities of a monitoring and evaluation system are the intended goals and effects of a solution, as well as inputs, activities, and outputs.

9.16.3   Elements

.1   Indicators

An indicator identifies a specific numerical measurement for a goal, impact, output, activity, or input. Each factor of interest has at least one indicator to measure it properly, but some may require several. A good indicator has five characteristics:

▶   **Clear:** precise and unambiguous

▶   **Relevant:** appropriate to the factor

▶   **Economical:** available at reasonable cost

▶   **Adequate:** provides a sufficient basis to assess performance

▶   **Quantifiable:** can be independently validated

In addition to these characteristics, stakeholder interests are also important. Certain indicators may help stakeholders perform or improve more than others. Over time, weaknesses in some indicators can be identified and improved.

Not all factors can be measured directly. Proxies can be used when data for direct indicators are not available or feasible to collect at regular intervals. For example, in the absence of a survey of client satisfaction, an organization might use the proportion of all contracts renewed as an indicator.

When establishing an indicator, its source, method of collection, collector, and the cost, frequency and difficulty of collection need to be considered. Secondary sources of data may be the most economical, but to meet the other characteristics of a good indicator, primary research, such as surveys, interviews or direct observations may be necessary. The method of data collection is the key driver of a monitoring, evaluation and reporting system's cost.

.2 Metrics

Metrics are quantifiable levels of indicators that are measured at a specified point in time. A target metric is the objective to be reached within a specified period. In setting a metric (usually one) for an indicator, it is important to have a clear understanding of the baseline starting point, resources that can be devoted to improving the factors covered by the indicator, and political concerns.

A metric can be a specific point, threshold or a range. A range can be useful if the indicator is new. The scope of time to reach the target metric can be multi-year to annual or quarterly, or even more frequent, depending on the need.

.3 Structure

Establishing a monitoring and evaluation system requires a data collection procedure, a data analysis procedure, a reporting procedure, and collection of baseline data. The data collection procedure covers units of analysis, sampling procedures, data collection instruments to use, collection frequency, and responsibility for collection. The analysis method specifies the procedures for conducting the analysis and the data consumer, who may have strong interests in how the analysis is conducted. Reporting procedure covers the report templates, recipients, frequency, and means of communication. Baseline information is that data provided immediately before or at the beginning of a period to measure. Baseline data is used to learn about recent performance and to measure progress from that point forward. It needs to be collected for each indicator, analyzed and reported.

There are three key factors in assessing the quality of indicators and their metrics—reliability, validity and timeliness. Reliability is the extent to which the data collection approach is stable and consistent across time and space. Validity is the extent to which data clearly and directly measure the performance the organization intends to measure. Timeliness is the fit of the frequency and latency of data to management's need for it.

.4 Reporting

Typically, reports compare the baseline, current metrics and target metrics to each other, with calculations of the differences presented in both absolute and relative terms. In most situations, trends are more credible and important than absolute metrics. Visual presentations tend to be more effective than tables, particularly when using qualitative text to explain the data.

9.16.4   **Usage Considerations**

.1   Advantages

Establishing a monitoring and evaluation system allows stakeholders to understand the extent to which a solution meets an objective, and how effective the inputs and activities of developing the solution (output) were.

Indicators, metrics and reporting also facilitate organizational alignment, linking goals to objectives, supporting solutions, underlying tasks, and resources.

.2   Disadvantages

Gathering excessive amounts of data beyond what is needed will result in unnecessary expense in collecting, analyzing and reporting. It will also distract project members from other responsibilities. On agile projects, this will be particularly relevant.

A bureaucratic metrics program fails from collecting too much data and not generating useful reports that will allow timely responsive action. Those charged with collecting metric data must be given feedback to understand how their actions are affecting the quality of the project results.

When metrics are used to assess performance, the individuals being measured are likely to act to increase their performance on those metrics, even if this causes suboptimal performance on other activities.

9.17   Non-functional Requirements Analysis

9.17.1   **Purpose**

The purpose of non-functional requirements is to describe the required qualities of a system, such as its usability and performance characteristics. These supplement the documentation of functional requirements, which describe the behavior of the system.

9.17.2   **Description**

Non-functional requirements document the qualities of a system that are important to:

▶ the user community, such as usability, learnability, reliability, etc.

▶ the development community, such as scalability, maintainability, reusability, etc.

Strictly speaking, the term "non-functional requirements" only applies when describing a software application. However, the various categories of non-functional requirements may be applicable to other solution components for which requirements can be developed. For example, reliability requirements for an organizational unit might include specified hours of service, and performance efficiency requirements for a business process might include cycle time to deal with a customer request and may be captured in a service level agreement (SLA). In these cases, an alternative term like "quality of service" requirements may be preferred.

9.17.3   **Elements**

The following elements are usually included in the description of non-functional requirements.

.1 Category

Non-functional requirements are usually organized into categories. Categorization supports the discovery of non-functional requirements by providing a mental checklist of characteristics to consider when performing requirements elicitation. The scheme listed here is based on ISO 9126, but other categorizations (such as FURPS+) may also be used.

Reliability: Is the software application available when needed? Reliability requirements include the ability of the application to recover from errors, uptime, or failures in the interfaces.

Performance Efficiency: Does the software application deliver acceptable performance levels given the resources available? Performance Efficiency requirements include the time taken to perform activities and the resource utilization levels.

Operability: Is the software application understandable to users? Operability requirements include the extent to which users can recognize whether an application will actually fulfill their needs, the ease of learning the application, and the usability of the application.

Security: Does the application prevent intentional misuse? Security requirements include the ability to ensure appropriate confidentiality of information, the integrity of information stored in the application, the ability to verify whether actions were taken and by whom, and the ability to authenticate users.

Compatibility: Can the application operate effectively with other applications in the same environment? Compatibility requirements include requirements for properly replacing another application, the ability to co-exist with other applications, and the ability to interact with other applications.

Maintainability: Can the application be effectively modified after implementation to meet changing needs? Maintainability requirements include the ability to change one component without affecting others, the ability to re-use components, whether the application can be effectively tested and problems can be properly diagnosed, the ease of making changes, and the ability to implement changes without causing unexpected failures.

Transferability: Can the application be installed and in another environment? Transferability requirements include the ease of installing and uninstalling the application, the kinds of different environments it can run in, and the ease of migrating it to a new environment.

.2 Measurement

The definition of a non-functional requirement should include an appropriate measure of success for each one so that it can be adequately tested. Some non-functional requirements may seem very subjective (e.g." intuitive interface") but careful thought can usually provide an appropriate success measurement.

.3 Documentation

Non-functional requirements are typically documented in text using declarative statements such as:

- ► Ninety percent of operators shall be able to use all the functionality of the system after no more than six hours of training.

- ► The system shall provide 90% of responses in no more than 2 seconds.

This documentation is presented as a part of the total set of requirements documentation, often in a section, or a separate document.

9.17.4 Usage Considerations

.1 Advantages

Success in meeting non-functional requirements will have a strong influence on whether or not a system is accepted by its users.

.2 Disadvantages

Non-functional requirements are often more difficult to define than functional requirements. Expectations regarding quality attributes may not be described and users of an application may find them difficult to articulate.

Overly stringent non-functional requirements may significantly impact the cost of developing a software application.

9.18 Observation

9.18.1 Purpose

Observation is a means of eliciting requirements by conducting an assessment of the stakeholder's work environment. This technique is appropriate when documenting details about current processes or if the project is intended to enhance or change a current process.

9.18.2 Description

Observation relies on studying people performing their jobs, and is sometimes called "job shadowing" or "following people around." For instance, some people have their work routine down to such a habit that they have difficulty explaining what they do or why. The observer may need to watch them perform their work in order to understand the flow of work. In certain projects, it is important to understand the current processes to better assess the process modifications that may be needed.

There are two basic approaches for the observation technique:

- ► **Passive/invisible:** In this approach, the observer observes the user working through the business routine but does not ask questions. The observer records what is observed, but otherwise stays out of the way. The observer waits until the entire process has been completed before asking any questions. The observer should observe the business process multiple times to ensure they understand how the process works today and why it works the way it does.

▶ **Active/visible:** In this approach, while the observer observes the current process and takes notes they may dialog with the user. When the observer has questions as to why something is being done as it is, they ask questions right away, even if it breaks the routine of the user.

Variations of the observation technique:

▶ In some cases, the observer might participate in the actual work to get a hands-on feel for how the business process works today. Of necessity this would be limited to activity that is appropriate for a non-expert to perform and whose results would not negatively impact the business.

▶ The observer becomes a temporary apprentice.

▶ The observer watches a demonstration of how a specific process and/or task is performed.

9.18.3   Elements

.1   Prepare For Observation

▶ Determine what sampling of users (e.g. experts and novices, just experts) to observe and which activities.

▶ Prepare questions to ask during or after the shadowing.

.2   Observe

▶ Observer introduces him- or herself to the person being observed and:

    ▷ Reassures the user that their work is not being questioned. Rather, the observation of the work and resulting documentation will serve as input to requirements analysis.

    ▷ Informs the user that the observer is present only to study their processes and will refrain from discussing future solutions to any problems.

    ▷ Explains to the user that they may stop the observation process at any time if they believe that it is interfering with their work.

    ▷ Suggests to the user that they may "think aloud" while they are working as a way to share their intentions, challenges, and concerns.

▶ Conduct observation.

    ▷ Take detailed notes.

    ▷ If using the active observation approach, ask probing questions about why certain processes and tasks are being performed as they are.

.3   Post Observation Wrap-Up – Documentation And Confirmation

▶ Obtain answers to original questions, or new questions that surfaced during the observations.

> ▶ Provide a summary of notes to the user, as soon as possible, for review and any clarification.

> ▶ When observing many users, compile notes at regular intervals to identify commonalties and differences among users. Review findings with the entire group to ensure that the final details represent the entire group, not selected individuals.

9.18.4   Usage Considerations

.1   Advantages:

> ▶ Provides realistic and practical insight into the business by getting a hands-on feel for how the business process works today.

> ▶ Elicits details of informal communication and ways people actually work around the system that may not be documented anywhere.

.2   Disadvantages

> ▶ Only possible for existing processes.

> ▶ Could be time-consuming.

> ▶ May be disruptive to the person being shadowed.

> ▶ Unusual exceptions and critical situations that happen infrequently may not occur during the observation.

> ▶ May not well work if the current process involves a high level of intellectual activity or other work that is not easily observable.

9.19   Organization Modeling

9.19.1   Purpose

Organization Modeling is used to describe the roles, responsibilities and reporting structures that exist within an organization and to align those structures with the organization's goals.

9.19.2   Description

An organizational model defines how an organization or organizational unit is structured. Organizational units bring together a group of people to fulfill a common purpose or goal. This purpose may be functional, meaning that the people in question share a common set of skills and knowledge, or to serve a particular market. An organizational model will define the scope of the organizational unit, the formal relationships between the people who are members of that unit, the roles those people fill, and the interfaces between that unit and other units or stakeholders.

9.19.3   Elements

.1   Organizational Purpose and Structure

Functions: Functionally-oriented organizations group together staff based on shared skills or areas of expertise. They are generally adopted in order to encourage a standardization of work or processes within the organization. Functional organizations facilitate cost management and reduce duplication of work, but are prone to develop communication and cross-functional co-ordination problems (known informally as "silos").

Markets: The term "market-oriented" covers a number of different possible ways of organizing an enterprise, all of which are based on serving a particular customer segment rather than on the common skills or expertise of the employee. Market-oriented structures enable the organization to be better oriented with the needs of its customers, but are prone to develop inconsistencies in how work is performed and to duplicate work in multiple divisions. A "market-oriented" organization may be organized around customer groups, geographical areas, projects, or processes.

Matrix: In this model, there are separate managers for each functional area and for each product, service, or customer group. Staff report into a line manager, who is responsible for the performance of a type of work and for identifying opportunities for efficiency in the work, and to a market (product/service/project/etc.) manager, who is responsible for managing the product, service, etc. across multiple functional areas.

.2 Roles

An organizational unit will include a number of defined roles. Each role will require a specific set of skills and knowledge, will have certain responsibilities, will perform certain kinds of work, and will have defined relationships with other roles in the organization.

.3 Interfaces

Each organizational unit will have interfaces with other organizational units. Interfaces may be in the form of work packages that the organizational unit receives or delivers to other units, communication with people in other roles, and so forth. Work packages should have defined requirements and quality standards that are agreed to by stakeholders affected by those packages. These requirements, standards, and expectations may be formally or informally defined, and may be negotiated on a case-by-case basis or allow for flexibility in how they are met.

.4 Org Charts

The fundamental diagram used in organization modeling is the org (organization) chart. There is no formal standard set for defining org charts, although there are certain standard conventions that most org charts follow. The org chart shows:

▶ **Organizational Units,** which may represent people, teams, departments, or divisions based on the level of abstraction of the org chart. Frequently, an org chart will mix organizational units, showing a mix of people, teams, and higher-level divisions.

▶ **Lines of Reporting,** which trace accountability and control between organizational units. A solid line typically denotes direct authority, while a dotted line indicates information transfer or situational authority. Lines of reporting visually depict the span of control of a particular manager or organizational unit (that is, the number of people that a manager is responsible for directing).

▶ **Roles and People.** An org chart should show the roles that exist within an organization and the people assigned to each of those roles.

Figure 9–7: Org Chart

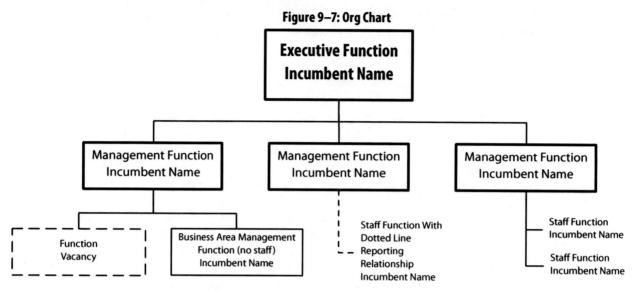

9.19.4   Usage Considerations

.1   Advantages

Organizational models are one of the few types of models any organization is almost certain to have defined. Even the simplest organization has to define the reporting structures among team members in order to co-ordinate work between its people.

.2   Disadvantages

The primary limitation of Organization Modeling is not the technique itself, but rather the implications of including organizational redesign in the scope of a project. Organizational redesigns are likely to be highly contentious and require significant executive support in order to be successful.

A secondary problem is that informal lines of authority and communication that are not reflected in the org chart are almost certain to exist within the organization.

9.20   Problem Tracking

9.20.1   Purpose

Problem tracking provides an organized approach to tracking, management, and resolution of defects, issues, problems, and risks throughout business analysis activities. Management of issues is important so that they can be resolved in a timely manner to ensure success.

9.20.2   Description

Problems may include issues, questions, risks, defects, conflicts, or other concerns that need to be tracked to resolution. A problem tracking system ensures that issues are not simply neglected or lost. For each problem, the tracking tool may include an identification of the problem, status updates, assigning of related actions that are required to team members and tracking expected resolution dates, resolution results, actions and decisions taken, priority, and impacts. The current status of problems should be communicated to all relevant stakeholders. Ensure problem tracking leads to:

▶ Resolution of problems in a timely manner that eliminate or minimize negative impacts.

▶ Allocation of resources to resolve problems.

▶ Identification of root causes of problems.

9.20.3 Elements

.1 Problem Record

A problem record may contain some or all of the following information:

▶ **Description:** A clear and concise description of the problem identified.

▶ **Raised By:** The person who identified the problem.

▶ **Date Identified**.

▶ **Impact:** The possible consequences if the problem is not resolved by the Need by Date. Impact may be assessed based on schedule, cost or scope, as examples.

▶ **Priority:** Determine the priority of the problem based on assessment by stakeholders. An example of a priority scale is: Critical, High, Medium, and Low.

▶ **Need by Date:** When the problem must be resolved by to avoid the consequences.

▶ **Owner:** One team member who is assigned to manage the problem to closure. This may not be the same person who identified the problem or the same person(s) who are assigned actions to resolve the problem.

▶ **Status:** The current status of the problem. Examples of statuses that can be used include Open, Assigned, Resolved, Cancelled.

▶ **Action Needed to Resolve**: Details of what action needs to be taken to resolve the problem. May be more than one.

▶ **Responsible for Action:** Person assigned to take the specific action.

▶ **Completion Date of Action**. Can be an estimated future date or an actual past date, if the problem is complete.

▶ **Outcome:** The results of the resolution.

.2 Problem Management

The problem must be tracked and managed until the problem is fixed or it is determined that no action will be taken. A regularly scheduled review of the problem report by all relevant parties ensures visibility and focus on the problems. If problems cannot be resolved in a reasonable period of time it may be necessary to escalate the matter.

.3   Metrics

An additional element that can be useful to gauge how the project is doing regarding problem resolution is to decide on a set of *metrics and key performance indicators (9.16)* and then measure and report on them. Examples of possible KPIs are:

▶ Number of problems by status and priority.

▶ Cycle time for each problem (number of days it took from Date Identified to Resolution Date).

9.20.4   Usage Considerations

.1   Advantages

Problem tracking provides an organized method for tracking and resolving risks, issues and defects. It provides a mechanism to communicate problems across the team and helps to maintain focus on open problems until they are resolved. The regular review of the problems together with the team also helps to maintain focus and ensure resolution.

.2   Disadvantages

In the following situations, it may be challenging to use the technique:

▶ If regular prioritization and management of problems is not done, the list becomes outdated and irrelevant.

▶ If key team members are not available on a regular basis to discuss the lists of problems and to determine actions to be taken, then progress to resolve them may become very slow to non-existent.

▶ If there is a strict deadline to deliver the solution, then problem management may become a lower priority. Often, root cause analysis of the problems can take more time and resources than are available.

9.21   Process Modeling

9.21.1   Purpose

To understand how work that involves multiple roles and departments is performed within an organization.

9.21.2   Description

A process describes how multiple people or groups collaborate over a period of time to perform work. Processes involve a number of activities that are linked by a sequence flow. A process is repeatable and may have multiple paths to completion.

A process is initiated by an event in the business domain, such as a sale of a product to a customer, a request for information by a senior executive, or a failure to complete a transaction. Events may be actions taken by a person, rules which cause action to be taken, or simply the passage of a period of time. The process model may involve manual activities, be completely automated, or a combination thereof. The process is complete when the objective or the goal of the process is completed.

A process model is a visual representation of the sequential flow and control logic of a set of related activities or actions. Process modeling is used to obtain a graphical representation of a current or future process within an organization. A model may be used at its highest level to obtain a general understanding of a process or at a lower level as a basis for simulation so that the process can be made as efficient as possible.

Figure 9–8: Flowchart

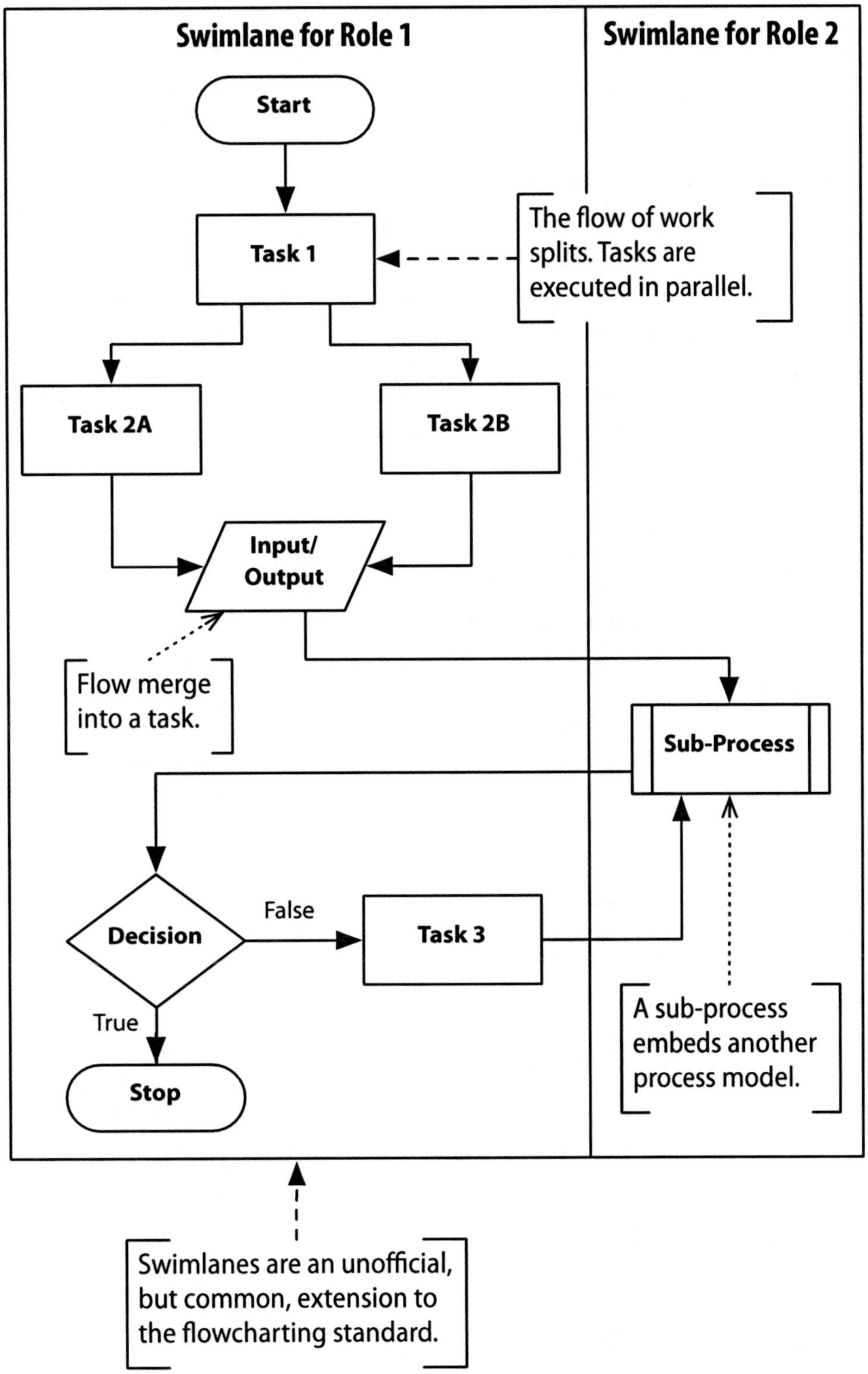

Figure 9–9: Activity Diagram

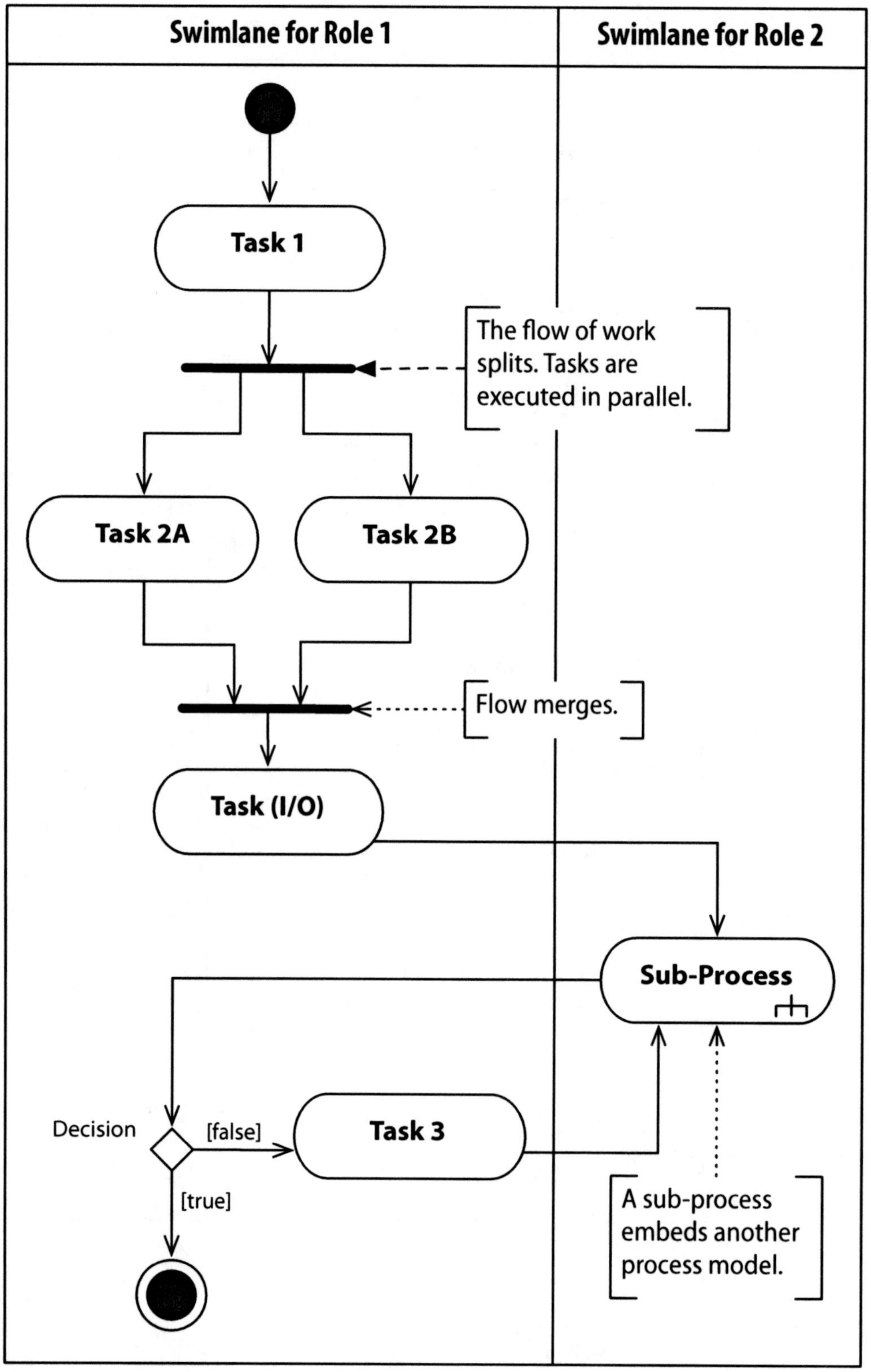

9.21.3   Elements

There are many different notations in use to depict process models. The most commonly used are flowcharts and UML activity diagrams, although BPMN has seen increasing adoption in recent years. Process models typically contain some or all of the following key elements:

.1   Notation Elements

Activities: The individual steps or pieces of work that must be completed in order to execute the business process. An activity may be a single task or may be further decomposed into a subprocess (with its own activities, flow, and other process elements).

Decisions: Forks where the flow of work proceeds in two or more flows and, optionally, where separate flows merge together. A decision may create mutually exclusive or parallel flows.

Events: Events occur outside the scope of a process and may be the result of actions taken, messages received, or the passage of time. Events may create, interrupt, or terminate processes.

Flow: Indicate the direction of the step-by-step sequence of the workflow. In general, diagrams are drawn from top to bottom or in the direction of reading to show the passage of time. The process flow may split to allow for activities to occur simultaneously and later merge.

Roles: Roles represent a type of person or group. Role definitions typically match those in the *organization model (9.19)*.

Swimlanes and Pools: Swimlanes are horizontal or vertical sections of a process model that show which activities are performed by a particular role. When the flow of work crosses the boundary of a swimlane, responsibility for that work then passes to another person or group within the organization.

A pool represents an organizational boundary. It may include a number of swimlanes. Commonly, a process will include one pool for the customer and a second pool for the organization, although it is possible for a process to include any number of pools.

Terminal Points: Terminal points represent the beginning or end of a process or process flow. A terminal point generally represents some kind of event that is visible to the organization or outside of it.

.2   Process Improvement

There are a number of frameworks and methodologies that focus on process improvement methods, such as Six Sigma, Lean, and a large number of proprietary BPM approaches. Methods for process improvement include value stream mapping, statistical analysis and control, process simulation, benchmarking, process frameworks, and others. Common changes to processes in order to improve them include:

► Analysis of a process to identify and remove activities that do not add value to a stakeholder, where possible.

▶ Reduction of the time required to complete a process (by reducing the time to perform a task or the wait time between tasks).

▶ Improving interfaces or handoffs between roles and organizational units to remove errors.

▶ Reduction or elimination of bottlenecks and backlogs.

9.21.4 Usage Considerations

.1 Advantages

▶ Most stakeholders are comfortable with the basic elements of and concepts behind a process model.

▶ Process models are effective at showing how to handle a large number of scenarios and parallel branches.

▶ Process models are likely to have value in their own right, as they will be used by business stakeholders for training and co-ordination of activities.

.2 Disadvantages

▶ Process models can become extremely complex and unwieldy if not structured carefully. Complex processes may involve enough activities and roles to make them almost impossible for a single individual to understand.

▶ Problems in a process cannot always be identified by looking at the model. It is usually necessary to engage stakeholders directly to find problems they have encountered while working with a process.

9.22 Prototyping

9.22.1 Purpose

Prototyping details user interface requirements and integrates them with other requirements such as use cases, scenarios, data and business rules. Stakeholders often find prototyping to be a concrete means of identifying, describing and validating their interface needs.

9.22.2 Description

Prototyping can be categorized in two ways:

Functional Scope. A horizontal prototype models a shallow, and possibly wide view of the system's functionality. It typically does not have any business logic running behind the visualization. A vertical prototype models a deep, and usually narrow slice of the entire system's functionality.

Usage Throughout System Development Lifecycle. A "Throw-away" prototype seeks to quickly uncover and clarify interface requirements using simple tools, sometimes just paper and pencil. As the name suggests, such a prototype is usually discarded when the final system has been developed. The focus is on functionality that is not easily elicited by other techniques, has conflicting viewpoints, or is difficult to understand. An "Evolutionary or Functional" prototype extends the initial interface requirements into a fully functioning system and requires a specialized prototyping tool or language. This prototype produces a working software application.

9.22.3 Elements

.1 Prepare For Prototyping

► Determine the prototyping approach: throw-away versus evolutionary / functional; vertical versus horizontal.

► Identify the functionality to be modeled.

.2 Prototype

Building the prototype is an iterative process. The initial efforts outline the high-level views. Subsequent iterations add detail depending on the functional scope (horizontal versus vertical),

When prototyping a report, the first iteration may produce a list of report requirements such as data attributes, selection criteria and derivation rules for totals. Further analysis may draft a detailed layout of the report.

When prototyping an interface that appears on a screen (whether on a computer screen or a device such as a cell phone, or a copy machine), a number of iterations may be useful. The initial focus is an end-to-end understanding of the interface flow. Add details as appropriate to the work.

► A Storyboard (also known as a Dialog Map, Dialog Hierarchy or Navigation Flow) portrays the navigation paths across the interface components. This visual includes abstractions of each screen along with directional arrows that indicate the allowable navigation flows.

► Screen prototypes provide data attributes, selection criteria and supporting business rules.

► A screen layout or mockup provides a graphical representation of the elements. At this detailed level, one would apply any organizational standards or style guides.

.3 Evaluate The Prototype

For detailed prototypes, verify that the logical interface elements trace to user requirements such as processes, data and business rules.

Validate that the prototype represents the user's needs. Scenarios are useful to 'test' the interfaces.

9.22.4 Usage Considerations

.1 Advantages

► Supports users who are more comfortable and effective at articulating their needs by using pictures, as prototyping lets them "see" the future system's interface.

► A prototype allows for early user interaction and feedback.

▶ A throw-away prototype can be an inexpensive means to quickly uncover and confirm a variety of requirements that go beyond just the interface such as processes, data, business rules.

▶ A vertical prototype can demonstrate what is feasible with existing technology, and where there may be technology gaps.

▶ An evolutionary / functional prototype provides a vehicle for designers and developers to learn about the users' interface needs and to evolve system requirements.

.2　　Disadvantages

▶ Depending on the complexity of the target system, using prototyping to elicit requirements can take considerable time if the process gets bogged down by the "how's" rather than "what's".

▶ Assumptions about the underlying technology may need to be made in order to initiate prototyping.

▶ A prototype may lead users to develop unrealistic expectations regarding the delivered system's performance, completion date, reliability and usability characteristics. This is because an elaborated, detailed prototype can look a lot like a functional system.

▶ Users may focus on the design specifications of the solution rather than the requirements that any solution must address. This can, in turn, constrain the solution design. Developers may believe that they must provide a user interface that precisely matches the prototype, even if superior technology and interface approaches exist.

9.23　Requirements Workshops

9.23.1　Purpose

A requirements workshop is a structured way to capture requirements. A workshop may be used to scope, discover, define, prioritize and reach closure on requirements for the target system.

Well-run workshops are considered one of the most effective ways to deliver high quality requirements quickly. They can promote trust, mutual understanding, and strong communications among the project stakeholders and project team and produce deliverables that structure and guide future analysis.

9.23.2　Description

A requirements workshop is a highly productive focused event attended by carefully selected key stakeholders and subject matter experts for a short, intensive period (typically one or a few days).

The workshop is facilitated by a team member or ideally, by an experienced, neutral facilitator. A scribe (also known as a recorder) documents the requirements elicited as well as any outstanding issues. A business analyst may be the facilitator or the scribe in these workshops. In situations where the business analyst is a subject matter expert on the topic, they may serve as a workshop participant. However, this must be approached with caution, as it can confuse others as to the role of business analyst. In addition, there may be suspicion that the business analyst who is also a participant may unduly bias the requirements documentation towards his or her own viewpoints and priorities.

A workshop may be used to generate ideas for new features or products, to reach consensus on a topic, or to review requirements. Other outcomes are often detailed requirements captured in models.

9.23.3   Elements

.1   Prepare for the Requirements Workshop

► Clarify the stakeholders needs, and the purpose of the workshop.

► Identify critical stakeholders who should participate in the workshop.

► Define the workshop's agenda.

► Determine what means will be used to document the output of the workshop.

► Schedule the session(s).

► Arrange room logistics and equipment, including seating, flipcharts, projectors, etc.

► Send materials in advance to prepare the attendees and increase productivity at the meeting.

► Conduct pre-workshop interviews with attendees. These are not full requirements interviews. Instead, they focus on ensuring that the purpose of the requirements workshop is understood and aligned with the needs of each attendee, and to ensure that any preparation needed for the session by that attendee is understood.

► Determine the number of stakeholders who should participate in the workshop.

.2   Conduct the Requirements Workshop

► Elicit, analyze and document requirements.

► Obtain consensus on conflicting views.

► Maintain focus by frequently validating the session's activities with the workshop's stated objectives.

The facilitator has the responsibility to:

► Establish a professional and objective tone for the meeting.

► Introduce the goals and agenda for the meeting.

► Enforce discipline, structure and ground rules for the meeting.

► Manage the meeting and keep the team on track.

► Facilitate a process for decision-making and build consensus, but avoid participating in the content of the discussion.

> ▶ Ensure that all stakeholders participate and have their input heard.

> ▶ Ask the right questions. This includes analyzing the information being provided, and following up with probing questions, if necessary.

The scribe's role is to document the requirements in the format determined prior to the workshop and keep track of any items or issues that are deferred during the session itself.

.3 Post Requirements Workshop Wrap-Up

> ▶ Follow up on any open action items that were recorded at the workshop.

> ▶ Complete the documentation and distribute it to the workshop attendees and the sponsor.

9.23.4 Usage Considerations

.1 Advantages

> ▶ A requirements workshop can be a means to elicit detailed requirements in a relatively short period of time.

> ▶ A requirements workshop provides a means for stakeholders to collaborate, make decisions and gain a mutual understanding of requirements.

> ▶ Requirements workshop costs are often lower than the cost of performing multiple interviews. A requirements workshop enables the participants to work together to reach consensus. This can be a cheaper and faster approach than doing serial requirements interviews, as interviews may yield conflicting requirements and the effort needed to resolve those conflicts across all interviewees can be very costly.

> ▶ Feedback is immediate. The facilitator's interpretation of requirements is provided immediately to the stakeholders and validated.

.2 Disadvantages

> ▶ Stakeholder availability may make it difficult to schedule the requirements workshop.

> ▶ The success of the requirements workshop is highly dependent on the expertise of the facilitator and knowledge of the participants.

> ▶ Requirements workshops that involve too many participants can slow down the workshop process. Conversely, collecting input from too few participants can lead to overlooking requirements that are important to users, or to specifying requirements that don't represent the needs of majority of the users.

9.24   Risk Analysis

9.24.1   Purpose

To identify and manage areas of uncertainty that can impact an initiative, solution, or organization.

9.24.2 Description

A risk describes an uncertain event or occurrence that may have an effect on the ability of the business analyst, project team, or organization to achieve an objective. Risks by their nature can be positive or negative. Risk analysis involves understanding the risk tolerance levels of the organization, assessing risks, and identifying responses.

9.24.3 Elements

.1 Risk Tolerance

A key factor in determining the response that a person or organization will select in regards to a risk is to understand their tolerance for risk. There is no correct or ideal response—a general strategy must be adapted to each particular circumstance. The three general categories of risk tolerance are:

▶ **Risk-Aversion.** A risk-averse person or organization will seek to reduce risks, particularly negative risks, and prefers to approach as close to certainty as possible. A reduction in potential benefits in return for a more certain outcome is seen as an acceptable tradeoff.

▶ **Neutrality.** A neutral approach to risk means that the probable benefits gained from the risk response must equal or outweigh the costs in order to justify action.

▶ **Risk-Seeking.** A risk-seeking person or organization will be willing to accept relatively high risks in order to maximize the potential benefit. Risk-seekers may accept low chances of success if the benefits of success are higher.

An individual or organization may exhibit different risk tolerances at different times. For instance, it has been demonstrated that most people will accept greater risks to avoid a perceived loss than they will to increase the payoff from a success, even when the financial outcomes are identical. The size and potential impact of the risk may also affect the risk tolerance.

.2 Assessment

Assessment involves determining the probability that the risk will occur and the impact if it does occur. Each of these factors is assessed on a common scale (High, Medium and Low, a number from 1–5, and so forth). This enables analysis to focus on the most important risks.

.3 Response

Response strategies determine how the organization will deal with a risk. For negative risks, strategies include:

▶ **Acceptance.** No effort to deal with the risk is made. The organization accepts the possibility that the risk will occur.

▶ **Transfer.** The responsibility for dealing with the risk and the possible effects of the risk are moved over to a third party.

▶ **Avoidance.** The organization takes measures to ensure that the risk cannot occur.

► **Mitigation.** The organization takes steps to reduce the probability of the risk occurring or the possible negative consequences of the risk occurring.

For positive risks, acceptance is also a viable strategy. Other strategies include:

► **Share.** Work with a third party to increase the probably the positive outcome will occur and agree to share in the benefits.

► **Enhance.** The organization takes steps to increase probability of the risk occurring and the potential benefit if the risk occurs.

► **Exploit.** The organization works to ensure that the event does occur.

9.24.4   Usage Considerations

.1   Advantages

Risk analysis enables an organization to prepare for the likelihood that at least some things will not go as planned.

.2   Disadvantages

The number of possible risks to most initiatives can easily become unmanageably large. It may only be possible to manage a subset of potential risks.

As risks are inherently uncertain, it may prove difficult to usefully estimate the impact of the risks.

9.25   Root Cause Analysis

9.25.1   Purpose

The purpose of root cause analysis is to determine the underlying source of a problem.

9.25.2   Description

Root cause analysis is a structured examination of the aspects of a situation to establish the root causes and resulting effects of the problem. A critical element of root cause analysis is to ensure that the current business thinking and processes are challenged. That is, do they still make sense or provide good business value in light of current realities?

9.25.3   Elements

Two commonly used root cause analysis methods include the Fishbone Diagram and the Five Whys:

.1   The Fishbone Diagram

A fishbone diagram (also known as an Ishikawa or cause-and-effect diagram) is used to identify and organize the possible causes of a problem. This tool helps to focus on the cause of the problem versus the solution and organizes ideas for further analysis. The diagram serves as a map depicting possible cause-and-effect relationships. Steps to develop a cause-and-effect diagram include:

► Capture the issue or problem under discussion in a box at the top of the diagram.

Figure 9–10: Fishbone Diagram

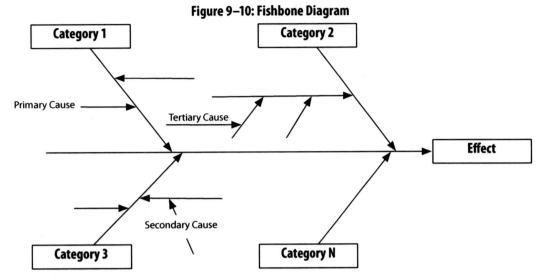

▶ Draw a line from the box across the paper or white board (forming the spine of the fishbone).

▶ Draw diagonal lines from the spine to represent categories of potential causes of the problem. The categories may include people, process, tools, and policies.

▶ Draw smaller lines to represent deeper causes.

▶ Brainstorm categories and potential causes of the problem and capture them under the appropriate category

▶ Analyze the results. Remember that the group has identified only potential causes of the problem. Further analysis is needed to validate the actual cause, ideally with data.

▶ Brainstorm potential solutions once the actual cause has been identified.

.2 Five Whys

The Five Whys is a question-asking process to explore the nature and cause of a problem. The Five Whys approach repeatedly asks questions in an attempt to get to the root cause of the problem. This is one of the simplest facilitation tools to use when problems have a human interaction component. To use this technique:

▶ Write the problem on a flip chart of white board.

▶ Ask: "Why do you think this problem occurs?" and capture the idea below the problem

▶ Ask: "Why?" again and capture that idea below the first idea

Continue with step 3 until you are convinced the actual root cause has been identified. This may take more or less than five questions—the technique is called the five whys because it often takes that many to reach the root cause, not because the question must be asked five times.

The Five Whys can be used alone, or as part of the fishbone diagram technique. Once all ideas are captured in the diagram, use the Five Whys approach to drill down to the root causes.

9.25.4   Usage Considerations

.1   Advantages

Root cause analysis provides a structured method to identify the root causes of identified problems, thus ensuring a complete understanding of the problem under review,

.2   Disadvantages

Root cause analysis works best when someone who has formal training or extensive experience facilitates a team of experts. The primary concern revolves around the ability of the facilitator to remain objective, a critical element to effective root cause analysis.

9.26   Scenarios and Use Cases

9.26.1   Purpose

Scenarios and use cases are written to describe how an actor interacts with a solution to accomplish one or more of that actor's goals, or to respond to an event.

9.26.2   Description

While the terms scenario and use case are often used loosely, a scenario is generally understood to describe just one way that an actor can accomplish a particular goal, while a use case describes all the possible outcomes of an attempt to accomplish a particular goal that the solution will support.

Scenarios are written as a series of steps performed by actors or by the solution that enable an actor to achieve a goal. A use case describes several scenarios in the form of primary and alternate flows. The primary or basic flow represents the simplest way to accomplish the goal of the use case. Special circumstances and exceptions that result in a failure to complete the goal of the use case are documented in alternate flows.

9.26.3   Elements

.1   Name

The scenario or use case must have a unique name within the project. The use case name should describe which goal or event it will deal with, and generally includes a verb (describing the action taken by the actor) and a noun (describing what is being done or the target of the action).

.2   Actor(s)

An actor is any person, system, or event external to the system under design that interacts with that system through a use case. Each actor must be given a unique name that represents the role they play in interactions with the system. This role does not necessarily correspond with a job title and should never be the name of an actual person. A particular person may fill the roles of multiple actors over time.

Caution: A temporal event is rarely modeled as an actor initiating a use case. The most common use of a temporal event as an actor is the use of a "Time" actor to trigger a use case that must be executed based on the calendar date (such as an end-of-month or end-of-year reconciliation of a system). Some authors recommend against this use.

.3 Preconditions

A precondition is any fact that the solution can assume to be true when the use case begins. This may include textual statements, such as "user must be logged in" or "Item must exist in catalogue", or the successful completion of other use cases.

.4 Flow of Events

Describes what the actor and the system do during the execution of the scenario or use case. Most use case descriptions will further break this down into a basic, or primary flow (representing the shortest successful path that accomplishes the goal of the actor) and a number of alternate flows that show more complex logic or error handling. If a circumstance still allows the actor to successfully achieve the goal of the use case, it is defined as an alternative. If the circumstance does not allow the actor to achieve their goal, the use case is considered unsuccessful and is terminated. This is defined as an exception.

.5 Post-Conditions

Any fact that must be true when the use case is complete. The post conditions must be true for all possible flows through the use case. The use case may describe separate post-conditions that are true for successful and unsuccessful executions of the use case.

.6 Relationships

Relationships between actors and use cases are called associations. Associations do not represent input, output, time or dependency. An association line only indicates that an actor has access (of some kind) to the functionality represented by the use case.

Relationships between use cases are known as stereotypes. There are two commonly used stereotypes:

Extend: allows for the insertion of additional behavior into a use case. The use case that is being extended must be completely functional in its own right. The extending use case does not need to be complete without reference to the base use case. An extension is functionally identical to an alternate flow, but is captured in a separate use case for convenience.

Include: allows for the base use case to make use of functionality present in another use case. The included use case does not need to be a complete use case in its own right, if it is not directly triggered by an actor. This relationship is most often used when some shared functionality is required by several use cases.

9.26.4 Usage Considerations

.1 Advantages

Use cases are good at clarifying scope and providing a high-level understanding of user behavioral goals, normal situations, alternatives or exception paths through an activity or business process.

Figure 9–11: Use Case Diagram

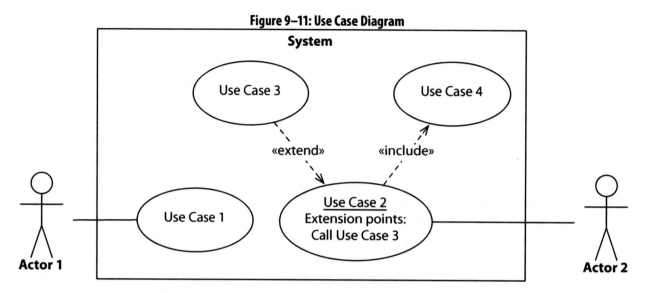

.2   Disadvantages

Business analysts are frequently tempted to describe most or all system behavior using use cases. Because many requirements can be captured in the use case format, there is frequently a temptation to use them to capture all requirements, even in situations where it is difficult to apply them or another analysis method might prove more effective.

Use cases do not have any features to support integration or the discovery of common elements, which is one of the reasons they are usually written at the highest-level of abstraction that is appropriate. Additional analysis and design is usually required after use case definition is complete to identify these common elements.

9.27   Scope Modeling

9.27.1   Purpose

Scope models are used to describe the scope of analysis or the scope of a solution.

9.27.2   Description

Scope models serve as a basis for defining and delimiting the scope of business analysis and project work. Scope models allow the definition of a "complete" scope—that is, the boundaries of the scope correspond with the natural boundaries of a business domain.

There are many different standards for scope modeling. In general, the scope model selected will depend on the analysis techniques selected to further explore the scope.

9.27.3   Elements

.1   Context Diagram

A context diagram is a top-level data flow diagram. It uses a single data process to describe the scope and shows the external entities and data stores that provide data to and receive data from the system. Context diagrams are still used on many projects that do not otherwise use data flow diagrams.

Figure 9–12: Context Diagram (Gane-Sarson Notation)

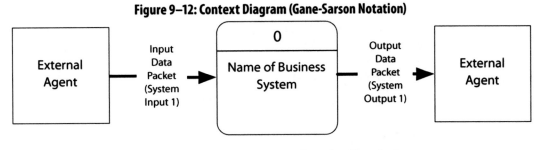

Figure 9–13: Context Diagram (Yourdon Notation)

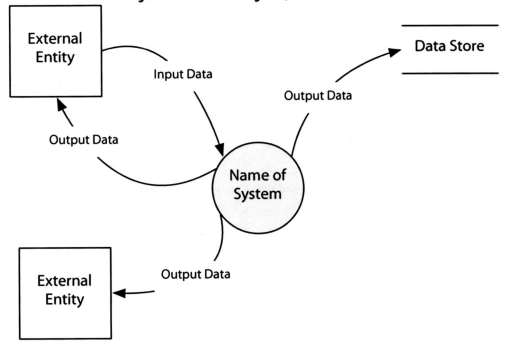

.2   Events

External events happen in an External Entity. They are external to the boundaries of the system being studied (a customer makes a request, a partner sends a message).

Temporal events are driven by time (e.g. monthly or annual reports). The time is determined by time-related business rules (e.g. produce this report at the end of every day, or prepare a tax return at the end of each tax period).

When events have been identified, the next question asked is "What processes are required to provide a complete response to this event?" The answers to this question identify the processes of the system. These processes may then be documented, and further analyzed, using an appropriate process modeling technique.

.3   Features

A feature is a service that the solution provides to fulfill one or more stakeholder needs. Features are high-level abstractions of the solution that must later be expanded into fully described functional and supplemental requirements. They allow for early priority and scope management and for validating the stakeholders' view of the solution.

.4   Use Case Diagram

A use case diagram visually depicts the use cases supported by a system, the actors who trigger those use cases, and relationships between the use cases.

.5   Business Process

A high-level business process model may also be used as a scope model.

9.27.4   Usage Considerations

.1   Advantages

A scope model will make it easier to determine what should be in and out of scope for a solution, even when new requirements are identified or requirements change.

.2   Disadvantages

A scope model will usually leave much of the detailed scope still needing to be investigated and detailed.

9.28   Sequence Diagrams

9.28.1   Purpose

Sequence diagrams are used to model the logic of usage scenarios, by showing the information passed between objects in the system through the execution of the scenario.

9.28.2   Description

A sequence diagram shows how classes and objects interact during a scenario. The classes required to execute the scenario are displayed on the diagram, as are the messages they pass to one another (triggered by steps in the use case). The sequence diagram shows how objects used in the scenario interact but not how they are related to one another. Sequence diagrams are also often used to show how user interface components or software components interact.

9.28.3   Key Features

The sequence diagram shows particular instances of each object with a lifeline beneath each object to indicate when the object is created and destroyed. The earliest events in the scenario are depicted at the top of the lifeline, with later events shown further down. The sequence diagram only specifies the ordering of events and not the exact timing.

The sequence diagram shows the stimuli flowing between objects. The stimulus is a message and the arrival of the stimulus at the object is called an event.

A message is shown as an arrow pointing from the lifeline of the object sending the message to the lifeline of the object receiving it. Message control flow describes the types of messages sent between objects.

► Procedural Flow transfers to the receiving object. The sender cannot act until a return message is received.

Figure 9–14: Sequence Diagram (UML)

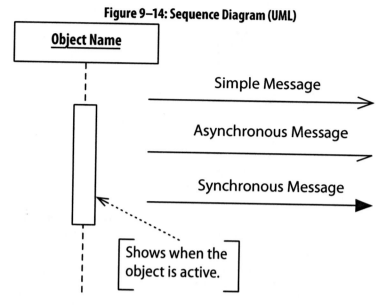

▶ Asynchronous Flow (also known as a signal) allows the object to continue with its own processing after sending the signal. The object may send many signals simultaneously, but may only accept one signal at a time.

9.28.4 Usage Considerations

.1   Advantages

The sequence diagram may be used in object-oriented analysis to validate *class diagrams* (described in 9.7) against *use cases (9.26)*, or to show the timing of interactions between entities within the system scope.

.2   Disadvantages

A sequence diagram must be defined for each possible scenario. Strictly speaking, a sequence diagram requires a fully defined class model (see Data Model), although less-formal sequence diagrams are often developed that represent user interface elements or interactions between actors.

9.29   State Diagrams

9.29.1   Purpose

A state diagram shows how the behavior of a concept, entity or object changes in response to events.

9.29.2   Description

A state diagram specifies a sequence of states that an object goes through during its lifetime, and defines which events cause a transition between those states. The allowable behavior of the object is dependent on its current state. There are many titles for the state diagram including State Machine Diagram, State Transition Diagram, and Entity Life Cycle Diagram.

Figure 9–15: State Machine Diagram (UML)

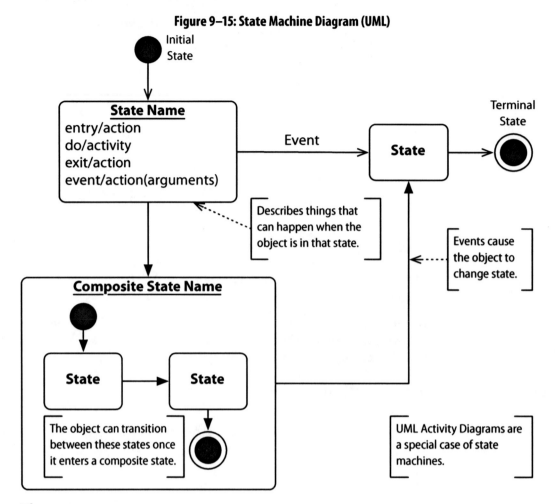

9.29.3   Elements

.1   States

A state represents a unique condition that an object can be in or status that it may have. All states for an object are mutually exclusive—an object can be in only one state at a time. The meaning of state is definable within the context of the business area being analyzed. Additional details of the state such as mandatory characteristics and relationships further describe the state. For example, a Canceled Project must have a cancellation date.

All state machines must have an initial state (representing the state of the object at creation) and may have any number of intermediate and end states.

.2   Transitions

A transition represents dynamic behavior that moves an item from one state to another. Transitions are triggered by activities completed, events, or other stimuli. An event may only cause a transition if the object is affected by the event in its current state. In addition, business rules may determine if an object responds to a particular event.

9.29.4   Usage Considerations

.1   Advantages

Domain SMEs should be intimately aware of life cycle states for their key concerns. Helping them list and describe the states and then draw the allowable transitions between states often uncovers missing data, control and behavioral requirements and may be helpful to clarify confusing or even conflicting requirements.

.2   Disadvantages

Since domain SMEs can understand and develop state diagrams very quickly, it is important not to unintentionally expand the scope. Each state (and associated transitions) should be validated to determine if it is relevant to the solution scope. There may be actual states an object goes through as part of its life cycle that do not have relevance to the domain. These states should not be modeled.

9.30   Structured Walkthrough

9.30.1   Purpose

Structured walkthroughs are performed to communicate, verify and validate requirements.

9.30.2   Description

A structured walkthrough is a working session where invited participants review and discuss a set of requirements. Participants are required to ask questions, and make comments and suggestions. Other issues may also be identified during the session. All questions, comments, concerns, and suggestions are recorded.

A walkthrough may result in revised requirements as well as issues that require investigation. A walkthrough may also be referred to as a requirements review. An inspection is similar, but follows a more formal process and uses checklists and other tools.

9.30.3   Elements

.1   Prerequisites

A complete requirements package. A requirements model or package must be complete in order to schedule a review. The review may cover only one requirement document, several related documents, or an entire requirements package.

A list of appropriate reviewers. Reviewers may be project stakeholders, business analysts, or other resources with specific expertise in the type of requirement being reviewed. Appropriate reviewers include:

► Knowledgeable representatives of stakeholders who contributed to the requirements.

► Knowledgeable representatives of stakeholders who will use the requirements in development of the solution.

▶ Reviewers representing the project's sponsor or end users. These individuals must be approved by management of those organizational units and be authorized to make decisions as their representative. This is a voting proxy delegation.

A meeting vehicle. A review may be held in a conference room with all participants present or it may be held using a technical facility allowing participants in remote locations to participate (i.e. collaboration tool, videoconference, internet meeting software).

.2   Process

Review Scope

Provide review participants with a checklist of items for which the reviewer should be looking. Examples of things that might be in a checklist for a particular session include requirements that are out of scope, requirements that are describe how the requirement will be implemented (solution specifications) instead of business or stakeholder requirements, or the accuracy of the description of the current business process.

Organize and Schedule Review

The Business Analyst must ensure that the requirements package is issued far enough in advance to allow all stakeholders to review it in advance. Stakeholders with approval authority should be present at the session. Reviewers need to understand that the purpose

Figure 9–15: Roles in a Structured Walkthrough

Role	Played By	Description
Author	Author of the requirements document, typically the business analyst. This role is mandatory. A review should not be conducted without the presence of the author.	Answers questions about the document, listens to suggestions, comments. Incorporates changes into the document after the review session.
Scribe	Any project team member who is familiar with the project may play this role. The author may play this role.	Person who documents all suggestions, comments, issues, concerns, outstanding questions that are raised during the review.
Moderator	A neutral facilitator. Often is played by a business analyst or a tester. This role is mandatory. It is best if the author of the document is not the moderator although resource constraints often necessitate this situation. When this is the case, the risk is lack of objectivity regarding the document.	Facilitates the working session, keeping participants focused each section of the requirements document as it is discussed. Verifies that all participants have reviewed the document before the session begins. Ensures that all participants are participating in the review.
Peer	This is another business analyst who has experience preparing similar requirements documents.	The peer reviews the document for its adherence to good requirements documentation standards.
Reviewer	Any stakeholder.	Reviews the document prior to the working session. Presents questions, comments, suggested changes and discusses them with the group.

of the review is to find and remove unclear, inconsistent and incorrect requirements.

Conduct the Review
The session itself should have the following structure:

▶ Introduction of parties attending presentation

▶ Statement of purpose of the reviewed deliverable

▶ Statement of review objectives

▶ Project background (if required for external parties)

▶ Formal walkthrough/review of deliverable

▶ Agreement of actions/changes required

▶ Review of deliverable status (e.g. signed-off, not signed off, etc.)

Compile Notes And Results Of The Review
Make sure that all participant comments are recorded and considered for revisions to the requirements document.

At the end of the review, it should be agreed whether:

▶ There are quality improvements that can be made to the requirements document

▶ The requirements document is acceptable in its current form

▶ Additional reviewers are required to comment on or approve the requirements document

Re-Review If Necessary
A decision will also be made as to whether another review/inspection is required if the deliverable has not been accepted.

.3   Rules To Be Followed During The Review
There are several rules that should be followed when conducting a structured walkthrough. The moderator is responsible for making sure that all participants adhere to the rules.

▶ Under normal circumstances, supervisors or managers (especially of the author) should exercise caution if they attend the review. Their organizational authority, specifically with regards to other review participants, can adversely affect the level of candor during the review. There may also be a temptation to exert their authority regarding decision points in an inappropriate manner.

▶ Reviewers must review and comment on the content, not on the author

▶ Participants must review the document before the session.

The business analyst must determine the appropriate project stakeholders who will participate in a structured walkthrough. The deliverable of a structured walkthrough is a list of questions, comments, concerns, and suggestions that are compiled during the working session. See *Problem Tracking (9.20)*.

9.30.4   Usage Considerations

.1   Advantages

▶ Promotes discussion of the requirements among stakeholders.

▶ Effective at identifying possible ambiguities and areas of misunderstanding.

.2   Disadvantages

Review sessions can lead to repeated revisions if changes are not carefully managed. The length of the revision and review cycle can result in a lengthy approval process.

9.31   Survey/Questionnaire

9.31.1   Purpose

A survey is a means of eliciting information from many people, sometimes anonymously, in a relatively short period of time. A survey can collect information about customers, products, work practices and attitudes. A survey may also be referred to as a questionnaire.

9.31.2   Description

A survey administers a set of written questions to the stakeholders and subject matter experts. Alternatively, respondents are provided with a series of statements and asked for their level of agreement or endorsement. Their responses are analyzed and distributed to the appropriate parties.

Questions in a survey are of two types:

▶ **Closed:** The respondent is asked to select from available responses. This is useful when the range of user's responses is fairly well understood, but the strength of each response category needs to be determined. The responses to closed questions are easier to analyze than those gained from open-ended questions, because they can be tied to numerical coefficients.

▶ **Open-ended:** The respondent is free to answer the questions as they wish. Useful when the issues are known but the range of user responses to them is not. The responses to open-ended questions may provide more detail and a wider range of responses than those gained from closed-ended questions. However, open-ended questions are more difficult to quantify and summarize as they often include qualitative, rather than quantitative, language.

9.31.3   Elements

.1   Prepare

A survey requires detailed preparation to ensure the needed information is obtained while minimizing the respondent's time to complete it.

▶ **Define the purpose of the survey and the target survey group.** Identify the objectives and the group to be surveyed. Confirm with the sponsor.

▶ **Choose the appropriate survey type.** Initial steps of a survey are the same as for an *interview (9.14)*, keeping in mind that semi-structured interviews are similar to open-ended surveys; and structured interviews are similar to closed-ended surveys.

▶ **Select the sample group.** Consider both the survey type (open-ended or close-ended) and the number of people in the identified user group in order to determine if the entire group needs to be surveyed. When the sample group is small, it may be practical to survey all members of the group. When the sample group is large and the desired survey type is open-ended, it may be necessary to identify a subset of users. It may also be important to survey all members of a large group is their user profile indicates wide variance due to geographic distribution, regulatory differences or lack of standardization in job function or business process. For such situations use of a statistical sampling method will help ensure that survey results are not biased.

▶ **Select the distribution and collection methods.** For each sample group determine the appropriate communication mode, such as hardcopy mail, email or web forum.

▶ **Project the desired level of response.** Determine what response rate would be acceptable. If the actual response rate is lower than the acceptable threshold, the use of the survey results may be limited. Offering an incentive can raise the response rate but the cost of the incentive must be justified and budgeted.

▶ **Determine if the survey should be supported with individual interviews.** As a survey does not provide the depth of data that can be obtained from individual interviews consider:

  ▷ Pre-survey interviews with key individuals may provide ideas for survey questions.

  ▷ Post-survey interviews can target specific survey responses or themes to elicit a greater level of detail.

▶ **Write the survey questions.**

  ▷ **Communicate the purpose.** Explain the objectives of the survey. If the stakeholders can see the reason for completing the survey, they are more likely to do so.

  ▷ **Be cognizant of the group's characteristics.** Understand the background of the target group, including their environment and specific terminology. Use this information when writing the questions. If there is significant diversity in the group's background it may be useful to divide a large group into smaller and homogeneous groups during the preparation stage and then produce variations of the survey that fit each subgroup's background.

  ▷ **Focus on the requirements:** All questions must be directed towards the stated objectives.

      ▷   Make the survey easy and fast to complete, ideally no more than five or 10 minutes. This implies limiting the number of survey items, and arranging them in an order that tells a story.

      ▷   Make sure that the question wording is clear and concise, using terminology that is familiar to the respondents.

      ▷   Each item must address a single point. Avoid double questions in a single question.

      ▷   Avoid the use of negative phrasing.

      ▷   Avoid complex branching structures, where the outcome of an "if" challenge is filtered further with subsequent "if"s.

      ▷   Avoid asking questions that may make respondents feel uncomfortable. Trying to elicit information that is restricted by regulations is likely to put respondents on the defensive.

►   **Test the survey.** Perform a usability test on the survey. Use the results to fine-tune the survey.

.2   Distribute The Survey

The distribution means should be selected according to:

►   Organizational policies

►   Urgency of obtaining the results

►   Level of security required

►   Geographic distribution of the respondents

.3   Document Survey Results

►   Collate the responses. For the responses to 'open-ended' questions, evaluate the details and identify any emerging themes.

►   Analyze and summarize the results.

►   Report findings to the sponsor.

9.31.4   Usage Considerations

.1   Advantages

►   When using closed-ended questions, surveys can be effective for obtaining quantitative data for use in statistical analysis.

►   When using open-ended questions, survey results may yield insights and opinions not easily obtainable through other elicitation techniques.

►   Does not typically require significant time from the responders.

- ► Effective and efficient when stakeholders are not located in one location.

- ► May result in large number of responses.

- ► Quick and relatively inexpensive to administer.

.2   Disadvantages

- ► Use of open-ended questions requires more analysis.

- ► To achieve unbiased results, specialized skills in statistical sampling methods are needed when the decision has been made to survey a subset of potential respondents.

- ► Some questions may be left unanswered or answered incorrectly due to their ambiguous nature.

- ► May require follow up questions or more survey iterations depending on the answers provided.

- ► Not well suited for collecting information on actual behaviors.

- ► The response rates for surveys are often too low for statistical significance. The use of incentives or enforcement means may be used to alleviate this.

9.32   SWOT Analysis

9.32.1   Purpose

A SWOT analysis is a valuable tool to quickly analyze various aspects of the current state of the business process undergoing change.

9.32.2   Description

SWOT is an acronym for Strengths, Weaknesses, Opportunities, and Threats. SWOT analysis is a framework for strategic planning, opportunity analysis, competitive analysis, business and product development.

9.32.3   Elements

The steps to conduct a SWOT analysis are as follows:

- ► Draw a grid or matrix.

- ► Describe the issue or problem under discussion at the top of the grid.

- ► Conduct a brainstorming session to complete each section in the grid. Strengths and Weaknesses are factors internal to the organization, organizational unit, or solution, while Opportunities and Threats are external factors.

  - ▷ **Strengths:** Anything that the assessed group does well. May include experienced personnel, effective processes, IT systems, customer relationships, or any other internal factor that leads to success.

- ▷ **Weaknesses.** Those things that the assessed group does poorly or not at all. Weaknesses are also internal.

- ▷ **Opportunities.** External factors that the assessed group may be able to take advantage of. May include new markets, new technology, changes in the competitive marketplace, or other forces. Opportunities exist beyond the scope of control of the assessed group; the choice is whether or not to take advantage of one when it is identified.

- ▷ **Threats.** External factors that can negatively affect the assessed group. They may include factors such as the entrance into the market of a new competitor, economic downturns, or other forces. Threats are also outside of the group's control.

- ▶ Facilitate a discussion to analyze the results. Remember that the group has identified only potential characteristics of the problem. Further analysis is needed to validate the actual characteristics, ideally confirmed with data.

- ▶ Once the characteristics of the issue or problem have been validated, the group brainstorms potential solutions to solve the problem. A standard practice for this is to compare internal strengths and weaknesses against external opportunities and threats and try to define strategies for each cell in the matrix.

Figure 9–16: SWOT Matrix

	Opportunities	**Threats**
Strengths	**SO Strategies** How can the group's strength be used to exploit potential opportunities? SO strategies are fairly straightforward to implement.	**ST Strategies** How can the group use its strengths to ward off potential threats? Can the threats be turned into opportunities?
Weaknesses	**WO Strategies** Can the group use an opportunity to eliminate or mitigate a weakness? Does the opportunity warrant the development of new capabilities?	**WT Strategies** Can the group restructure itself to avoid the threat? Should the group consider getting out of this market? WT strategies involve worst-case scenarios.

9.32.4 Usage Considerations

.1 Advantages

The SWOT analysis helps quickly analyze various aspects of the current state of the organization and its environment prior to identifying potential solution options.

.2 Disadvantages

The SWOT analysis is a very high-level view; more detailed analysis is almost always needed.

9.33 User Stories

9.33.1 Purpose

User Stories are a brief description of functionality that users need from a solution to meet a business objective.

9.33.2 Description

A user story is a textual description of things that the solution needs to allow users to do. User stories are typically a sentence or two that describes who uses the story, the goal they are trying to accomplish, and any additional information that may be critical to understanding the scope of the story.

9.33.3 Key Features

A user story includes a short description of the problem to be solved. This is from the perspective of the user. The only detail that needs to be included is information that reduces the risk of misunderstanding by developers that create the estimate.

A user story includes:

► **Actor:** Stakeholder who benefits from the user story.

► **Description:** A high-level overview of what functionality the user story includes.

► **Benefit:** The business value the story delivers.

A user story should also have defined *Acceptance and Evaluation Criteria (9.1)*.

9.33.4 When to Use

.1 Advantages

User stories create an environment of customer ownership of features and prioritizations in an incremental, iterative development environment. They may eliminate the need to provide functional requirements in some environments. User stories also require that the value delivered by the story be clearly articulated.

.2 Disadvantages

They may not be the best technique for some environments with regulatory restrictions or when an organization mandates documentation. This modeling technique may not be effective when participants are not co-located. This technique does not explicitly address how to document non-functional requirements.

9.34   Vendor Assessment

9.34.1   Purpose

To assess the ability of a potential vendor to meet commitments regarding a product or service.

9.34.2   Description

When solutions are in part provided by external vendors (who may be involved in design, construction, implementation, or maintenance of the solution or solution components), or when the solution is outsourced, there may be specific requirements in regard to the involvement of that third party.

For example, there may be a need to ensure that the supplier is financially secure, capable of maintaining specific staffing levels, committing appropriately skilled staff to support the solution, and so forth. *Non-functional requirements (9.17)* can be used to define the service levels expected of a third party. Vendor assessment is conducted to ensure that the vendor is reliable and that service levels will meet an organization's expectations.

9.34.3   Elements

.1   Knowledge and Expertise

A common reason for using third-party vendors is that they can provide knowledge and expertise not available within the organization. In such cases, the business analyst should consider whether that expertise will need to be transferred and how capable the supplier is of performing that transfer. It may be desirable to target vendors with particular expertise in methodologies or technologies, with the goal of having that expertise transferred to people within the enterprise.

.2   Licensing and Pricing Models

In cases when a solution or solution component is purchased from or outsourced to an outside vendor, the licensing or pricing model will need to be taken into account. In many cases, solutions that offer similar functionality may differ greatly in their licensing models, requiring an analysis of different usage scenarios to determine which option will provide the best cost/benefit ratio under the scenarios likely to be encountered in the enterprise.

.3   Product Reputation and Market Position

How many customers are currently using the product or service? Is the product widely accepted or used in similar organizations? Is there a regular update schedule and roadmap of features that are planned for delivery?

.4   Terms and Conditions

Are the services provided by the vendor to be temporary or permanent? The business analyst should investigate whether the vendor's licensing terms and technology infrastructure are likely to present challenges if the organization later chooses to transition to another supplier. There may also be considerations regarding the vendor's use of and responsibility for protecting the integrity of the organization's confidential data. In addition, the terms under which customizations of the product should be considered.

.5   Vendor Experience and Reputation

The vendor's experience with other customers may provide valuable information on how likely it is that they will be able to meet their contractual and non-contractual obligations. The vendor can also be evaluated for conformance and compliance with external relevant standards for quality, security, and professionalism.

.6   Vendor Stability

How certain is it that the vendor will be able to provide the required services in the future? It may be necessary to request that steps be taken to ensure that there are no risks if the vendor encounters financial difficulties and that it will be possible to maintain and enhance the solution even if the vendor's situation changes radically.

9.34.4   Usage Considerations

.1   Advantages

An effective vendor assessment reduces the risk of the organization developing a relationship with an unsuitable vendor and is likely to improve long-term satisfaction with the decision.

.2   Disadvantages

Can be time-consuming to gather sufficient information on multiple vendors. Some information may not be readily available. Vendors with new and innovative products may score poorly because they do not have a significant history in the market.

Glossary

Activity Diagram

A *model* that illustrates the flow of processes and/or complex use cases by showing each *activity* along with information flows and concurrent activities. Steps can be superimposed onto horizontal *swimlanes* for the roles that perform the steps.

Activity

A unit of work performed as part of an *initiative* or *process*.

Actor(s)

The human and nonhuman *roles* that interact with the *system*.

Allocation

See *requirements allocation*.

Analyst

A generic name for a role with the responsibilities of developing and managing *requirements*. Other names include *business analyst*, business integrator, requirements analyst, requirements engineer, and systems analyst.

Association

A link between two elements or objects in a diagram.

Assumption

Assumptions are influencing factors that are believed to be true but have not been confirmed to be accurate.

Attribute

A data element with a specified data type that describes information associated with a concept or entity.

Baseline

A point-in-time view of *requirements* that have been reviewed and agreed upon to serve as a basis for further development.

Benchmarking

A comparison of a *process* or *system*'s cost, time, *quality*, or other metrics to those of leading peer *organizations* to identify opportunities for improvement.

Black Box Tests

Tests written without regard to how the software is implemented. These tests show only what the expected input and outputs will be.

Brainstorming

Brainstorming is a team activity that seeks to produce a broad or diverse set of options through the rapid and uncritical generation of ideas.

Business Analysis

Business analysis is the set of tasks and *techniques* used to work as a liaison among *stakeholders* in order to understand the structure, *policies* and operations of an *organization*, and recommend *solutions* that enable the organization to achieve its *goals*.

Business Analysis Approach

The set of *processes*, templates, and *activities* that will be used to perform *business analysis* in a specific context.

Business Analysis Communication Plan

A description of the types of communication the *business analyst* will perform during *business analysis*, the recipients of those communications, and the form in which communication should occur.

Business Analysis Plan

A description of the planned activities that the *business analyst* will execute in order to perform the business analysis work involved in a specific *initiative*.

Business Analyst

A practitioner of *business analysis*.

Business Architecture

A subset of the *enterprise architecture* that defines an *organization*'s current and future state, including its strategy, its *goals* and *objectives*, the internal environment through a process or functional view, the external environment in which the business operates, and the *stakeholders* affected by the organization's activities.

Business Case

An assessment of the costs and benefits associated with a proposed *initiative*.

Business Constraint(s)

Business *constraints* are limitations placed on the *solution* design by the *organization* that needs the solution. Business constraints describe limitations on available solutions, or an aspect of the current state that cannot be changed by the deployment of the new solution. See also *technical constraint*.

Business Domain

See *domain*.

Business Domain Model

A conceptual view of all or part of an *enterprise* focusing on *products*, *deliverables* and *events* that are important to the mission of the *organization*. The domain model is useful to validate the solution scope with the business and technical *stakeholders*. See also *model*.

Business Event

A system trigger that is initiated by humans.

Business Goal

A state or condition the business must satisfy to reach its *vision*.

Business Need(s)

A type of high-level *business requirement* that is a statement of a business *objective*, or an impact the *solution* should have on its environment.

Business Policy

A business policy is a non-actionable directive that supports a *business goal*.

Business Process

A set of defined ad-hoc or sequenced collaborative *activities* performed in a repeatable fashion by an *organization*. Processes are triggered by *events* and may have multiple possible outcomes. A successful outcome of a process will deliver value to one or more *stakeholders*.

Business Requirement

A higher level business rationale that, when addressed, will permit the *organization* to increase revenue, avoid costs, improve service, or meet regulatory requirements.

Business Requirements Document

A Business Requirements Document is a *requirements package* that describes *business requirements* and *stakeholder requirements* (it documents requirements of interest to the business, rather than documenting business requirements).

Business Rule(s)

A business rule is a specific, actionable, testable directive that is under the control of the business and supports a *business policy*.

Capability

A function of an *organization* that enables it to achieve a *business goal* or *objective*.

Cardinality

The number of occurrences of one entity in a *data model* that are linked to a second entity. Cardinality is shown on a data model with a special notation, number (e.g., 1), or letter (e.g., M for many).

Cause and Effect Diagram

See *fishbone diagram*.

Change Control Board (CCB)

A small group of *stakeholders* who will make decisions regarding the disposition and treatment of changing *requirements*.

Change-driven Methodology

A *methodology* that focuses on rapid delivery of *solution* capabilities in an incremental fashion and direct involvement of *stakeholders* to gather feedback on the solution's performance.

Checklist

A *quality control* technique. They may include a standard set of quality elements that reviewers use for *requirements verification* and *requirements validation* or be specifically developed to capture issues of concern to the project.

Class

A descriptor for a set of system objects that share the same attributes, operations, relationships, and behavior. A class represents a concept in the system under design. When used as an analysis *model*, a class will generally also correspond to a real-world entity.

Class Model

A type of *data model* that depicts information groups as classes.

Code

A system of programming statements, symbols, and rules used to represent instructions to a computer.

Commercial-off-the-Shelf Software (COTS)

Software developed and sold for a particular market.

Competitive Analysis

A structured *process* which captures the key characteristics of an industry to predict the long-term profitability prospects and to determine the practices of the most significant competitors.

Constraint

A constraint describes any limitations imposed on the *solution* that do not support the business or stakeholder needs.

Context Diagram

An analysis *model* that illustrates *product scope* by showing the system in its environment with the external entities (people and systems) that give to and receive from the system.

Cost Benefit Analysis

Analysis done to compare and quantify the financial and non-financial costs of making a change or implementing a *solution* compared to the benefits gained.

Customer

A *stakeholder* who uses products or services delivered by an *organization*.

Data Dictionary

An analysis *model* describing the data structures and attributes needed by the system.

Data Entity

A group of related information to be stored by the system. Entities can be people, roles, places, things, organizations, occurrences in time, concepts, or documents.

Data Flow Diagram (DFD)

An analysis *model* that illustrates processes that occur, along with the flows of data to and from those processes.

Data Model

An analysis *model* that depicts the logical structure of data, independent of the data design or data storage mechanisms.

Decision Analysis

An approach to decision-making that examines and models the possible consequences of different decisions. Decision analysis assists in making an optimal decision under conditions of uncertainty.

Decision Tables

An analysis *model* that specifies complex business rules or logic concisely in an easy-to-read tabular format, specifying all of the possible conditions and actions that need to be accounted for in business rules.

Decision Tree

An analysis model that provides a graphical alternative to *decision tables* by illustrating conditions and actions in sequence.

Decomposition

A technique that subdivides a problem into its component parts in order to facilitate analysis and understanding of those components.

Defect

A deficiency in a *product* or *service* that reduces its quality or varies from a desired attribute, state, or functionality. See also *requirements defect*.

Deliverable

Any unique and verifiable work *product* or *service* that a party has agreed to deliver.

Design Constraints

Software requirements that limit the options available to the system designer.

Desired Outcome

The business benefits that will result from meeting the *business need* and the end state desired by *stakeholders*.

Developer

Developers are responsible for the construction of software applications. Areas of expertise include development languages, development practices and application components.

Dialog Hierarchy

An analysis *model* that shows user interface dialogs arranged as hierarchies.

Dialog Map

An analysis *model* that illustrates the architecture of the system's user interface.

Discovery Session

See *requirements workshop*.

Document Analysis

Document analysis is a means to elicit *requirements* of an existing system by studying available documentation and identifying relevant information.

Domain

The problem area undergoing analysis.

Domain Subject Matter Expert (SME)

A person with specific expertise in an area or domain under investigation.

Elicitation

An activity within requirements development that identifies sources for *requirements* and then uses elicitation techniques (e.g., interviews, prototypes, facilitated workshops, documentation studies) to gather requirements from those sources.

Elicitation Workshop

See *requirements workshop*.

End User

A person or system that directly interacts with the *solution*. End users can be humans who interface with the system, or systems that send or receive data files to or from the system.

Enterprise

An *organizational unit, organization,* or collection of organizations that share a set of common *goals* and collaborate to provide specific *products* or services to *customers*.

Enterprise Architecture

Enterprise architecture is a description of an *organization*'s business processes, IT software and hardware, people, operations and projects, and the relationships between them.

Entity-Relationship Diagram

An entity-relationship diagram is a graphical representation of the entities relevant to a chosen problem domain, the *relationships* between them, and their *attributes*.

Evaluation

The systematic and objective assessment of a *solution* to determine its status and efficacy in meeting objectives over time, and to identify ways to improve the solution to better meet objectives. See also *metric, indicator* and *monitoring*.

Event

An event is something that occurs to which an *organizational unit, system,* or *process* must respond.

Event Response Table

An analysis *model* in table format that defines the *events* (i.e., the input stimuli that trigger the system to carry out some function) and their responses.

Evolutionary Prototype

A *prototype* that is continuously modified and updated in response to feedback from users.

Exploratory Prototype

A *prototype* developed to explore or verify *requirements*.

External Interfaces

Interfaces with other systems (hardware, software, and human) that a proposed *system* will interact with.

Feasibility Analysis

See *feasibility study*.

Feasibility Study

An evaluation of proposed alternatives to determine if they are technically possible within the constraints of the *organization* and whether they will deliver the desired benefits to the organization.

Feature

A cohesive bundle of externally visible functionality that should align with *business goals* and *objectives*. Each feature is a logically related grouping of *functional requirements* or *non-functional requirements* described in broad strokes.

Fishbone Diagram

A diagramming technique used in *root cause analysis* to identify underlying causes of an observed problem, and the *relationships* that exist between those causes.

Focus Group

A focus group is a means to elicit ideas and attitudes about a specific *product*, *service* or opportunity in an interactive group environment. The participants share their impressions, preferences and needs, guided by a moderator.

Force Field Analysis

A graphical method for depicting the forces that support and oppose a change. Involves identifying the forces, depicting them on opposite sides of a line (supporting and opposing forces) and then estimating the strength of each set of forces.

Functional Requirement(s)

The *product* capabilities, or things the product must do for its users.

Gap Analysis

A comparison of the current state and desired future state of an *organization* in order to identify differences that need to be addressed.

Glossary

A list and definition of the business terms and concepts relevant to the *solution* being built or enhanced.

Goal

See *business goal*.

Horizontal Prototype

A *prototype* that shows a shallow, and possibly wide, view of the system's functionality, but which does not generally support any actual use or interaction.

Impact Analysis

An impact analysis assesses the effects that a proposed change will have on a *stakeholder* or stakeholder group, *project*, or *system*.

Implementation Subject Matter Expert (SME)

A *stakeholder* who will be responsible for designing, developing, and implementing the change described in the requirements and have specialized knowledge regarding the construction of one or more solution components.

Included Use Cases

A use case composed of a common set of steps used by multiple use cases.

Incremental Delivery

Creating working software in multiple releases so the entire product is delivered in portions over time.

Indicator

An indicator identifies a specific numerical measurement that indicates progress toward achieving an impact, output, activity or input. See also *metric*.

Initiative
Any effort undertaken with a defined *goal* or *objective*.

Inspection
A formal type of *peer review* that utilizes a predefined and documented process, specific participant roles, and the capture of defect and process *metrics*. See also *structured walkthrough*.

Interface
A shared boundary between any two persons and/or systems through which information is communicated.

Interoperability
Ability of systems to communicate by exchanging data or services.

Interview
A systematic approach to elicit information from a person or group of people in an informal or formal setting by asking relevant questions and documenting the responses.

Iteration
A *process* in which a *deliverable* (or the *solution* overall) is progressively elaborated upon. Each iteration is a self-contained "mini-project" in which a set of activities are undertaken, resulting in the development of a subset of project *deliverables*. For each iteration, the team plans its work, does the work, and checks it for quality and completeness. (Iterations can occur within other iterations as well. For example, an iteration of requirements development would include elicitation, analysis, specification, and validation activities.)

Knowledge Area
A group of related tasks that support a key function of *business analysis*.

Lessons Learned Process
A process improvement technique used to learn about and improve on a *process* or *project*. A lessons learned session involves a special meeting in which the team explores what worked, what didn't work, what could be learned from the just-completed iteration, and how to adapt processes and techniques before continuing or starting anew.

Metadata
Metadata is information that is used to understand the context and validity of information recorded in a *system*.

Methodology
A set of processes, rules, templates, and working methods that prescribe how *business analysis*, solution development and implementation is performed in a particular context.

Metric
A metric is a quantifiable level of an *indicator* that an organization wants to accomplish at a specific point in time.

Model(s)
A representation and simplification of reality developed to convey information to a specific audience to support analysis, communication and understanding.

Monitoring
Monitoring is a continuous process of collecting data to determine how well a *solution* is implemented compared to expected results. See also *metric* and *indicator*.

Need(s)
See *business need*.

Non-functional Requirement(s)
The quality attributes, design and implementation constraints, and external interfaces that the *product* must have.

Objective
A target or *metric* that a person or organization seeks to meet in order to progress towards a *goal*.

Object Oriented Modeling
An approach to software engineering where software is comprised of components that are encapsulated groups of data and functions which can inherit behavior and attributes from other components; and whose components communicate via messages with one another. In some organizations, the same approach is used for business engineering to describe and package the logical components of the business.

Observation

Observation is a means to elicit *requirements* by conducting an assessment of the *stakeholder*'s work environment.

Operational Support

A *stakeholder* who helps to keep the *solution* functioning, either by providing support to *end users* (trainers, help desk) or by keeping the solution operational on a day-to-day basis (network and other tech support).

Operative Rule(s)

The *business rules* an *organization* chooses to enforce as a matter of policy. They are intended to guide the actions of people working within the business. They may oblige people to take certain actions, prevent people from taking actions, or prescribe the conditions under which an action may be taken.

Opportunity Analysis

The process of examining new business opportunities to improve organizational performance.

Optionality

Defining whether or not a relationship between entities in a *data model* is mandatory. Optionality is shown on a data model with a special notation.

Organization

An autonomous unit within an *enterprise* under the management of a single individual or board, with a clearly defined boundary that works towards common goals and objectives. Organizations operate on a continuous basis, as opposed to an *organizational unit* or project team, which may be disbanded once its *objectives* are achieved.

Organization Modeling

The analysis technique used to describe roles, responsibilities and reporting structures that exist within an *organization*.

Organizational Process Asset

All materials used by groups within an *organization* to define, tailor, implement, and maintain their *processes*.

Organizational Readiness Assessment

An assessment that describes whether *stakeholders* are prepared to accept the change associated with a *solution* and are able to use it effectively.

Organizational Unit

Any recognized association of people in the context of an *organization* or *enterprise*.

Peer Review

A validation technique in which a small group of *stakeholders* evaluates a portion of a work product to find errors to improve its quality.

Plan-driven Methodology

Any *methodology* that emphasizes planning and formal documentation of the processes used to accomplish a *project* and of the results of the project. Plan-driven methodologies emphasize the reduction of risk and control over outcomes over the rapid delivery of a solution.

Prioritization

The process of determining the relative importance of a set of items in order to determine the order in which they will be addressed.

Problem Statement

A brief statement or paragraph that describes the problems in the current state and clarifies what a successful *solution* will look like.

Process

See *business process*.

Process Map

A business model that shows a *business process* in terms of the steps and input and output flows across multiple functions, organizations, or job roles.

Process Model

A visual *model* or representation of the sequential flow and control logic of a set of related activities or actions.

Product

A *solution* or component of a solution that is the result of a *project*.

Product Backlog

A set of *user stories*, *requirements* or *features* that have been identified as candidates for potential implementation, prioritized, and estimated.

Product Scope

The *features* and functions that characterize a *product*, *service* or result.

Project

A temporary endeavor undertaken to create a unique *product*, *service* or result.

Project Charter

A document issued by the project initiator or *sponsor* that formally authorizes the existence of a project, and provides the *project manager* with the authority to apply organizational resources to project activities.

Project Manager

The *stakeholder* assigned by the performing organization to manage the work required to achieve the project *objectives*.

Project Scope

The work that must be performed to deliver a *product*, *service*, or result with the specified features and functions. See also *scope*.

Prototype

A partial or preliminary version of the system.

Quality

The degree to which a set of inherent characteristics fulfills requirements.

Quality Assurance

Activities performed to ensure that a process will deliver products that meet an appropriate level of quality.

Quality Attributes

The subset of *nonfunctional requirements* that describes properties of the software's operation, development, and deployment (e.g., performance, security, usability, portability, and testability).

Questionnaire

See *survey*.

Regulator

A *stakeholder* with legal or governance authority over the solution or the process used to develop it.

Relationship

A defined *association* between concepts, classes or entities. Relationships are usually named and include the *cardinality* of the association.

Relationship Map

A business *model* that shows the organizational context in terms of the *relationships* that exist among the organization, external customers, and providers.

Repository

A real or virtual facility where all information on a specific topic is stored and is available for retrieval.

Request For Information (RFI)

A requirements document issued to solicit vendor input on a proposed process or product. An RFI is used when the issuing organization seeks to compare different alternatives or is uncertain regarding the available options

Request For Proposal (RFP)

A requirements document issued when an *organization* is seeking a formal proposal from vendors. An RFP typically requires that the proposals be submitted following a specific *process* and using sealed bids which will be evaluated against a formal evaluation methodology.

Request For Quote (RFQ)

An informal solicitation of proposals from vendors.

Requirement

1. A condition or capability needed by a *stakeholder* to solve a problem or achieve an objective.

2. A condition or *capability* that must be met of possessed by a *solution* or *solution component* to satisfy a contract, standard, specification or other formally imposed documents.

3. A documented representation of a condition or capability as in 1) or 2).

Requirement(s) Attribute

Metadata related to a requirement used to assist with requirements development and management.

Requirement(s) Defect

An error in requirements caused by incorrect, incomplete, missing, or conflicting requirements.

Requirements Allocation

The process of apportioning requirements to subsystems and components (i.e., people, hardware, and software).

Requirements Discovery Session

See *requirements workshop*.

Requirements Document

See *requirements package*.

Requirements Iteration

An iteration that defines requirements for a subset of the solution scope. For example, an iteration of requirements would include identifying a part of the overall product scope to focus upon, identifying requirements sources for that portion of the product, analyzing *stakeholders* and planning how to elicit requirements from them, conducting elicitation techniques, documenting the requirements, and validating the requirements.

Requirements Management

The activities that control requirements development, including requirements change control, requirements attributes definition, and requirements traceability.

Requirements Management Plan

A description of the *requirements management* process.

Requirements Management Tool

A software tool that stores requirements information in a database, captures requirements attributes and associations, and facilitates requirements reporting.

Requirements Model

A representation of requirements using text and diagrams. Requirements models can also be called user requirements models or analysis models and can supplement textual requirements specifications.

Requirements Package

A requirements package is a set of requirements grouped together in a document or presentation for communication to *stakeholders*.

Requirements Quality

See *requirements validation* and requirements verification.

Requirements Risk Mitigation Strategy

An analysis of requirements-related risks that ranks risks and identifies actions to avoid or minimize those risks.

Requirements Signoff

Formal approval of a set of requirements by a sponsor or other decision maker.

Requirements Trace Matrix

A matrix used to track requirements' relationships. Each column in the matrix provides requirements information and associated project or software development components.

Requirements Traceability

The ability to identify and document the lineage of each requirement, including its derivation (backward traceability), its allocation (forward traceability), and its relationship to other requirements.

Requirements Validation

The work done to ensure that the *stated requirements* support and are aligned with the *goals* and *objectives* of the business.

Requirements Verification

The work done to evaluate requirements to ensure they are defined correctly and are at an acceptable level of quality. It ensures the requirements are sufficiently defined and structured so that the solution development team can use them in the design, development and implementation of the *solution*.

Requirements Workshop

A requirements workshop is a structured meeting in which a carefully selected group of *stakeholders* collaborate to define and or refine *requirements* under the guidance of a skilled neutral facilitator.

Retrospective

See *lessons learned process*.

Return on Investment

A measure of the profitability of a project or investment.

Risk

An uncertain event or condition that, if it occurs, will affect the goals or objectives of a proposed change.

Risk Mitigation Strategy

See *requirements risk mitigation strategy*.

Root Cause Analysis

Root cause analysis is a structured examination of an identified problem to understand the underlying causes.

Scenario

An analysis *model* that describes a series of actions or tasks that respond to an event. Each scenario is an instance of a *use case*.

Scope

The area covered by a particular activity or topic of interest. See also *project scope* and *solution scope*.

Scope Model

A *model* that defines the boundaries of a business domain or solution.

Secondary Actor

An *actor* who participates in but does not initiate a *use case*.

Sequence Diagram

A type of diagram that shows objects participating in interactions and the messages exchanged between them.

Service

Work carried out or on behalf of others.

Software Engineer

See *developer*.

Software/Systems Requirements Specification

A requirements document written primarily for *Implementation SME*s describing functional and nonfunctional requirements.

Solution

A solution meets a *business need* by resolving a problem or allowing an *organization* to take advantage of an opportunity.

Solution Requirement

A characteristic of a *solution* that meets the business and stakeholder requirements. May be subdivided into functional and non-functional requirements.

Solution Scope

The set of capabilities a *solution* must deliver in order to meet the *business need*. See also *scope*.

Span of Control

Span of control is the number of employees a manger is directly (or indirectly) responsible for.

Sponsor

A *stakeholder* who authorizes or legitimizes the product development effort by contracting for or paying for the project.

Stakeholder

A group or person who has interests that may be affected by an *initiative* or influence over it.

Stakeholder Analysis

The work to identify the *stakeholders* who may be impacted by a proposed *initiative* and assess their interests and likely participation.

Stakeholder List, Roles, and Responsibility Designation

A listing of the stakeholders affected by a business need or proposed solution and a description of their participation in a project or other initiative.

Stakeholder Requirement

Stakeholder requirements are statements of the needs of a particular stakeholder or class of stakeholders. They describe the needs that a given stakeholder has and how that stakeholder will interact with a solution. Stakeholder requirements serve as a bridge between *business requirements* and the various categories of *solution requirements*.

State Diagram

An analysis *model* showing the life cycle of a data entity or class.

State Machine Diagram

See *state diagram*.

State Transition Diagram

See *state diagram*.

Stated Requirements

A requirement articulated by a stakeholder that has not been analyzed, verified, or validated. Stated requirements frequently reflect the desires of a stakeholder rather than the actual need.

Structural Rule

Structural rules determine when something is or is not true or when things fall into a certain category. They describe categorizations that may change over time.

Storyboard

See *dialog hierarchy* and *dialog map*.

Structured Walkthrough

A structured walkthrough is an organized *peer review* of a deliverable with the objective of finding errors and omissions. It is considered a form of *quality assurance*.

Subject Matter Expert (SME)

A *stakeholder* with specific expertise in an aspect of the problem domain or potential solution alternatives or components.

Supplier

A *stakeholder* who provides products or services to an organization.

Survey

A survey administers a set of written questions to *stakeholders* in order to collect responses from a large group in a relatively short period of time.

Swimlane

The horizontal or vertical section of a *process model* that show which activities are performed by a particular actor or role.

SWOT Analysis

SWOT is an acronym for Strengths, Weaknesses, Opportunities and Threats. It is a model used to understand influencing factors and how they may affect an initiative.

System

A collection of interrelated elements that interact to achieve an objective. System elements can include hardware, software, and people. One system can be a sub-element (or subsystem) of another system.

Technical Constraint(s)

Technical *constraints* are limitations on the design of a solution that derive from the technology used in its implementation. See also *business constraint*.

Technique

Techniques alter the way a business analysis task is performed or describe a specific form the output of a task may take.

Temporal Event

A system trigger that is initiated by time.

Tester

A *stakeholder* responsible for assessing the quality of, and identifying defects in, a software application.

Throw-away Prototype

A *prototype* used to quickly uncover and clarify interface requirements using simple tools, sometimes just paper and pencil. Usually discarded when the final system has been developed.

Timebox
A fixed period of time to accomplish a *desired outcome*.

Traceability
See *requirements traceability*.

Transition Requirement(s)
A classification of *requirements* that describe capabilities that the *solution* must have in order to facilitate transition from the current state of the enterprise to the desired future state, but that will not be needed once that transition is complete.

Unified Modeling Language (UML)
A non-proprietary modeling and specification language used to specify, visualize, and document deliverables for object-oriented software-intensive systems.

Use Case
An analysis *model* that describes the tasks that the system will perform for *actors* and the *goals* that the system achieves for those actors along the way.

Use Case Diagram
A type of diagram defined by UML that captures all *actors* and *use cases* involved with a *system* or *product*.

User
A *stakeholder*, person, device, or system that directly or indirectly accesses a system.

User Acceptance Test
Test cases that users employ to judge whether the delivered system is acceptable. Each acceptance test describes a set of system inputs and expected results.

User Requirement
See *stakeholder requirement(s)*.

User Requirements Document
A *requirements document* written for a user audience, describing user requirements and the impact of the anticipated changes on the users.

User Story
A high-level, informal, short description of a solution capability that provides value to a *stakeholder*. A user story is typically one or two sentences long and provides the minimum information necessary to allow a developer to estimate the work required to implement it.

Validated Requirements
Requirements that have been demonstrated to deliver business value and to support the business *goals* and *objectives*.

Validation
The process of checking a product to ensure that it satisfies its intended use and conforms to its requirements. Validation ensures that you built the correct solution. Also see *requirements validation*.

Variance Analysis
Analysis of discrepancies between planned and actual performance, to determine the magnitude of those discrepancies and recommend corrective and preventative action as required.

Verification
The process of checking that a deliverable produced at a given stage of development satisfies the conditions or specifications of the previous stage. Verification ensures that you built the solution correctly. Also see *requirements verification*.

Verified Requirements
Requirements that have been shown to demonstrate the characteristics of requirements quality and as such are cohesive, complete, consistent, correct, feasible, modifiable, unambiguous, and testable.

Vertical Prototype
A *prototype* that dives into the details of the interface, functionality, or both.

Vision Statement (product vision statement)
A brief statement or paragraph that describes the why, what, and who of the desired software product from a business point of view.

Walkthrough

A type of peer review in which participants present, discuss, and step through a work product to find errors. Walkthroughs of requirements documentation are used to verify the correctness of requirements. See also *structured walkthrough*.

Work Breakdown Structure (WBS)

A deliverable-oriented hierarchical decomposition of the work to be executed by the project team to accomplish the project objectives and create the required deliverables. It organizes and defines the total scope of the project.

Work Product

A document or collection of notes or diagrams used by the business analyst during the requirements development process.

Bibliography

*The following works were referenced by contributors to the **BABOK® Guide** during the development of this version or of previous versions. In cases where multiple editions of a work were consulted, only the most recent edition is listed.*

*In addition to the works listed here, many other sources of information on business analysis were consulted by contributors and reviewers or otherwise or influenced the development of the **BABOK® Guide**, including articles, white papers, websites, blog postings, online forums, seminars, workshops, and conferences.*

*With only a very few exceptions, the ideas and concepts found in the **BABOK® Guide** were not created for or original to it. The **BABOK® Guide** is a synthesis of decades of research into how organizations work and methods that can be used to identify potential improvements. The works listed below themselves build on the thoughts and research of many others.*

Aaker, David A. 1995. *Developing Business Strategies*. John Wiley & Sons Inc.

Adelman, Sid, Larissa Moss, and Majid Abai. 2005. *Data Strategy*. Addison-Wesley Professional.

Alexander, Ian, and Neil Maiden. 2004. *Scenarios, Stories, Use Cases: Through the Systems Development Life-Cycle*. John Wiley & Sons Inc.

Alexander, Ian, and Richard Stevens. 2002. *Writing Better Requirements*. Addison-Wesley Professional.

Altier, William J. 1999. *The Thinking Manager's Toolbox: Effective Processes for Problem Solving and Decision Making*. Oxford University Press.

Ambler, Scott W. 2004. *The Object Primer: Agile Model-Driven Development with UML 2.0*. Cambridge University Press.

Armour, Frank, and Granville Miller. 2000. *Advanced Use Case Modeling: Software Systems*. Addison-Wesley Professional.

Association of Business Process Management Professionals. 2008. *Guide to the Business Process Management Common Body of Knowledge*. ABPMP.

Baird, Jim, A. Ross Little, Valerie LeBlanc, and Louis Molnar. 2001. *Business Requirements Analysis: Applied Best Practices, 4th Edition*. The Information Architecture Group.

Bechtold, Richard. 2007. *Essentials of Software Project Management, 2nd Edition*. Management Concepts.

Bensoussan, Babette E., and Craig S. Fleisher. 2008. *Analysis Without Paralysis: 10 Tools to Make Better Strategic Decisions*. FT Press.

Berman, Jeff. 2006. *Maximizing Project Value: Defining, Managing, and Measuring for Optimal Return*. Amacom.

Berman, Karen, and Joe Knight. 2008. *Financial Intelligence for IT Professionals*. Harvard Business School Press.

Bittner, Kurt, and Ian Spence. 2002. *Use Case Modeling*. Addison-Wesley Professional.

Boar, Bernard H. 2001. *The Art of Strategic Planning for Information Technology*. John Wiley & Sons Inc.

Boehm, Barry, and Richard Turner. 2003. *Balancing Agility and Discipline: A Guide for the Perplexed*. Addison-Wesley Professional.

Brache, Alan P. and Sam Bodley-Scott. 2005. *Implementation: How to Transform Strategic Initiatives into Blockbuster Results*. McGraw-Hill.

Brassard, Michael, Lynda Finn, and Dana Ginn. 2002. *The Six SIGMA Memory Jogger II: A Pocketguide of Tools for Six SIGMA Improvement Teams*. Goal/QPC.

Bridgeland, David M., and Ron Zahavi. 2008. *Business Modeling: A Practical Guide to Realizing Business Value*. Morgan Kaufmann.

Brooks, Frederick P. 1995. *The Mythical Man-Month: Essays on Software Engineering, Anniversary Edition*. Addison-Wesley Professional.

Brown, Dan. 2006. *Communicating Design: Developing Web Site Documentation for Design and Planning.* New Riders Press.

Burton, Richard M., Gerardine DeSanctis, and Børge Obel. 2006. *Organizational Design: A Step-by-Step Approach.* Cambridge University Press.

Carkenord, Barbara A. 2009. *Seven Steps to Mastering Business Analysis.* J. Ross Publishing.

Carnegie Mellon University. 1995. *The Capability Maturity Model: Guidelines for Improving the Software Process.* Addison-Wesley Professional.

Chrissis, Mary Beth, Mike Konrad, and Sandy Shrum. 2006. *CMMI®: Guidelines for Process Integration and Product Improvement (2nd Edition).* Addison-Wesley Professional.

Cimperman, Rob. 2006. *UAT Defined: A Guide to Practical User Acceptance Testing.* Addison-Wesley Professional.

Clemen, Robert T. 1996. *Making Hard Decisions: An Introduction to Decision Analysis.* Wadsworth Publishing Company.

Cockburn, Alistair. 2000. *Writing Effective Use Cases.* Addison-Wesley Professional.

Cockburn, Alistair. 2004. *Crystal Clear: A Human-Powered Methodology for Small Teams.* Addison-Wesley Professional.

Cohn, Mike. 2004. *User Stories Applied: For Agile Software Development.* Addison-Wesley Professional.

Constantine, Larry L., and Lucy A.D. Lockwood. 1999. *Software for Use: A Practical Guide to the Models and Methods of Usage-Centered Design.* Addison-Wesley Professional.

Craig, Malcolm. 2000. *Thinking Visually: Business Applications of Fourteen Core Diagrams.* Continuum International Publishing Group.

Davis, Alan M. 1995. *201 Principles of Software Development.* McGraw-Hill, Inc.

Davis, Alan M. 2005. *Just Enough Requirements Management: Where Software Development Meets Marketing.* Dorset House.

Demarco, Tom, and Timothy Lister. 2003. *Waltzing With Bears: Managing Risk on Software Projects.* Dorset House.

Denney, Richard. 2005. *Succeeding with Use Cases: Working Smart to Deliver Quality.* Addison-Wesley Professional.

Dye, Lowell D., and James S. Pennypacker. 2003. *Project Portfolio Management: Selecting and Prioritizing Projects for Competitive Advantage.* Ctr for Business Practices.

Dymond, Kenneth M. 1995. *A Guide to the CMM®: Understanding the Capability Maturity Model for Software.* Process Inc. U.S.

Eckerson, Wayne W. 2005. *Performance Dashboards: Measuring, Monitoring, and Managing Your Business.* John Wiley & Sons Inc.

Eriksson, Hans-Erik, and Magnus Penker. 2000. *Business Modeling with UML: Business Patterns at Work.* John Wiley & Sons Inc.

Fisher, Roger. 1991. *Getting to Yes: Negotiating Agreement Without Giving In.* Penguin.

Fitzpatrick, Jody L, James R Sanders, and Blaine R Worthen. 2003. *Program Evaluation: Alternative Approaches and Practical Guidelines.* Allyn & Bacon.

Forsberg, Kevin, Hal Mooz, and Howard Cotterman. 2005. *Visualizing Project Management: Models and Frameworks for Mastering Complex Systems.* Wiley.

Fowler, Martin. 2003. *UML Distilled: A Brief Guide to the Standard Object Modeling Language.* Addison-Wesley Professional.

Freedman, Daniel P., and Gerald M. Weinberg. 1990. *Handbook of Walkthroughs, Inspections, and Technical Reviews: Evaluating Programs, Projects, and Products.* Dorset House.

Gause, Donald C., and Gerald M. Weinberg. 1989. *Exploring Requirements: Quality Before Design.* Dorset House.

George, Michael L., John Maxey, David T. Rowlands, and Malcolm Upton. 2004. *The Lean Six Sigma Pocket Toolbook: A Quick Reference Guide to 70 Tools for Improving Quality and Speed.* McGraw-Hill.

Goldsmith, Robin F. 2004. *Discovering Real Business Requirements for Software Project Success.* Artech.

Goodpasture, John C. 2001. *Managing Projects for Value.* Project Management Institute.

Gottesdiener, Ellen. 2002. *Requirements by Collaboration: Workshops for Defining Needs.* Addison-Wesley Professional.

Gottesdiener, Ellen. 2005. *The Software Requirements Memory Jogger: A Pocket Guide to Help Software and Business Teams Develop and Manage Requirements.* Goal/QPC.

Gygi, Craig, Neil DeCarlo, and Bruce Williams. 2005. *Six Sigma For Dummies.* Wiley Publishing, Inc.

Hadden, Rita Chao. 2003. *Leading Culture Change in Your Software Organization: Delivering Results Early.* Management Concepts.

Hammer, Michael, and James Champy. 2003. *Reengineering the Corporation: A Manifesto for Business Revolution.* HarperCollins Publishers.

Hammond, John S, Ralph L Keeney, and Howard Raiffa. 1998. *Smart Choices.* Harvard Business School Press.

Harmon, Paul. 2007. *Business Process Change: A Guide for Business Managers and BPM and Six Sigma Professionals.* Morgan Kaufmann.

Harvard Business Review. 1998. *Harvard Business Review on Measuring Corporate Performance.* Harvard Business School Press.

Harvard Business Review. 2007. *Harvard Business Review on Making Smarter Decisions.* Harvard Business School Press.

Hass, Kathleen B. 2007. *The Business Analyst as Strategist: Translating Business Strategies into Valuable Solutions.* Management Concepts.

Hass, Kathleen B., Don J. Wessels, and Kevin Brennan. 2007. *Getting it Right: Business Requirements Analysis Tools and Techniques.* Management Concepts Inc.

Havey, Michael. 2005. *Essential Business Process Modeling.* O'Reilly Media.

Hay, David C. 2002. *Requirements Analysis: From Business Views to Architecture.* Prentice Hall.

Hetzel, Bill. 1993. *The Complete Guide to Software Testing.* Wiley.

Hiatt, Jeffrey M., and Timothy J. Creasey. 2003. *Change Management.* Prosci Research.

Hohmann, Luke. 1996. *Journey of the Software Professional: The Sociology of Computer Programming.* Prentice Hall.

Hopkins, Richard, and Kevin Jenkins. 2008. *Eating the IT Elephant: Moving from Greenfield Development to Brownfield.* IBM Press.

Hubbard, Douglas W. 2007. *How to Measure Anything: Finding the Value of "Intangibles" in Business.* Wiley.

IEEE Computer Society. 1990. *IEEE Std. 610-12-1990: IEEE Standard Glossary of Software Engineering Terminology.* Institute of Electrical and Electronics Engineers.

IEEE Computer Society. 1998. *IEEE Std. 1233–1998: IEEE Guide for Developing System Requirements Specifications*. Institute of Electrical and Electronics Engineers.

IEEE Computer Society. 1998. *IEEE Std. 830–1998: IEEE Recommended Practice for Software Requirements Specifications.* Institute of Electrical and Electronics Engineers.

IEEE Computer Society. 2004. *Guide to the Software Engineering Body of Knowledge, 2004 Version.* Institute of Electrical and Electronics Engineers.

International Organization for Standardization. 2008. *ISO/IEC CD 25010: Software engineering – Software product Quality Requirements and Evaluation (SQuaRE) – Software and quality in use models Requirements and Evaluation (SQuaRE) Quality Model, Version 0.55.* ISO/IEC.

Jackson, M. 1995. *Software Requirements And Specifications.* Addison-Wesley Professional.

Jacobson, Ivar, and Pan-Wei Ng. 2004. *Aspect-Oriented Software Development with Use Cases.* Addison-Wesley Professional.

Jalote, Pankaj. 1999. *CMM® in Practice: Processes for Executing Software Projects at Infosys.* Addison-Wesley Professional.

Jonasson, Hans. 2007. *Determining Project Requirements.* Auerbach Publications.

Jones, Morgan D. 1998. *The Thinker's Toolkit: 14 Powerful Techniques for Problem Solving.* Three Rivers Press.

Jones, T. Capers. 1998. *Estimating Software Costs.* McGraw-Hill.

Juran, J. M. 1992. *Juran on Quality by Design: The New Steps for Planning Quality into Goods and Services.* Free Press.

Kaplan, Robert S., and David P. Norton. 1996. *The Balanced Scorecard: Translating Strategy into Action.* Harvard Business School Press.

Kessler, Carl, and John Sweitzer. 2007. *Outside-in Software Development: A Practical Approach to Building Successful Stakeholder-based Products.* IBM Press.

Khoshafian, Setrag. 2006. *Service Oriented Enterprises.* Auerbach Publications.

Kit, Edward. 1995. *Software Testing In The Real World: Improving The Process.* Addison-Wesley Professional.

Kotonya, Gerald, and Ian Sommerville. 1998. *Requirements Engineering: Processes and Techniques.* Wiley.

Kotter, John P. 1996. *Leading Change.* Harvard Business School Press.

Kovitz, Benjamin L. 1998. *Practical Software Requirements: A Manual of Content and Style.* Manning Publications.

Larman, Craig. 2004. *Applying UML and Patterns: An Introduction to Object-Oriented Analysis and Design and Iterative Development.* Prentice Hall.

Lauesen, Soren. 2001. *Software Requirements: Styles & Techniques.* Addison-Wesley Professional.

Lawson, Raef, Denis Desroches, and Toby Hatch. 2007. *Scorecard Best Practices: Design, Implementation, and Evaluation.* Wiley.

Leffingwell, Dean, and Don Widrig. 2003. *Managing Software Requirements: A Use Case Approach, 2nd Edition.* Addison-Wesley Professional.

Leffingwell, Dean. 2007. *Scaling Software Agility: Best Practices for Large Enterprises.* Addison-Wesley Professional.

Lepsinger, Richard, and Anntoinette D. Lucia. 1999. *The Art and Science of Competency Models: Pinpointing Critical Success Factors in Organizations.* Jossey-Bass/Pfeiffer.

Lowy, Alex. 2007. *No Problem.* Authorhouse.

Maister, David H., Charles H. Green, and Robert M. Galford. 2001. *The Trusted Advisor.* Free Press.

Martin, James. 1989. *Information Engineering Book I: Introduction.* Prentice Hall.

Martin, James. 1990. *Information Engineering Book II: Planning & Analysis.* Prentice Hall.

Martin, James. 1990. *Information Engineering Book III: Design and Construction.* Prentice Hall.

McConnell, Steve. 1996. *Rapid Development.* Microsoft.

Mintzberg, Henry, and James Brian Quinn. 1995. *The Strategy Process: Concepts, Context and Cases.* Prentice Hall.

Morabito, Joseph, Ira Sack, and Anilkumar Bhate. 1999. *Organization Modeling: Innovative Architectures for the 21st Century.* Prentice Hall.

Moss, Larissa T., and Shaku Atre. 2003. *Business Intelligence Roadmap: The Complete Project Lifecycle for Decision-Support Applications.* Addison-Wesley Professional.

Myers, Glenford J. 2004. *The Art of Software Testing, 2nd Edition.* Wiley.

Nielsen, Jakob. 1993. *Usability Engineering.* Morgan Kaufmann.

Niven, Paul R. 2008. *Balanced Scorecard: Step-by-Step for Government and Nonprofit Agencies.* Wiley.

Object Management Group. 2007. *Business Motivation Model (BMM) Specification.* Object Management Group, Inc.

Object Management Group. 2008. *Business Process Maturity Model (BPMM), Version 1.0.* Object Management Group, Inc.

Object Management Group. 2008. *Business Process Modeling Notation, V1.2.* Object Management Group, Inc.

Ould, Martyn A. 2005. *Business Process Management: A Rigorous Approach.* Meghan Kiffer Pr.

Page-Jones, Meilir. 1988. *Practical Guide to Structured Systems Design.* Prentice Hall.

Paul, Debra, and Donald Yeates. 2006. *Business Analysis*. British Computer Society.

Perry, William E. 2000. *Effective Methods for Software Testing, 2nd Edition*. John Wiley & Sons.

Porter, Michael E. 1980. *Competitive Strategy: Techniques for Analyzing Industries and Competitors*. Free Press.

Porter, Michael. 1985. *Competitive Advantage*. Free Press.

Pressman, Roger S. 2000. *Software Engineering: A Practitioner's Approach*. McGraw-Hill.

Project Management Institute. 2008. *A Guide to the Project Management Body of Knowledge, 4th Edition*. Project Management Institute.

Rad, Parviz F., and Ginger Levin. 2002. *The Advanced Project Management Office: A Comprehensive Look at Function and Implementation*. CRC Press.

Roam, Dan. 2008. *Back Of The Napkin*. Penguin Group.

Robertson, Suzanne, and James C. Robertson. 2004. *Requirements-Led Project Management: Discovering David's Slingshot*. Addison-Wesley Professional.

Robertson, Suzanne, and James C. Robertson. 2006. *Mastering the Requirements Process, 2nd Edition*. Addison-Wesley Professional.

Ross, Jeanne W, Peter Weill, and David C. Robertson. 2006. *Enterprise Architecture as Strategy*. Harvard Business School Press.

Ross, Ronald G. 2003. *Principles of the Business Rule Approach*. Addison-Wesley Professional.

Ross, Ronald G. 2005. *Business Rule Concepts - Getting to the Point of Knowledge, 2nd Edition*. Business Rule Solutions Inc.

Ruble, David. 1997. *Practical Analysis and Design for Client/Server and GUI Systems*. Prentice Hall.

Rumbaugh, James, Ivar Jacobson, and Grady Booch. 2004. *The Unified Modeling Language Reference Manual, 2nd Edition*. Addison-Wesley Professional.

Rummler, Geary A., and Alan P. Brache. 1995. *Improving Performance: How to Manage the White Space in the Organization Chart*. Jossey-Bass.

Scholtes, Peter R. 1997. *The Leader's Handbook: Making Things Happen, Getting Things Done*. McGraw-Hill.

Schwaber, Ken. 2004. *Agile Project Management With Scrum*. Microsoft.

Senge, Peter M. 1990. *The Fifth Discipline*. Doubleday.

Senge, Peter M. 1999. *The Dance of Change*. Doubleday.

Sharp, Alec, and Patrick McDermott. 2001. *Workflow Modeling: Tools for Process Improvement and Application Development*. Artech House.

Sodhi, Jag, and Prince Sodhi. 2001. *IT Project Management Handbook*. Management Concepts.

Sodhi, Jag, and Prince Sodhi. 2003. *Managing IT Systems Requirements*. Management Concepts.

Software Engineering Institute. 2006. *CMMI ® for Development, Version 1.2*. Carnegie Mellon University.

Software Engineering Institute. 2007. *CMMI ® for Acquisition, Version 1.2*. Carnegie Mellon University.

Sommerville, Ian, and Pete Sawyer. 1997. *Requirements Engineering: A Good Practice Guide*. Wiley.

Stanford, Naomi. 2007. *Guide to Organisation Design: Creating High-Performing and Adaptable Enterprises*. Profile Books.

Stevens, Richard, Peter Brook, Ken Jackson, and Stuart Arnold. 1998. *System Engineering, Coping with Complexity*. Pearson Education.

Streibel, Barbara J., Brian L. Joiner, and Peter R. Scholtes. 2003. *The Team Handbook: Third Edition*. Joiner/Oriel Inc.

Tarantino, Anthony. 2008. *Governance, Risk, and Compliance Handbook: Technology, Finance, Environmental, and International Guidance and Best Practices*. Wiley.

Tayntor, Christine B. 2005. *Successful Packaged Software Implementation*. CRC Press.

Thayer, Richard H. 1997. *Software Engineering Project Management*. Wiley-IEEE Computer Society Press.

Thayer, Richard H., and Merlin Dorfman. 1996. *Software Engineering*. Wiley-IEEE Computer Society Press.

Thayer, Richard H., and Merlin Dorfman. 1997. *Software Requirements Engineering, 2nd Edition.* Wiley-IEEE Computer Society Press.

Thorp, John, and Fujitsu Consulting's Center for Strategic Leadership. 2003. *The Information Paradox: Realizing the Business Benefits of Information Technology, Revised Edition.* McGraw-Hill.

Tockey, Steve. 2004. *Return on Software: Maximizing the Return on Your Software Investment.* Addison-Wesley Professional.

Ury, William. 1993. *Getting Past No: Negotiating in Difficult Situations.* Bantam.

Van Assen, Marcel, Gerben Van den Berg, and Paul Pietersma. 2008. *Key Management Models: The 60+ models every manager needs to know.* Pearson Education Canada.

Van Bon, Jan, Arjen de Jong, and Axel Kolthof. 2007. *Foundations of IT Service Management Based on ITIL V3.* Van Haren Publishing.

Von Halle, Barbara. 2001. *Business Rules Applied: Building Better Systems Using the Business Rules Approach.* Wiley.

Ward, John L., and Elizabeth Daniel. 2006. *Benefits Management: Delivering Value from IS & IT Investments.* Wiley.

Weill, Peter, and Jeanne W Ross. 2004. *IT Governance.* McGraw-Hill Europe.

Weinberg, Gerald M. 1998. *The Psychology of Computer Programming: Silver Anniversary Edition.* Dorset House.

White, Stephen A., Derek Miers, and Layna Fischer. 2008. *BPMN Modeling and Reference Guide.* Future Strategies Inc.

Wiegers, Karl E. 2003. *Software Requirements, 2nd Edition.* Microsoft.

Wiegers, Karl E. 2006. *More About Software Requirements: Thorny Issues and Practical Advice.* Microsoft Press.

Wiegers, Karl E. 2007. *Practical Project Initiation: A Handbook with Tools.* Microsoft.

Young, Ralph R. 2001. *Effective Requirements Practices.* Addison-Wesley Professional.

Young, Ralph R. 2004. *Requirements Engineering Handbook.* Artech House.

Yourdon, Edward. 1978. *Structured Walkthroughs, 2nd Edition.* Yourdon Press.

Contributors

C.1 Version 2.0

C.1.1 Body of Knowledge Committee

Content for this release was primarily developed by the Body of Knowledge Committee:

▶ Kevin Brennan, CBAP, OCEB, PMP, Vice President, Professional Development (*Requirements Analysis*, *Underlying Competencies*, Final Revision)

▶ Barbara A. Carkenord, MBA, CBAP (*Requirements Management and Communication*, *Solution Assessment and Validation*)

▶ Mary Gorman, CBAP (*Elicitation*)

▶ Kathleen B. Hass, PMP (*Enterprise Analysis*)

▶ Brenda Kerton, MA (*Glossary*)

▶ Elizabeth Larson, CBAP, PMP (*Business Analysis Planning and Monitoring*)

▶ Richard Larson, CBAP, PMP (Review Committee Chair)

▶ Jason Questor (Editor, Graphics Team Lead)

▶ Laura Paton, MBA, CBAP, PMP (Project Manager)

C.1.2 Content Contributors

The following individuals contributed additional content used in this revision:

Tony Alderson
James Baird
Jake Calabrese, CBAP
Bruce C. Chadbourne, PgMP, PMP
Karen Chandler
Carrolynn Chang
Richard Fox, CBAP
Rosemary Hossenlopp
Peter Gordon, CBAP
Ellen Gottesdiener

Monica Jain
Cherifa Mansoura Liamani, Ph.D.
Karen Little
Laura Markey
Richard Martin
Gillian McCleary
William B. Murray
Angie Perris, CBAP
David Wright

The Graphics Team developed graphics and graphics standards:

Carl Gosselin
Perry McLeod, CBAP, PMP
Alexandre Romanov

Patricia Sandino
Maggie Yang

Version 2.0 also includes content developed for previous versions of the *BABOK® Guide*.

C.1.3   Expert Advisory and Review Group

The following industry experts generously provided IIBA® with advice and guidance on the scope and content of version 2.0 of the *BABOK® Guide* during its planning and development, and helped to shape the content and direction of this release.

Scott Ambler	Kent J. McDonald
James Baird	Mark McGregor
Kurt Bittner	Meilir Page-Jones
Rafael Dorantes	James Robertson
Robin F. Goldsmith, JD	Suzanne Robertson
Ellen Gottesdiener	Ronald G. Ross
Paul Harmon	David Ruble
Dean Leffingwell	Steve Tockey
Gladys S.W. Lam	

C.1.4   Practitioner Reviewers

The following individuals participated in the practitioner review of version 2.0, and provided feedback used in the revision of the Public Review Draft:

Sharon M. Aker	Barbara Koenig
Betty H. Baker, CBAP	Steven R. Koss, MBA
B. D. Barnes PhD, PE, PMP, CSSBB	Douglas Kowalczyk
Jennifer S. Battan, CBAP	Robert Lam, MBA, ISP
Subrahmanya Gupta Boda	Richard Larson, CBAP, PMP
Craig W. Brown, MPM, CSM	Karen Little, CBAP
Cathy Brunsting	Joy Matthews
Peter Burg, PMP	Perry McLeod, CBAP, PMP
Greg Busby, CBAP	Holly M. Meyer
Diana Cagle, MBA, CBAP	Michael Mohammed
Duncan Cairns	Brian Monson, PMP
Bruce Chadbourne, PgMP, PMP	Nancy A. Murphy, PMP, CBAP
Carrollynn Chang	Richard L. Neighbarger, CSQA, CSQE
Patricia Chappell, CBAP, MBA	Tony Newport, CBAP
Mark Cheek, PMP	Samia Osman
Huai-Ling Ch'ng, CBAP	Cecilia Rathwell
Desirée Purvis (née Chu), CBAP	Suzanna Etheridge Rawlins, PMP
Pauline Chung	Helen Ronnenbergh
Joseph Da Silva	Zoya Roytblat
Nitza Dovenspike	Christopher Ryba
James Downey, Ph.D., PMP	Julian Sammy
Tamer El-Tonsy, CISA, PRINCE2, ITIL	Keith Sarre, CBAP
Steve Erlank, BSc, BCom (Hons)	Laura Schleicher
Margaret Gaino Ewing, MBA, CBAP	Fred Seip
Stephanie Garwood, CBAP	Thomas Slahetka, CBAP
Joe Goss	Warren Steger
Karen Gras, CBAP	Leah Sturm, CBAP
Kwabby Gyasi	James M. Szuch
Bob Hillier, PMP	Robin Tucker
Billie Johnson, CBAP	Krishna Vishwanath
Peter Johnson, CBAP	A. S. Umashankar
Hans Jonasson, CBAP, PMP	

The following individuals also served as review team leads:

- Cathy Brunsting

- Patricia Chappell, CBAP, MBA

- Stephanie Garwood, CBAP

- Robert Lam, MBA, ISP

C.1.5 Other Significant Contributors

The following IIBA® volunteers and staff contributed ideas and support during the planning, development process, and release of this version.

- Kathleen Barret, President and CEO

- Angela Barrington-Foote, Chair, Role Delineation Committee (Present)

- Suzanne Bertschi, Certification Manager

- Michael Gladstone, CBAP, Vice President, Certification

- Sandra Micallef, Program Manager

- Indy Mitra, Secretary and Head of Operational Compliance

- Cleve Pillifant, Chair, Role Delineation Committee (Former)

- Lynda Sydney, Head of Communications

- Katie Wise, Graphic Design

C.1.6 Additional Thanks

IIBA® and the Body of Knowledge Committee would like to thank all those practitioners of business analysis how have provided us with comments and feedback over the years, as well as those who provided us with feedback on the Public Review Draft, and to Dave Revell, SVP, BMO Financial Group, for his active support during our formative years.

C.1.7 Production and Publication

Layout and DTP: Kevin Brennan and Jeff Mackintosh. **Cover:** Kim Koehler. **Index:** Rita Tatum.

C.2 Version 1.6

C.2.1 Body of Knowledge Committee

- Kathleen Barret (President)

- Kevin Brennan, CBAP, PMP (Vice-President, Body of Knowledge (at time of publication) and Chair, Requirements Analysis & Documentation and BA Fundamentals Sub-committees

- Barbara Carkenord, MBA, CBAP (Chair, Requirements Communication Sub-committee and Solution Assessment and Validation Sub-committee)

- Mary Gorman, CBAP (Chair, Requirements Elicitation Sub-committee)

- Kathleen B. Hass, PMP (Chair, Enterprise Analysis Sub-committee)

- Brenda Kerton (Chairperson, Body of Knowledge Committee (during development))

- Elizabeth Larson, CBAP, PMP (Co-chair, BOK Review Sub-committee)

- Richard Larson, CBAP, PMP (Co-chair, BOK Review Sub-committee)

- Dulce Oliveira (Chair, Requirements Planning & Management Sub-committee)

- Cleve Pillifant (Member, Accreditation – liaison to Body of Knowledge Committee)

C.2.2   Contributors to Version 1.6

Tony Alderson

Finny Barker

Neil Burton

Karen Chandler

Richard Fox, CBAP

Rosemary Hossenlopp

Peter Gordon, CBAP

Monica Jain

Peter Kovaks

Chris Matts

Laura Markey

Patricia Martin

Richard Martin

Rosina Mete

William Murray

Harish Pathria

Kathleen Person

Tony Rice

John Slater

Mark Tracy

Jacqueline Young

C.2.3   Reviewers of Version 1.6

Sharon Aker

Betty H. Baker, CBAP

Jo Bennett

Cathy Brunsting

Carrollynn Chang, CBAP

Patricia Chappell, CBAP, MBA

Pauline Chung

Joseph R. Czarnecki

Stephanie Garwood, CBAP

May Jim, CBAP

Day Knez

Barb Koenig

Robert Lam

Cherifa Mansoura Liamani, Ph.D.

Gillian McCleary

Kelly Piechota

Howard Podeswa

Leslie Ponder

Cecilia Rathwell

Jennifer Rojek

Keith Sarre, CBAP

Jessica Gonzalez Solis

Jim Subach

Diane Talbot

Krishna Vishwanath

Marilyn Vogt

Scott Witt

Summary of Changes from Version 1.6

appendix   **D**

D.1   Overview

Version 2.0 of the *BABOK® Guide* is extensively revised, restructured, and rewritten by comparison to version 1.6. This appendix provides a overview of where topics covered in version 1.6 may be found in version 2.0. This summary is not a complete description of the changes, and in some cases the scope of a task or technique has changed significantly at a lower level.

D.2   Enterprise Analysis

The tasks *Define Business Need* (5.1) and *Assess Capability Gaps* (5.2) have no direct equivalent in 1.6.

1.6 Task or Technique	2.0 Task or Technique
Creating and Maintaining the Business Architecture (2.2)	Not directly addressed in version 2.0. Business analysis at the enterprise-wide or strategic level will be addressed in a separate application area extension.
Conducting Feasibility Studies (2.3)	*Determine Solution Approach* (5.3) See also *Chapter 9: Techniques* for some of the referenced techniques.
Determining Project Scope (2.4)	*Determine Solution Scope* (5.4). The project management content in this task has been removed. See also *Chapter 9: Techniques* for some of the referenced techniques.
Preparing the Business Case (2.5)	*Define Business Case* (5.5) See also *Chapter 9: Techniques* for some of the referenced techniques.
Conducting the Initial Risk Assessment (2.6)	*Define Business Case* (5.5) *Risk Analysis* (9.24)
Preparing the Decision Package (2.7)	*Prepare Requirements Package* (4.4) *Communicate Requirements* (4.5)
Selecting and Prioritizing Projects (2.8)	Not directly addressed in version 2.0. Business analysis at the enterprise-wide or strategic level will be addressed in a separate application area extension.
Launching New Projects (2.9)	No directly equivalent task.
Managing Projects for Value (2.10)	*Define Business Case* (5.5). In version 2.0, there are no separate tasks for re-evaluating or updating work done by another task. These situations are treated as another instance of the original task.
Tracking Project Benefits (2.11)	*Evaluate Solution Performance* (7.7)

D.3　Requirements Planning and Management

This Knowledge Area underwent considerable revision. It was determined that it attempted to cover three distinct topics:

▶ Management of a team of business analysts, which was determined to fall outside the scope of business analysis itself.

▶ Management of requirements, which was moved to the *Requirements Management and Communication* Knowledge Area.

▶ Planning and managing the execution of business analysis activities, which was moved to the *Business Analysis Planning and Monitoring* Knowledge Area.

The task *Plan Requirements Management Process* (2.4) has no direct equivalent in 1.6.

1.6 Task or Technique	2.0 Task or Technique
Understand Team Roles for the Project (3.2)	*Conduct Stakeholder Analysis* (2.2). The version 2.0 task is explicitly limited to analyzing roles and responsibilities in regard to stakeholder participation in business analysis activities. See also *Document Analysis* (9.9), *Interview* (9.14) and *Survey/Questionnaire* (9.31) for techniques described in this task.
Define Business Analyst Work Division Strategy (3.3)	No equivalent in 2.0.
Define Requirements Risk Approach (3.4)	No directly equivalent task. Risks are identified through elicitation activities and can be communicated and managed. See techniques *Problem Tracking* (9.20) and *Risk Analysis* (9.24).
Determine Planning Considerations (3.5)	*Plan Business Analysis Approach* (2.1)
Select Requirements Activities (3.6)	*Plan Business Analysis Activities* (2.3). Section 3.6.3 corresponds to *Plan Business Analysis Communication* (2.4).
Estimate Requirements Activities (3.7)	*Plan Business Analysis Activities* (2.3) and *Estimation* (9.10).
Manage Requirements Scope (3.8)	Multiple tasks: see below
·　*Establish Requirements Baseline* (3.8.1)	·　*Manage Solution Scope and Requirements* (4.1)
·　*Structure Requirements for Traceability* (3.8.2)	·　*Manage Requirements Traceability* (4.2)
·　*Identify Impacts to External Systems and/or Other Areas of the Project* (3.8.3)	·　*Assess Organizational Readiness* (7.3)
·　*Identify Scope Change Resulting from Requirement Change (Change Management)* (3.8.4)	·　*Manage Solution Scope and Requirements* (4.1)
·　*Maintain Scope Approval* (3.8.5)	·　*Manage Solution Scope and Requirements* (4.1)
Measure and Report on Requirements Activity (3.9)	*Manage Business Analysis Performance* (4.5). The discussion of metrics in the version 2.0 task is explicitly limited to metrics for business analysis activities and deliverables.
Manage Requirements Change (3.10)	*Manage Solution Scope and Requirements* (4.1)

D.4   Requirements Elicitation

The name of this Knowledge Area was changed to *Elicitation*.

1.6 Task or Technique	2.0 Task or Technique
Elicit Requirements (4.2)	*Prepare for Elicitation (3.1)* *Conduct Elicitation Activity (3.2)* *Document Elicitation Results (3.3)* *Confirm Elicitation Results (3.4)*
Brainstorming (4.3)	*Brainstorming (9.3)*
Document Analysis (4.4)	*Document Analysis (9.9)*
Focus Group (4.5)	*Focus Groups (9.11)*
Interface Analysis (4.6)	*Interface Analysis (9.13)*
Interview (4.7)	*Interviews (9.14)*
Observation (4.8)	*Observation (9.18)*
Prototyping (4.9)	*Prototyping (9.22)*
Requirements Workshop (4.10)	Requirements Workshop (9.23)
Reverse Engineering (4.11)	Not included in 2.0.
Survey/Questionnaire (4.12)	*Survey/Questionnaire (9.31)*

D.5   Requirements Analysis and Documentation

The name of this Knowledge Area was changed to *Requirements Analysis. Prioritize Requirements* (6.1) has no direct equivalent in version 1.6.

1.6 Task or Technique	2.0 Task or Technique
Structure Requirements Packages (5.2)	The purpose of this task most closely relates to *Organize Requirements* (6.2), but the actual content maps most closely to *Functional Decomposition* (9.12)
Create Business Domain Model (5.3)	*Organize Requirements* (6.2) and *Specify and Model Requirements* (6.3)
Analyze User Requirements (5.4)	*Organize Requirements* (6.2) and *Specify and Model Requirements* (6.3)
Analyze Functional Requirements (5.5)	*Organize Requirements* (6.2) and *Specify and Model Requirements* (6.3)
Analyze Quality of Service Requirements (5.6)	*Organize Requirements* (6.2), *Specify and Model Requirements* (6.3), and *Non-functional Requirements Analysis* (9.17)
Determine Assumptions and Constraints (5.7)	*Define Assumptions and Constraints (6.4)*
Determine Requirements Attributes (5.8)	Determining which attributes are used is covered in *Plan Requirements Management Process* (4.4). Capturing attributes for a particular requirement is covered in *Specify and Model Requirements* (6.3).
Document Requirements (5.9)	*Prepare Requirements Package (4.4)*
Validate Requirements (5.10)	*Validate Requirements (6.6)*

1.6 Task or Technique	2.0 Task or Technique
Verify Requirements (5.11)	*Verify Requirements* (6.5)
Data and Behavior Models (5.12)	No equivalent for this grouping. Many of the individual techniques are present in version 2.0 as described below:
• 　*Business Rules* (5.12.1)	• 　*Business Rules Analysis* (9.4)
• 　*Class Model* (5.12.2)	• 　*Data Modeling* (9.7)
• 　*CRUD Matrix* (5.12.3)	• 　Not described in version 2.0.
• 　*Data Dictionary* (5.12.4)	• 　*Data Dictionary and Glossary* (9.5)
• 　*Data Transformation and Mapping* (5.12.5)	• 　*Define Transition Requirements* (7.4)
• 　*Entity Relationship Diagrams* (5.12.6)	• 　*Data Modeling* (9.7)
• 　*Metadata Definiton* (5.12.7)	• 　*Data Modeling* (9.7)
Process/Flow Models (5.13)	No equivalent for this grouping. Many of the individual techniques are present in version 2.0 as described below:
• 　*Activity Diagram* (5.13.1)	• 　*Process Modeling* (9.21)
• 　*Data Flow Diagram* (5.13.2)	• 　*Data Flow Diagrams* (9.6)
• 　*Event Identification* (5.13.3)	• 　Not described in version 2.0. Events are described in relation to a number of other techniques, and may be used as a basis for *Scope Modeling* (9.27)
• 　*Flowchart* (5.13.4)	• 　*Process Modeling* (9.21)
• 　*Sequence Diagram* (5.13.5)	• 　*Sequence Diagrams* (9.28)
• 　*State Machine Diagram* (5.13.6)	• 　*State Diagrams* (9.29)
• 　*Workflow Models* (5.13.7)	• 　*Process Modeling* (9.21)
Usage Models (5.14)	No equivalent for this grouping. Many of the individual techniques are present in version 2.0 as described below:
• 　*Prototyping* (5.14.1)	• 　*Prototyping* (9.22)
• 　*Storyboards/Screen Flows* (5.14.2)	• 　*Prototyping* (9.22)
• 　*Use Case Description* (5.14.3)	• 　*Scenarios and Use Cases* (9.26)
• 　*Use Case Diagram* (5.14.4)	• 　*Scenarios and Use Cases* (9.26). Use case diagrams may also be used for *Scope Modeling* (9.27).
• 　*User Interface Designs* (5.14.5)	• 　*Prototyping* (9.22)
• 　*User Profiles* (5.14.6)	• 　No direct equivalent in 2.0. This technique would fall within *Conduct Stakeholder Analysis* (2.2).
• 　*User Stories* (5.14.7)	• 　*User Stories* (9.33)

D.6   Requirements Communication

This Knowledge Area was combined with requirements management tasks moved from *Requirements Planning and Management* into *Requirements Management and Communication*. The task *Maintain Requirements for Re-use* (4.3) has no direct equivalent in 1.6.

1.6 Task or Technique	2.0 Task or Technique
Create a Requirements Communication Plan (6.2)	*Plan Business Analysis Communication (2.4)*
Manage Requirements Conflicts (6.3)	*Manage Solution Scope and Requirements (4.1)*
Determine Appropriate Requirements Format (6.4)	*Plan Business Analysis Communication (2.4) and Prepare Requirements Package (4.4)*
Create a Requirements Package (6.5)	*Prepare Requirements Package (4.4)*
Conduct a Requirements Presentation (6.6)	*Communicate Requirements (4.5)*
Conduct a Formal Requirements Review (6.7)	*Structured Walkthrough (9.30)*
Obtain Requirements Signoff (6.8)	*Manage Solution Scope and Requirements (4.1)*

D.7   Solution Assessment and Validation

The text for these tasks was incomplete at the time version 1.6 was published. The tasks in version 2.0 use a very different conceptual structure and therefore the tasks can only match in a very approximate fashion.

1.6 Task or Technique	2.0 Task or Technique
Develop Alternate Solutions (7.2)	*Allocate Requirements (7.2)*
Evaluate Technology Options (7.3)	*Assess Proposed Solution (7.1)*
Facilitate the Selection of a Solution (7.4)	*Assess Proposed Solution (7.1)*
Ensure the Usability of the Solution (7.5)	*Validate Solution (7.5)*
Support the Quality Assurance Process (7.6)	*Validate Solution (7.5)*
Support the Implementation of the Solution (7.7)	*Define Transition Requirements (7.4)*
Communicate Solution Impacts (7.8)	*Assess Organizational Readiness (7.3)*
Post Implementation Review and Assessment (7.9)	*Manage Business Analysis Performance (2.5) and Evaluate Solution Performance (7.6)*

D.8   Underlying Fundamentals

No content had been created for this section at the time that version 1.6 was published. This Knowledge Area broadly equates to the *Underlying Competencies* Knowledge Area in version 2.0, but the individual topics are structured very differently.

Index

References are to section numbers except where specified as figure numbers.

absolute reference, for requirement, 2.5.4.3
abstraction, levels of, 6.2.4.1
acceptance, 9.1, 9.24.3.3
acceptance criteria, 2.2.5.1, 9.12
acceptance and evaluation criteria
    definition: description, 9.1.2; elements, 9.1.3;
       organizational readiness assessment, 7.3.5.1;
       purpose, 9.1.1; requirements allocation, 7.2.5
    requirements: validation, 6.6.5; verification, 6.5.5.1
    solution: assessment, proposed, 7.1.5; validation,
       7.5.5
    usage considerations, 9.1.4
active/visible observation, 9.18.2
activities, 9.21.3.1
activity description, 2.3.4.4
activity list, 2.3.4.4
actor, 9.26.3.2, 9.33.3
agile, 1.5.2
    planning activities, 2.3.4.3
    planning approach, 2.1.2, 2.1.4
    planning communication, 2.4.4.3
    planning requirements management, 2.5.4.5
    See also Change-Driven Approaches.
alternative generation, 5.3.4.1
analogous estimation, 9.10.3.1
analytical thinking, 1.7, 8.1
    creative thinking, 8.1.1
    decision making, 8.1.2
    learning, 8.1.3
    problem solving, 8.1.4
    systems, 8.1.5
approaches, ranking and selection of, 5.3.3.3
assessment
    organizational readiness, 7.3
    proposed solution, 7.1.7
assumption, 2.3.4.4, 5.3.4.2, 6.4.4.1
    business case, defined, 5.5.3
    defined, 6.4: description, 6.4.2, elements, 6.4.4,
       input, 6.4.3, input/output, figure 6-5, purpose,
       6.4.1, stakeholders, 6.4.5, techniques, 6.4.5
    identification, 6.6.4.1
    solution: assessment, proposed, 7.1.3, scope,
       defined, 5.4.3
attributes, 9.7.3.2
author, of requirement, 2.5.4.3
automated systems, 2.2.4.2
available resources, 7.2.4.1
average rate of return, 9.8.3.1
avoidance, of risk, 9.24.3.3

baselining, 4.1.5.2
behavioral characteristics, 1.7, 8.2
    ethics, 8.2.1

    personal organization, 8.2.2
    trustworthiness, 8.2.3
benchmarking, 9.2
    business need, defined, 5.1.5
    description, 9.2.2
    elements, 9.2.3
    purpose, 9.2.1
    solution approach, 5.3.5.1
benefit, 5.5.4.1, 9.33.3
benefits realization dependencies, 6.6.4.4
body of knowledge, defined, 1.1
bottom-up estimation, 9.10.3.3
brainstorming, 2.2.5.1, 3.3.5, 9.3
    business need, defined, 5.1.5
    description, 9.3.2
    elements, 9.3.3
    preparation, 9.3.3.1
    purpose, 9.3.1
    session, 9.3.3.2
    solution approach, 5.3.5.1
    usage considerations, 9.3.4
    wrap-up, 9.3.3.3
budgeting, 6.1.5.3
business analysis
    approach, 2.3.3: communications input, 2.4.3,
       output, 2.1.7
    communication plan, 2.4.7, 4.4.3, 4.5.3
    defined, 1.2
    deliverables, 2.3.4.3
    information sources, 1.8
    input, 2.6.3
    performance: description, 2.6.2; elements, 2.6.4; in-
       put/output diagram, figure 2-10; management,
       2.6; output, 2.6.7; purpose, 2.6.1; stakeholders,
       2.6.8; techniques, 2.6.5
    performance assessment, 2.3.3, 2.6.7
    performance metrics, 2.6.3
    planning: monitoring, 1.4; process, 2.1.4.5
    planning activities, 2.3: description, 2.3.2; deter-
       mining, 2.3.4.4; elements, 2.3.4; input, 2.3.3;
       input/output diagram, figure 2-7; output, 2.3.7;
       purpose, 2.3.1; stakeholders, 2.3.6; techniques,
       2.3.5
    planning approach, 2.1: description, 2.1.2, ele-
       ments, 2.1.4; inputs, 2.1.3, figure 2-2; output,
       2.1.7; purpose, 2.1.1; stakeholders, 2.1.6; tech-
       niques, 2.1.5
    planning communication, 2.4: description, 2.4.2;
       elements, 2.4.4; input, 2.4.3, figure 2-8; purpose,
       2.4.1; stakeholders, 2.4.6; techniques, 2.4.5
    plans, 2.3.7, 2.4.3, 2.6.3
    process assets, 2.6.7
    stakeholders attitude towards, 2.2.4.3
    standards, 2.1.2

A Guide to the *Business Analysis Body of Knowledge®*

A Guide to the *Business Analysis Body of Knowledge*®

About IIBA®

International Institute of Business Analysis (IIBA®) is an independent non-profit professional association formed in 2003 to serve the growing field of business analysis. For individuals working in a broad range of roles – business analysis, systems analysis, requirements analysis or management, project management, consulting, process improvement and more – **IIBA® can help you do your job better and enhance your professional life.**

The mission of IIBA® is to develop and promote the business analysis profession. We want to help Business Analysts like you obtain a higher level of knowledge, advance your skills and provide added value to your everyday work. Members benefit from:

► Professional development with webinars, quick tips, educational tools, plus newsletters and other BA information

► Access to the IIBA® Community Network

► Opportunity to become a member of an IIBA® Chapter to network and share knowledge with peers in your community

► Opportunity to influence and contribute to the business analysis profession

► Free access to PDF and eBook editions of the *BABOK® Guide*

► Discounted fee for the CBAP® exam

To become an IIBA® member, sign up through our website at http://www.theiiba.org/join/.

Chapters

Ongoing professional development is a key benefit of IIBA® membership and is supported at the chapter level through activities, meetings, and educational programs. IIBA® chapters advance the mission and objectives of the organization by promoting professional standards and practices at the local level. A list of IIBA® chapters can be found at http://www.theiiba.org/chapters/.

Certified Business Analysis Professional™ (CBAP®)

IIBA® has created the Certified Business Analysis Professional™ (CBAP®), a designation awarded to candidates who have successfully demonstrated their expertise as practitioners of business analysis.

Benefits to the individual from acquiring and maintaining CBAP® certification may include:

► Demonstrated knowledge of the skills necessary to be an effective Business Analyst.

► A proven level of competence in the principles and practices of business analysis.

► Participation in a recognized professional group.

► Recognition of professional competence by professional peers and management.

► Advanced career potential due to recognition as a professional Business Analysis practitioner.

► Demonstrated commitment to the field of Business Analysis, increasingly recognized as a vital component of any successful project.

Benefits to the organization resulting from employees acquiring CBAP® certification may include:

► Establishment and implementation of best practices in business analysis by individuals acknowledged as knowledgeable and skilled.

► More reliable, higher quality results produced with increased efficiency and consistency.

► Identification of professional Business Analysts to clients and business partners.

► Professional development and recognition for experienced Business Analysts.

► Demonstrated commitment to the field of Business Analysis, increasingly recognized as a vital component of any successful project.

CPSIA information can be obtained at www.ICGtesting.com
Printed in the USA
BVOW06s0606011214

376865BV00002B/16/P